Bourgeois Nightmares

Bourgeois Nightmares

Suburbia, 1870–1930

Robert M. Fogelson

Yale University Press • New Haven and London

Frontispiece: Subdivision plan, Palos Verdes Estates, California, ca. 1923

Part 1 illustration: Billboard in the Country Club District, Kansas City (ca. 1910), J. C. Nichols Company Scrapbooks (KC54) 1:124, Western Historical Manuscript Collection, University of Missouri-Kansas City Archives

Part 2 illustration: From *Gasoline Stations or Brendonwood* (promotional brochure, ca. 1920), Loeb Library, Harvard University

Printed in the United States of America by Sheridan Books Inc.

Library of Congress Cataloging-in-Publication Data
Fogelson, Robert M.
Bourgeois nightmares : suburbia, 1870–1930 / Robert M. Fogelson.
    p.   cm.
ISBN 0-300-10876-1 (alk. paper)
  1. Suburbs—United States—History. 2. Real covenants— United States. 3. Suburban life—United States—History. I. Title.
HT352.U6F64 2005
307.76′0973—dc22   2005009023

A catalogue record for this book is available from the British Library.

The paper in this book meets the guidelines for permanence and durability of the Committee on Production Guidelines for Book Longevity of the Council on Library Resources.

10 9 8 7 6 5 4 3 2 1

To Maria Alvarez, Joshua Fogelson, and Camille Ballard

and to David Handlin, who asked the question that

prompted me to write a book I had never thought of writing

"Suppose I [meaning a man of means and refinement] come here [from the city to one of its suburbs], what grounds of confidence can I have that I shall not by-and-by find a dram-shop on my right, or a beer-garden on my left, or a factory chimney or warehouse cutting off this view of the water? Is this charming road sure not to be turned also into a common town street, strewn with garbage, and in place of these lovely woods, can I be certain that here also there will not soon be a field of stumps with shanties and goats and heaps of cinders?"

Frederick Law Olmsted et al.
"Report to the Staten Island Improvement Commission of a Preliminary Scheme of Improvements," 1871

Contents

Introduction

Early in the 1950s, a couple of years before I finished high school, my parents made a down payment on a house to be built in Bayberry, a residential development in New Rochelle, one of New York City's rapidly growing suburbs. Like many of their neighbors, most of whom were second-generation immigrants, professionals, and small-business men who had prospered after World War II, they were unhappy with the apartment house in the West Bronx into which they had moved during the Great Depression. Although they did not tell me (or my two younger brothers) why, I later learned that they found their two-bedroom apartment too small to raise three boys—though it was much bigger than the Manhattan tenements in which their parents had raised even larger families. They were also fed up with paying rent and tired of fighting with the landlord. They wanted to be homeowners, not tenants, to live in a single-family house on a good-sized lot, with a well-tended lawn and plenty of shade trees, surrounded by other single-family houses. Now that many of their neighbors were on the move, they saw no reason to stay put. A few of the neighbors moved east, to Queens and Long Island. But just as they had once headed north from Manhattan to the Bronx, so most now moved north from the Bronx to Westchester County, to New Rochelle, Mount Vernon, and, if they could afford it, Scarsdale. My parents followed suit, confident that in a year or so we too would be living happily in suburbia.

Their confidence, it turned out, was misplaced. They soon discovered that houses were going up everywhere in Bayberry—everywhere, that is, but on their lot. When my father complained about the lack of progress, the developer gave him one excuse after another, none of which made much sense. More than a little suspicious, he asked a friend who was in the construction business to look into the situation. He found our property was at the spot in the first tier of lots through which the developer was moving his materials and workers to the second tier. Our house would eventually be built, but not until all the others were done. When the developer admitted as much, my father took back his down payment. A few years later my parents did move—but to another apartment in the Bronx, not to a house in suburbia; and in time they returned to Manhattan, first as tenants and then as owners of a cooperative apartment. Although I did not know it at the time, Bayberry would be as close to living in suburbia as I ever came. After spending four years in dormitories at Columbia College and five in Cambridge apartments and Harvard's Winthrop House, I returned to New York, where I taught at Columbia for four years and rented an apartment in a townhouse on the Upper East Side. When I went to MIT in 1968, I moved into an apartment house on the fringe of one of Cambridge's suburban neighborhoods. I still live there. I have also spent the past thirty summers on a farm in a part of Martha's Vineyard that has thus far pretty much withstood the pressures of suburbanization.

Although I have never lived in suburbia, I have spent a good deal of time there. I have visited my brothers, both of whom live in the suburbs—one in Scarsdale, the other in Hermosa Beach, a suburb of Los Angeles. Most of my relatives also live in the suburbs, as do many of my friends and colleagues. I have gone to suburban restaurants, movie theaters, and shopping centers. I have read about the suburbs in novels and short stories and seen them portrayed in movies and on television. As a historian of urban America, I have also taught about suburbia, its past and present, its politics, society, and culture. And though I cannot claim to have succeeded, I have tried to keep up with the vast outpouring of books, articles, and theses about the history of suburbia: about the history of suburbs in general, of which the best known are Kenneth T. Jackson's *Crabgrass Frontier,* John R. Stilgoe's *Borderlands,* and Robert Fishman's *Bourgeois Utopias,* the inspiration for the title of this book; about the history of types of suburbs, including the streetcar suburbs of Boston, the lakeshore suburbs of Chicago, and the working-class suburbs of Los Angeles; about the history of individual suburbs, of Baltimore's Roland Park, Houston's River Oaks, and Kansas City's Country Club District; and about the history of suburbia and mass transit, suburbia and city planning, suburbia and domestic architecture.

The literature is so vast that it is easy to forget that almost all of it has appeared in the past forty-five years. Indeed, it is so vast that historians have already begun writing articles about the historiography of suburbia, the history of its history. This literature is also very rich, so rich that historians now know more about suburbia than about any other part of the American metropolis. We know about the origins of the suburbs in the early and mid nineteenth century and about their growth in the late nineteenth and early twentieth. We know about the subdividers, the businessmen who transformed rural acreage into suburban lots, and their customers, the families that bought the lots and built houses on them. We know how fears of disease, crime, immorality, poverty, immigration, and public disorder drove many Americans from the center of the city to the periphery. And we know how railroads and streetcars and later els, subways, and highways facilitated their exodus. We have learned why subdividers gave way after World War II to developers like William J. Levitt, who not only laid out the lots but also put up the houses. We have also learned how the developers, with the help of financial institutions, real estate associations, local zoning boards, and federal housing agencies, built the modern metropolis in which most people now live, work, shop, and amuse themselves on the periphery.

As good as this literature is, it has missed something central not only to the history of suburbia but also to the history of American society. It has overlooked what are known as restrictive covenants, or deed restrictions. Legal devices that were widely used in real estate transactions, contracts that bound the seller and buyer (and, until the restrictions expired, subsequent sellers and buyers), these covenants did more than bar the owners from selling and leasing their property to non-Caucasians. They also imposed a host of highly onerous restrictions on how the owners could use their property. I first came across these restrictions roughly forty years ago while doing research for a book about Los Angeles. I found that during the late nineteenth and early twentieth centuries it was common for subdividers to impose restrictive covenants on suburban tracts, especially upper-middle-class tracts, and even to use the restrictions as a marketing tool. If real estate was, next to poker, the "great American game," as Thorstein Veblen once wrote, why, I wondered, were Americans willing to play by such stringent rules? This question, I later realized, led to other questions, the answers to which tell us much about the history of suburbia and the society of which it was an integral part.

Of the many Los Angeles suburbs, none raised these questions more sharply than Palos Verdes Estates. A subdivision whose restrictions ran thirty pages, it covered thirty-two hundred acres of the Palos Verdes Peninsula, a spectacular site standing high above the Pacific Ocean at the southwestern edge of the metropolis. The modern history of the peninsula began in 1913, when a syndicate of eastern financiers and railroad executives bought most of what had once been El Rancho de Los Palos Verdes from George Bixby for $1.5 million. The ranch had been carved out of El Rancho San Pedro—one of the immense ranches into which the Spaniards had divided much of southern California—in 1846; in 1882 it was partitioned into seventeen parcels, the largest of which, the Palos Verdes Peninsula, was awarded to Jotham Bixby, from whom his son George inherited it in 1894. Leading the syndicate was Frank A. Vanderlip, whose career reads like a Horatio Alger story. The son of a midwestern farmer whose death forced the sale of the family homestead, Vanderlip worked as a lathe operator and, after a year of college and a job as a financial analyst, turned to journalism. He spent a few years as a reporter and editor and then as private secretary to Lyman Gage, a Chicago banker who had been appointed secretary of the Treasury. Following a stint as assistant secretary, Vanderlip joined the National City Bank of New York, one of the country's largest, as vice president; eight years later he was named president. For what was small change to Vanderlip and his associates, all of whom were millionaires, the syndicate acquired a huge parcel about twenty miles from downtown Los Angeles. Covering sixteen thousand acres, or twenty-five square miles, it was more than half the size of San Francisco, the largest city on the Pacific Coast, and slightly larger than Manhattan, where Vanderlip and many of the other investors worked.[1]

Hard as it is to believe, Vanderlip bought the Palos Verdes Peninsula, in his words, "sight unseen"—although he did send two of "his trusted younger men" to look at it beforehand, his son later recalled. He may have thought that the deal was too good to pass on, that at less than a hundred dollars an acre the property "certainly could be sold for more." But not long after, he was overcome by "an unusual lassitude and an occasional dizziness" that kept him in bed for a month. When he recovered, he followed his doctor's advice to take a break from the bank and went to California to visit Palos Verdes. What he saw bowled him over. Palos Verdes, he wrote, was like a "beautiful empire," with "miles of seacoast," "gleaming crescent beaches," "picturesque rolling hills and occasionally more picturesque canyons." It reminded him of "the Sorrentine Peninsula and the Amalfi Drive." But Palos Verdes had no whitewashed houses and medieval churches, only herds of sheep and cattle, fields of grain, and rows of peas, beans, and tomatoes, cultivated by Japanese-American truck farmers. All this was "here in America," Vanderlip wrote, "an unspoiled sheet of paper to be written on with loving care." To help figure out what to write on it, to make sure that it would not be spoiled "by greedy real estate operations and crowded architectural horrors," as much of the Los Angeles coast had been, he called on Olmsted Brothers, a firm of planners, designers, and landscape architects in Brookline, Massachusetts.[2]

Olmsted Brothers was the foremost firm of its kind in the country. Its principals were John Charles Olmsted and Frederick Law Olmsted, Jr., the stepson and son, respectively, of the late Frederick Law Olmsted, the dean of American landscape architects. As well as being the designer, with Calvert Vaux, of Central Park, Olmsted, Sr., was the founder of the New York firm that moved to Brookline in 1884 and changed its name to Olmsted Brothers in 1898. Although best known for its design of parks, parkways, private estates, and public institutions, the firm was well regarded for its work on several of the country's most admired suburban subdivisions. It was this work that brought the firm to Vanderlip's attention. A year or so before he bought Palos Verdes, Vanderlip had hired the Olmsteds to lay out the grounds for an eighteen-acre subdivision adjacent to Beechwood, his large country estate in Scarborough-on-the-Hudson, a small village in northern Westchester County. Although the Olmsteds had never worked on a subdivision as large as Palos Verdes—indeed, there had never been a subdivision as large to work on—Vanderlip turned to them again. Before long they came up with a plan for what the *Boston Evening Transcript* called "the country's most fashionable and exclusive residence colony," designed for a select group of the country's richest people. A California version of Tuxedo Park—a residential retreat for wealthy New Yorkers that had been developed by Pierre Lorillard IV, heir to a great tobacco fortune, in the mid-1880s—the plan featured large estates for the fortunate few (as well as a country club, golf clubs, yacht club, tennis courts, swimming pools, and polo grounds) and three "model villages," wrote the *Transcript*, to house the mechanics, gardeners, and laborers who worked for them.[3]

Work got under way in 1914. Under Olmsted Brothers' supervision, Koebig & Koebig, a Los Angeles engineering firm, made an extensive survey of the property. Plans were also drawn for more than one hundred miles of roads and a fourteen-mile highway along the bluffs. And architects Howard Shaw of Chicago and Myron Hunt of Los Angeles did the preliminary drawings for a magnificent clubhouse. But work came to a halt when war broke out in Europe. It started again in 1916, only to be put on hold a year later when the United States entered the war and the project's leaders joined the war effort. Taking leave from the bank, Vanderlip went to Washington, D.C., where, as one of the many "Dollar-a-Year" men, he chaired the Treasury Department's War Savings Committee. Frederick Law Olmsted served as a member of the Commission on Emergency Construction of the War Industries Board and as the manager of the Town Planning Division of the United States Housing Corporation, which had been set up to build low-cost housing for defense workers. His brother John, who had been in charge of the firm's work in Palos Verdes, was not involved in the war effort because he was seriously ill— and, it turned out, had only a few years to live.[4] By the time the war was over, it was clear that the original plan was deeply flawed. For all the many virtues of Palos Verdes—its spectacular scenery, breathtaking views, and balmy climate—it was too far from the East Coast. Few New Yorkers or Bostonians who could afford a second (or third) home were going to take a three-day train ride to Palos Verdes when in a matter of hours (or at most a day) they could travel to Bar Harbor, Cape Cod, Newport, the Hamptons, and other fashionable resorts.

Vanderlip returned to the bank after the war, but he resigned in 1919. Although he now had time to devote to Palos Verdes, he lost interest in developing it himself. And in August 1921, at the beginning of the greatest real estate boom in southern California history, he gave E. G. Lewis an option to buy the property for $5 million, just over $300 an acre. Lewis was one of the many colorful characters who dazzled Americans during the Gilded Age. The son, grandson, and great-grandson of Episcopalian clergymen, he was an amalgam of visionary and con man. Above all, he was a salesman, who started out peddling mosquito repellents and patent medicines and went on to make and lose fortunes as a publisher and a real estate developer. He spent much of his life one step ahead of his creditors, who forced him into bankruptcy twice, and two steps ahead of postal officials, who finally caught up with him in the late 1920s, when he was convicted of mail fraud and sentenced to five years in federal prison. Why Vanderlip, a hard-headed banker and businessman, gave an option to Lewis—a man, wrote one journalist a few years later, who had "a twenty-year record of broken promises and unfulfilled pledges"—is hard to say. Perhaps he was impressed by Lewis's accomplishments as the developer of University City, St. Louis, and Atascadero, California. Or perhaps he was taken in by what the same journalist described as Lewis's "unshakable optimism," "his contagious self-confidence," and "[his] natural aptitude for the kind of sleight-of-hand performance which before the eyes of a spellbound crowd produces a towering pyramid resting on its apex."[5]

Lewis had a vision for Palos Verdes. It would be "the Riviera [sic] of the Pacific coast"—"a great Acropolis, the most beautiful residential city in the world, overshadowing the greatest metropolis in all the world," he told a crowd of investors and potential investors, to whom he promised dividends of 700 to 1,500 percent within three or four years. To help create this "New City," he assembled a team of engineers, lawyers, planners, and landscape architects, probably the most influential of whom were Frederick Law Olmsted, Jr., and Charles H. Cheney, a prominent

California planner who was a strong advocate of restrictive covenants. Lewis had experts galore. What he did not have was money. He did not have the $5 million to pay for the land, much less an estimated $30 million to make the streets, parks, sewers, utilities, and other improvements. Hence he formed a trust, which issued notes, some of which, known as convertible notes, could later be exchanged for property in Palos Verdes. In effect, Lewis was selling land in order to raise the money to buy and improve it. Exploiting his knack as a salesman (and the boom in the real estate market), he raised a great deal of money, perhaps as much as $15 million, but not enough under the terms of the trust. In February 1923 the trustee, Title Insurance and Trust Company, pulled out of the project and offered the investors their money back. Vanderlip and his associates, to whom the property reverted, then set up another trust, which managed to salvage $1 million from what was left of the capital. With the money, the new trust bought thirty-two hundred acres from the syndicate, one-fifth of its holdings, and named it Palos Verdes Estates.[6]

Before he was forced to step down, Lewis made considerable progress. Following the Olmsted Brothers plan, his staff built roads and sewers, installed water mains and other utilities, laid out parks and a golf course, and planted trees and shrubs. They also subdivided the land and priced the lots. Under the leadership of Jay Lawyer, who replaced Lewis as general manager of the project, the new owners picked up where Lewis left off. They also launched a major advertising campaign and, though Palos Verdes Estates was far from finished, opened it to the public in June 1923. Even by southern California standards, the opening was stupendous. Indeed, said one newspaper, it was "without parallel in the history of real estate projects on the Pacific Coast." More than thirty thousand people came. Some drove; others took the Pacific Electric railway to Redondo Beach and from there a motor coach to Palos Verdes. Most wanted to find out what the fuss was all about and enjoy a free outing on a pleasant summer day. After Boy Scouts raised the flag and veterans of the Grand Army of the Republic fired a salute, the festivities got under way. Highlighted by concerts, aerial stunts, aquaplaning demonstrations, novelty races, a baseball game, a yacht race, a tug-of-war, and day-long dancing, the opening was a veritable "three-ring circus," said the *Los Angeles Express*. Along with Jay Lawyer and Henry Clarke, the director of sales, more than a hundred employees were on hand to greet the visitors and, if asked, to show them the site. For perhaps the only time in the history of Palos Verdes Estates, no effort was made to sell anything. "Business was laid aside," observed the *Los Angeles Times*, "and the day was given over to pleasure and study."[7]

For all the inflated rhetoric, Palos Verdes Estates was not a "New City." Indeed, it was not a city at all. It was a suburb, a suburb designed "predominantly for fairly prosperous people wanting detached houses and a garden setting but unwilling to burden themselves with the care of extensive grounds," wrote Olmsted, Jr. It was "a model residential suburb," said Cheney, and "the largest single piece of city planning by private enterprise ever undertaken in this country for permanent development." In accord with principles formulated long ago by Olmsted, Sr., the streets were laid out to fit into the contour of the hilly site, with the lots arranged to preserve the expansive views. Through traffic was concentrated on a few wide streets, Olmsted, Jr., wrote, "leaving the great majority of local residence streets indirect, comparatively free from traffic, quiet and safe for children." Hundreds of acres were reserved for parks, playgrounds, bridle trails, and a golf course. Also set aside were several miles of seashore. Palos Verdes was a place not only "to invest, but to *live*," read one of its ads. As one of the promotional brochures put it: "Palos Verdes is typical of that proverbial suburban community of which the city dweller often dreams but seldom sees; uncommon in its abundance of natural beauty, restful in its quiet peace, and warm in its spirit of easy friendliness and charm. A community, compact and secluded[,] which has succeeded in shutting out all din and confusion of modern metropolitan life."[8] As well as any suburb in the country, Palos Verdes Estates embodied the vision of the "bourgeois utopia" so brilliantly described by historian Robert Fishman.

Through newspaper ads and promotional brochures, Lawyer and his associates hammered away at the point that Palos Verdes Estates stood, in Olmsted's words, *"head and shoulders"* above any other residential community. They pointed to its natural beauty, especially its unspoiled coastline and rolling hills, its open spaces, its recreational facilities, and its unsurpassed climate, warm in winter, cool in summer, sunny and dry almost all year round. Also highlighted were its extensive improvements—an abundant water supply, a system of roads on which traffic would flow freely and pedestrians move safely, and a subdivision plan that provided ocean views for most lots. Although it was anything but, Palos Verdes, claimed its promoters, was conveniently located, forty minutes from downtown Los Angles, thirty-five from Wilshire Boulevard, one of the city's main outlying shopping districts; and with a handful of fine shops and stores within Palos Verdes it was not even necessary to leave the peninsula for everyday goods and services. Palos Verdes was a splendid place to raise a family, read the ads. It had—or would soon have—good schools, churches, and clubs. Growing up in Palos Verdes, "your little girl may skate along the sidewalk, safely ride her bicycle or play a game of old fashioned 'hopscotch,'" and "that lad of yours" will be spared the memory of "emotional sex movies, concrete backyards, lawns not made for summersaults and streets that are danger lanes of traffic." Lots were not cheap, but prices "are far below what you may expect," said another ad. And property values were bound to go up.[9]

The ads and brochures portrayed Palos Verdes as a world of beautiful houses overlooking the ocean, sturdy boys playing pirates on the beach, a well-dressed girl riding her pony, a man returning home from a round of golf, greeted by his children, one on each arm, and his wife, picking flowers from the garden. But without meaning to, the ads and brochures revealed that this Pacific paradise had a dark side as well. Nowhere was this side more clearly revealed than in the repeated assurances that its residents would be protected, in the words of Olmsted, Jr., against "encroachment by any possible developments of an adverse sort," especially developments that jeopardized the "stability and permanence" of the community. They would be protected against "undesirable neighbors." Against "oil derricks, tank farms, lumber yards, warehouses," and other industrial enterprises. Against commercial garages, funeral parlors, and other objectionable businesses that had blighted many once fashionable neighborhoods. Against apartment houses and single-family houses built on top of one another. Even against "unsightly structures," including "the inartistic, the injurious in design." The residents would be protected not only by the natural setting and topography, by the ocean on three sides and the hills on the fourth, but also by what Olmsted Brothers called an "unusually complete, inclusive and elaborate" set of restrictive covenants. "Permanent protective restrictions, officially recorded, cover every foot of the entire City," read one of the ads.[10]

There was never much doubt that some restrictions would be imposed on Palos Verdes whether it was developed as an exclusive colony for the very wealthy or as a garden suburb for the moderately well-to-do. Vanderlip, whose subdivision in Scarborough-on-the-Hudson was highly restricted, was very much in favor of them. So were the Olmsted brothers, who had drafted the restrictions not only for Vanderlip's small subdivision but also for several much larger subdivisions all over the country. Lewis was convinced that restrictions would enhance the desirability of Palos Verdes as a residential community, as was Cheney, who took a large hand in drafting the restrictions for the Palos Verdes project. H. T. Cory, the project's chief engineer, and Frank James, its general counsel, had reservations, but in time they came around— or went along. Drawing heavily on restrictions imposed on other upper-middle-class subdivisions, some of which had been drafted by Olmsted Brothers, Lewis's team eventually came up with a long list of its own, a list, said the Olmsted firm, that had "run the gauntlet of legal criticism by a number of able attorneys." The restrictions were written into the contract between Lewis and the Title Insurance and Trust Company in 1921. And a year or two later the Commonwealth Trust Company, acting on behalf of the new owners, filed substantially the same restrictions, the Palos Verdes Estates Protective Restrictions, in the Los Angeles County courthouse.[11]

Imposed on every lot, incorporated into every deed, forming part of the contract between buyer and seller and as binding legally as any other part, the restrictions severely limited what the owners could do with their property. What were called, most likely by Cheney, "the usual restrictions" forbade an owner to sell or rent a lot or house to anyone "not of the white or Caucasian race." Except in the case of chauffeurs, gardeners, or domestic servants who lived on the same premises as their employers, an owner was even forbidden to permit an African- or Asian-American to use or occupy the property. Far from being thought repugnant, these restrictions were central to Lewis's vision that Palos Verdes would bring together "the cream of the manhood and womanhood of the greatest nation that has ever lived, the greatest race that has ever lived, the Caucasian race and the American nation." Although desperately short of capital, Lewis was so wedded to this vision that he would not even allow non-Caucasians to invest in the Palos Verdes project. Other restrictions barred the owners from using their property for a wide range of activities, some of which were nuisances and others which, if not nuisances, were considered objectionable in residential communities. Among them were slaughterhouses, oil refineries, iron foundries, and coal yards, reform schools, mental asylums, sanitariums, and cemeteries, and saloons and places for the manufacture of "malt, vinous or spirituous liquors." (It is interesting to note that at a time when the Los Angeles Chamber of Commerce was working hard to persuade eastern manufacturers to set up branch factories in southern California, Palos Verdes Estates barred any trade or business "obnoxious or offensive by reason of the emission of odor, smoke, gas, dust or noise"—indeed "any noxious trade or business" whatsoever.)[12]

Even an owner who had no intention of using the property for a coal yard or a mental asylum, much less to sell or rent it to an

African- or Asian-American, was subject to a host of other restrictions. Suppose he or she wanted to build a single-family house—the only type of house permitted on more than 90 percent of the lots. The restrictions spelled out where on the lot it could stand, how much of the lot it could cover, and how high above the ground it could rise. They even specified how much it had to cost. This cost, which included architect's fees and builder's profits, but not garages or other outbuildings, varied according to the lot, the view, and the neighborhood and ranged from moderately to extremely expensive. But as Lewis pointed out, an expensive house was not necessarily a well-designed house. Hence he included in the restrictions a provision about which Jay Lawyer was initially skeptical. Prior to construction, every owner had to submit the plans to the Palos Verdes Art Jury, without whose approval nothing could be built. The jury, whose members included Myron Hunt and other prominent architects, required not only that the design be "reasonably good" but that in most cases it conform to what was known as "California architecture"—a distinctive type of architecture that derived "its chief inspiration directly or indirectly from Latin types, which developed under similar climatic conditions along the Mediterranean." Whether the design was approved depended on such things as the color (generally "light in tone"), the materials (as a rule plaster, stucco, concrete, or "an approved artificial stone"), and even the pitch of the roof—"preferably not steeper than thirty (30) degrees and never to exceed thirty-five (35)."[13]

If the Art Jury gave its approval, the owners could begin building, though they could not use any "old or second hand material"; nor could the buyers or anyone else occupy the house or any part of it until construction was finished. Even after a family moved in, they were subject to still more restrictions. Suppose they wanted fresh eggs for breakfast or believed it would be instructive and enjoyable for their children to tend to a handful of domestic animals. They were out of luck. The restrictions banned not only cows and hogs but even chickens and rabbits. Suppose a homeowner thought a sturdy wooden fence would give the family more privacy or keep the neighbor's dog off the lawn and out of the flower garden. Under the restrictions a fence could not be erected without permission from the Palos Verdes Homes Association, the community's governing body, and approval by the Palos Verdes Art Jury. And all fences (as well as hedges, walls, and poles) were limited to "a reasonable height." Or suppose a homeowner wanted to take down, cut back, or just trim a tree that was obstructing the view of the ocean. If it was more than twenty feet tall, permission from the Homes Association was needed. (If a tree was so tall that it blocked a neighbor's view, the Association could cut it back against the owner's wishes.) And suppose the owner decided to move and put the house on the market, a routine decision for residents of greater Los Angeles. Under the Palos Verdes restrictions the seller could not even post a "For Sale" sign on the property.[14]

For an owner who viewed property in Palos Verdes more as an investment than as a homesite, the restrictions were even more onerous. Suppose the owner wanted to capitalize on the growing demand for housing in Los Angeles by erecting multifamily units on the lot. It was out of the question. The restrictions barred two-family houses and apartment buildings of any kind outside the few districts that served as buffers between the small business centers and the surrounding single-family communities. The same was true for an owner who hoped to take advantage of the growing demand for shops and stores, which were barred outside the business centers. Palos Verdes Estates might have been a good investment for someone who was happy with a gradual increase in property values, but not for someone looking for a windfall spurred by changes in land use. The restrictions also prevented owners from generating income from their property. At a time when the outdoor advertising industry was booming, many companies were ready to pay good money to rent space for billboards on well-located lots. But the restrictions banned billboards. Even signs for the few shops and stores needed the approval of the Art Jury. At a time when oil companies were making one spectacular strike after another in the Los Angeles basin, some not far from Palos Verdes, their representatives were offering landowners handsome royalties in return for mineral rights. But the restrictions banned drilling for oil and natural gas too.[15]

The Palos Verdes Estates Protective Restrictions were not a gimmick. Rather they were guidelines, designed to regulate the development of the community in the decades ahead. To be effective, they had to be enforced in a conscientious way. So long as the trustee owned most of the property, it could be counted on to do so, but once most of the lots were sold, it would no longer have much of a stake in the community. Anticipating this problem, Lewis and his associates created the Palos Verdes Homes Association, a nonprofit organization that was run by a five-member board elected by the property owners. Among its many tasks, which included managing the waterworks and maintaining the grounds, it was authorized to enforce the restrictions. To abate a violation, it was empowered to enter the premises, even over the owner's objection, and, if need be, to apply for an injunction. To be effective, the restrictions also had to be imposed for a long time. But Lewis and his associates were afraid that if extended in perpetuity they would not survive a legal challenge. So they came up with what they thought was the next best arrangement. The restrictions would remain in force until 1960, or for thirty-seven years. Then they would be automatically renewed for successive twenty-year periods unless the owners of more than one-half of the property, exclusive of streets, parks, and other public lands, agreed in writing to abolish or modify them.[16] In spirit, if not in law, the restrictions extended more or less in perpetuity.

Palos Verdes Estates was not a utopian community. It had little in common with the many cooperative and communitarian settlements that had sprung up in California in the late nineteenth century. Indeed, it had as little in common with these settlements as Shaker Heights had with the Shaker colony that had once occupied the site on which the Van Sweringen brothers, Oris T. and Mantis J., later developed Cleveland's most fashionable suburb. Nor was Palos Verdes Estates a philanthropic or quasi-philanthropic enterprise—akin, say, to the Russell Sage Foundation's Forest Hills Gardens, a middle-class subdivision in Queens, one of New York City's outer boroughs, or the City and Suburban Homes Company's York Avenue Estate, a dozen model tenements on Manhattan's Upper East Side. For all the rhetoric of "a great Acropolis" and "the New City," Palos Verdes Estates was a real estate subdivision, albeit an exceptionally large, well-planned, and high-priced one. For Vanderlip and Lewis, it was a commercial venture. Although intent on doing as good a job as possible, Olmsted and Cheney saw it much the same way. So did the investors, many of whom were assured that nonconvertible notes in the Palos Verdes project were "an investment without parallel in the history of land development."[17] To succeed, Lewis and his successors did what other subdividers before them had done. They spent a lot of money, preferably other people's money, to buy, improve, and subdivide the land and then put the lots on the market, hoping that the sales would generate enough revenue to recover the capital and yield a substantial profit.

If Palos Verdes Estates had to sell lots—and to sell them before property taxes and other carrying charges depleted the remaining capital and threatened the solvency of the entire enterprise—why did Vanderlip, Lewis, and their associates impose so many restrictions on how prospective purchasers could use their property (and, to a lesser degree, dispose of it)? Also, why did they impose some restrictions that were so drastic that Frank James told Lewis that he "wouldn't live in such a place"? And why did they impose these restrictions at a time when the residential real estate market in Los Angeles was so fiercely competitive—a time when more than one hundred new subdivisions were opening every month, many of which were more conveniently located than Palos Verdes, some of which had sites almost as spectacular? If the restrictions were so far-reaching and, in some instances, so burdensome, why did the hard-headed businessmen in charge of Palos Verdes Estates publicize and even celebrate them? Why did the newspaper ads stress that Palos Verdes Estates was more highly restricted than other residential communities? Why did Lawyer and Clarke use "rigid restrictions" as a marketing tool, as valuable a one as the splendid setting, superb design, and expensive improvements? In other words, why did the developers assume the restrictions would make Palos Verdes Estates more appealing to prospective purchasers?[18]

Assuming the developers knew what they were doing, this

question raises many others. Like most Americans, the residents of Los Angeles strongly believed in the sanctity of private property—which, wrote the New Jersey Supreme Court in 1923, was "the keystone of the arch of civilization." Although they went along with a rudimentary zoning law in 1908 and a more sophisticated one thirteen years later, why would they choose to move into a subdivision that limited in so many ways their "natural right" to use and dispose of their property as they saw fit? These people also lived in a city where, one journalist wrote, real estate speculation "permeates all walks of life"; as a character in *The Boosters*, a novel about Los Angeles in the 1920s, observes, "no matter what a man's business, he is almost certain to dabble in real estate on the side." Why would such people submit to so many constraints on their wheeling and dealing? What makes these questions so perplexing is that Palos Verdes Estates was designed for the well-to-do. The price of the lots, plus the minimum cost of the houses, put it far beyond the reach of everyone else. Moreover, it was designed for homeowners, not for tenants, who, as a rule, had to put up with many onerous restrictions on how they used someone else's property. They either took the premises on the landlord's terms or did not take it at all. Why would those residents of Los Angeles who could afford to live virtually anywhere in the metropolitan area—and who, in all likelihood, subscribed to the popular view that a man's home was *"His Castle"*—buy and build in so highly restricted a subdivision as Palos Verdes Estates?[19]

If restrictive covenants were found nowhere in Los Angeles but in Palos Verdes—if they were a product of, say, the size of the subdivision or the influence of the Olmsteds—they would be only moderately intriguing. But this was not the case. At about the same time Palos Verdes was opened, scores of other restricted subdivisions came on the market all over greater Los Angeles. Bel-Air, "the Suburb Supreme," high up in the hills above west Los Angeles, was "highly restricted." So was Hancock Park, a subdivision off Wilshire Boulevard that was so exclusive it did not mention the price of the lots in its ads. (As J. P. Morgan supposedly said when asked about the cost of his yacht, "if you have to ask you can't afford it.") Beverly Crest, another hillside subdivision, boasted of "rigid restrictions," as did Flintridge Highlands, which was in the San Gabriel Valley. Santa Monica's Canyon Vista Park stressed its "high grade restrictions," nearby Boulevard Terrace its "high-class restrictions." West Van Nuys, a San Fernando Valley subdivision, took pride in its "Wise Restrictions." So did Silver Lake Terrace, which was located between Los Angeles and Pasadena. Other subdivisions had "carefully worked-out restrictions," "desirable restrictions," "sensible restrictions," and "adequate restrictions." Still others had "strict race restrictions and moderate building restrictions," or building restrictions that were "high enough to prevent poor surroundings, still not too high for a modest home." By the early 1920s, if not earlier, so many subdivisions were restricted in one way or another that some property owners thought it necessary to mention it in ads when they had unrestricted lots for sale.[20]

Restrictive covenants would also be only moderately intriguing if they were found nowhere in the United States but in Los Angeles, a city with a well-deserved reputation for outlandish fads of all kinds. But again this was not the case. By the time Palos Verdes Estates was opened, hundreds of restricted subdivisions had gone on the market all over the country. The Olmsteds worked on dozens of them, the best known of which were Guilford, Maryland, Forest Hills Gardens, Great Neck Hills, in New York's Nassau County, and Colony Hills, in Springfield, Massachusetts. Cheney, Cory, and Elvon Musick, counsel to the Title Insurance and Trust Company, visited what Cory called "high class [meaning highly restricted] developments" in a dozen cities, among them Baltimore's Roland Park and Kansas City's Country Club District. It was this trip, Cory told a group of prospective investors, that dispelled his and Musick's doubts about the value of tough restrictions. Indeed, in drafting the Palos Verdes Protective Restrictions, Cheney drew heavily on the experience of Roland Park, Forest Hills Gardens, the Country Club District, and St. Francis Wood in San Francisco. Like Palos Verdes Estates, these subdivisions used restrictions as a marketing tool, stressing that they were "rigid," "thorough," and "wise" and, in the case of Chatham Crescent, Savannah's "finest resident section," promising that "they will be rigidly enforced." To make sure everyone got the point, J. C. Nichols included at the top of most ads for his Country Club District the phrase "1000 Acres Restricted," a phrase that was copied by River Oaks, Houston's most exclusive subdivision.[21]

A nationwide phenomenon, restrictive covenants were found not only in much-heralded subdivisions designed for the well-to-do. They were also found, albeit not as often, in little-known tracts intended for the less affluent—even, in some cases, for workingmen and their families. They were found, too, in cooperative apartment houses built for the very rich in New York and a few other cities in the early twentieth century (and sometimes in the exclusive watering spots where they spent their summers).[22] But these covenants reveal more about the suburbs, where by the 1920s they were the rule, than about the cities, where they were the exception. They tell us much not only about the dreams of suburbanites, which have been vividly described by many other historians, but about their nightmares; not only about their hopes but about their fears. About their fear of others, of racial minorities and poor people, once known as "the dangerous classes," and their fear of people like themselves. About their fear of change and their fear of the market, of which they were among the chief beneficiaries. The restrictions reveal that suburbia reflected, in Fishman's words, more than "the alienation of the middle classes from the urban-industrial world they themselves were creating."[23] It also reflected a host of deep-seated fears that permeated much of American society in the late nineteenth and early twentieth centuries. Better than anything else, these restrictions illuminated the dark side of the "bourgeois utopia."

one

Suburbia, 1870–1930:
The Quest for Permanence

The Problem of Unwanted Change

Frederick Law Olmsted, Sr., had nothing to do with the planning of Palos Verdes Estates—and in all likelihood he never even saw the Palos Verdes Peninsula.[1] By the time Vanderlip and his associates bought the property from Bixby and hired Olmsted Brothers to help subdivide it, Olmsted had been dead for more than a decade. But had he lived long enough, he would probably have approved of how his sons designed Palos Verdes Estates— how, in line with principles he had formulated, they enhanced the natural beauty by reserving hundreds of acres for parks and open spaces, how they preserved the breathtaking views by laying out the streets and lots to fit into the contour of the hilly terrain, and how they rendered the streets quiet and safe by funneling traffic into a few wide thoroughfares. He would also have approved of how the Olmsteds and Cheney restricted Palos Verdes Estates—how, in an attempt to ensure its *"stability* and *permanence,"* they imposed a set of sweeping and stringent restrictions on what the owners could do with their property. For much like the restrictions in other upper-middle-class subdivisions in the late nineteenth and early twentieth centuries, the Palos Verdes Estates Protective Restrictions were designed to solve a problem that Olmsted had noticed as early as the 1860s and 1870s, a problem that raised strong doubts about the future of suburbs in the United States. Although Olmsted was not the only American who was aware of this problem, no one else spelled it out so vividly and perceptively.

As a designer, consultant, and writer, Olmsted devoted much of his prodigious energy to trying to ameliorate some of the worst features of America's cities. But by the 1860s he began to doubt that it was possible to build in these cities "a convenient and tasteful" house "adapted to the civilized requirements of a single family, except at a cost which even rich men find prohibitive." Given the natural tendency of people to "flock together" in cities, a return to the country was out of the question. So was an exodus to "the sterile parts of the great West." But a move to the suburbs was not. For most Americans, Olmsted argued, the suburbs offered the benefits of city life without the congestion, tumult, noise, crime, and vice, and the pleasures of country life without the inconvenience, isolation, and lack of amenities. As he wrote to Edward Everett Hale, a Boston clergyman best known today as the author of "The Man Without a Country," the suburbs provided "elbow room about a house without going into the country, without sacrifice of butchers, bakers, & theatres." In a society racked by class conflict, "a suburban yeomanry," in the words of two Olmsted scholars, also served as a much-needed balance wheel. Well-planned and well-designed suburbs, Olmsted wrote in the late 1860s, were "the most attractive, the most refined and the most soundly wholesome forms of domestic life."[2]

But as Olmsted pointed out, few suburbs were well planned and well designed, much less "attractive," "refined," and "soundly wholesome." With the subdividers driven by short-term pecuniary goals, most suburbs were built "little by little, without any general plan"; and where the subdivisions were laid out in a methodical way, "no intelligent design has been pursued to secure any distinctly rural attractiveness." The result, Olmsted observed, was that most suburbs were "as yet little better than rude overdressed villages, or fragmentary half-made towns." More often than not, the roads were "untidy, shabby, uninviting, and completely contradictory to the ideal which most townspeople have in view when they seek to find a pleasant site for a suburban home"—a site at once sylvan and picturesque. Sometimes the lots were "in themselves attractive," Olmsted conceded. But all too often they were located next to "rough clearings in old wood land with blocks of gaunt trees left standing; patches of waste land and ill kept fields[,] raw banks by the side of the road, puddles and swamps[,] roadside taverns and beer gardens[,] shanties, dilapidated stables or small groups of buildings such as are to be looked for in the most repulsive outskirts of cities with cinders and garbage strewn before them New York fashion." Even worse, some suburbs were "malarious or otherwise unhealthy." No wonder, Olmsted wrote in the mid-1880s, there was little demand for suburban lots near New York City and many of them "can be bought at half their original cost."[3]

Even more disturbing than the sorry state of what Olmsted called "catch-penny speculations" was the rapid deterioration of once fashionable suburbs. As he wrote in the early 1870s, "Numerous suburbs of New York, which a few years ago were distinguished for their rural beauty and refined society, have thus, through the gradual development of various uncongenial elements, entirely lost their former character." What were once "charming villas and cottages" have been sold "at less than half their cost" and turned into "boarding and tenement houses." These suburbs were "laid waste almost as by an invading army." To Olmsted, it was plain that the success of suburbia led to its undoing. Attracted to a new subdivision by the expansive views and wooded grounds, a few families bought lots and then built houses and made other improvements, which detracted from the natural setting. For a while the suburb retained many of the qualities that first drew people to it. But before long other families moved in. Through "ignorance, incompetence, bad taste, or knavery," Olmsted wrote, the newcomers destroyed "just those circumstances of the locality which have really constituted the chief parts of its value to cultivated townspeople." Far from happy with the changes, some owners lost interest in their property or found other uses for it. "Rural buildings and fences are allowed to fall into decay, woods and orchards to be cut down, shops, brick-yards, breweries, factories to be brought in, and a poor semblance of the scattering outskirts of a large town to overgrow what had been a beautiful countryside."[4]

Olmsted had observed this deterioration on a tract of about a thousand to fifteen hundred acres on Staten Island, where he had worked on and off as a gentleman farmer in the late 1840s and early 1850s. A tract that was once "the most attractive of any on the island, or even perhaps of any on this side of the Atlantic," it had been covered by farms and villages, whose residents lived in cozy cottages alongside pretty roads, "winding among the great trees, crossing clear brooks and skirting the clean meadows." Then a wharf was built, and a ferry began running between the island and the city. New roads were constructed, and old farms were di-vided into suburban lots, "inviting to a good class of residents." But no provision was made for proper drainage, and no care was given to protecting the natural setting. Soon the growing suburb attracted not only the well-to-do but also servants, laborers, and what would now be called day-trippers. To tap the new market, one businessman opened a beer garden; others set up shops and stables and built small dwellings, "to make room for which fine trees were often felled." "At length," Olmsted wrote, "two or three factories were established in the neighborhood, increasing the de-mand for small lots for lodging houses, stores, and dram shops" and making the place less attractive for single-family houses. Polluted by household wastes and left stagnant by road construction, the once sparkling brooks became "disgusting and dangerous." The once beautiful woodlands, cleared by builders (and then stripped by the poor for fuel), were replaced by "bare, unsightly wastes" and "pestiferous swamps." To Olmsted, it was extremely troubling that "a suburban district of great beauty" that was easily accessible to the city could deteriorate so rapidly.[5]

Things were just as bad in the cities, where rapid deterioration was spreading over many once attractive residential communities. Five years earlier, Olmsted wrote in the early 1860s, New York's Washington Heights was a neighborhood of "nothing but elegance & fashion." Now it showed "the unmistakable signs of the advance guard of squalor." Homeowners were eager to sell, but no one other than saloon keepers were willing to buy. The same process was under way in Brooklyn, Philadelphia, and other cities. A case in point was Boston's South End. In only two or three decades, it went from a well-to-do residential community, featuring handsome houses and private parks, to a port of entry for working-class immigrants, full of taverns, factories, and, in one sociologist's words, "women of dubious character." (In John P. Marquand's novel *The Late George Apley*, the hero's father leaves the South End after he sees "a man in his shirt sleeves" on the steps of a brownstone across the street.) Residential deterioration was not just an East Coast phenomenon. It also took place on Cleveland's Euclid Avenue and Kansas City's Quality Hill, a fashionable residential neighborhood before it was abandoned by the elite in the late nineteenth century. To Olmsted, unwanted change was bad enough in the cities, but even worse in the suburbs—where, one journalist wrote in the 1920s, "population attracts business; business begets more business, and soon what was once a residence community becomes a city, and a part of the population starts moving again, out toward that fringe of green that will always be the ideal setting for the home."[6]

Other Americans shared Olmsted's concern. Brookline had once been "the garden of Boston," wrote town historian Harriet Woods in 1874. But lately "greedy speculators" were wiping out "every vestige of rural beauty" and the other qualities "which have for years made our town proverbial for its charms." A *Brookline Chronicle* writer made a similar point. Ever since the railroad and the Irish, "who never object to living in close quarters," came to Brookline, he said five years later, "there seems to be a *mania* for destroying everything that is old or beautiful or natural." George E. Kessler, another prominent landscape architect, complained in the mid-1890s about what he called "the erratic tendency" of shops and stores to follow residents to the periphery, where they formed "a large sprawling [and unattractive] combination of city and village." This litany continued well into the twentieth century. "Choose any city you please," wrote J. C. Nichols, subdivider of Kansas City's Country Club District, in 1923. Go into the part "that was ultra-fashionable a dozen or a score of years ago; there you will find mansions turned into boarding houses and modiste shops, or remodeled or razed for office and store buildings; or if some homes have not been used in that way, you will find their original residence values destroyed by the establishment of stores, shops, undertaking parlors, and the like, in proximity."[7]

For someone of means and refinement who was thinking of moving from the city to the suburbs this created a serious problem, Olmsted pointed out, one that raised hard questions about any parcel, no matter how attractive it was at first glance.

"Suppose I come here, what grounds of confidence can I have that I shall not by-and-by find a dram-shop on my right, or a beer-garden on my left, or a factory chimney or warehouse cutting off this view of the water? Is this charming road sure not to be turned also into a common town street, strewn with garbage, and in place of these lovely woods, can I be certain that here also there will not soon be a field of stumps with shanties and goats and heaps of cinders? If so, what is likely to be the future average value of land in this vicinity? . . . Looking either with reference to enjoyment of it as a place of residence, or as an investment for my children, I must be cautious not to be too much affected by superficial appearances. *What improvements have you here that tend to insure permanent healthfulness and permanent rural beauty?*"[8]

Without satisfactory answers to these questions, most Americans were not likely to move. They were not likely to leave for suburbia if before long it was doomed to lose the very qualities that made it so attractive to them. They were not likely to uproot their families if before long they would be forced to uproot them yet again. They were not likely to invest their hard-earned money in suburban real estate if before long they would have to sell at a loss. To put it another way, few Americans were likely to move to suburbia unless they saw it as more than a stopgap in the quest for a wholesome domestic environment. Whatever else suburbia had to offer, it had to offer permanence. Somehow a solution to the problem of unwanted change had to be found.

The Search for a Solution

The very rich had little trouble finding a solution. To prevent what they regarded as undesirable people and undesirable activities from spoiling their suburban retreats, they built homes on estates of scores, hundreds, and even thousands of acres. They made sure that no nearby buildings would deteriorate by making sure that there would be no buildings nearby. One case in point was Woodburne, the estate of William Minot, who was reputedly Boston's largest landowner. Another was Druim Moir, the home of Henry Howard Houston, a very wealthy Philadelphia businessman, investor, and railroad director. Even more impressive than Woodburne and Druim Moir were the huge estates, many with hundred-room mansions (and their own golf courses and race tracks), that were built on Long Island's North Shore by the Pratts, Vanderbilts, Guggenheims, and other magnates. Perhaps the most impressive was Greentree, the 660-acre estate of Payne Whitney, who paid more in income taxes in the mid-1920s than any other American except Henry Ford and John D. Rockefeller. After visiting the White House with their mother (who was a granddaughter of Franklin D. Roosevelt), two of Whitney's great grandchildren remarked that it was "nice enough, but hardly on a par with Greentree." Even larger than Greentree were some of Chicago's North Shore estates. Westleigh, the estate of meat-packer Louis Swift, covered more than 1,500 acres. Melody Farm, the estate of Swift's rival J. Ogden Armour, was half as large but had a private siding to the Milwaukee railroad. Even the largest of these estates were dwarfed by Rockefeller's compound at Pocantico Hills in Tarrytown, New York, which by the 1920s covered more than 6,000 acres, nearly ten square miles, almost twice as large as Palos Verdes Estates.[9]

But this solution was well beyond the means of all but a handful of Americans, all but a few thousand out of tens of millions. Even the well-to-do could not afford to buy such large tracts, much less build such huge houses. Nor could they afford to retain the staffs of landscapers, gardeners, handymen, laborers, cooks, and domestics needed to run these places and cater to the demands of the owners and their guests. According to Olmsted, Sr., it took more than just "very unusual wealth" to create great estates. It took "quite exceptional tastes" as well. As a rule, he wrote, even if a site is well chosen and "the *surrounding circumstances are favorable*," a "space of private ground of many acres . . . is entirely undesirable." (Presumably Biltmore, George W. Vanderbilt's enormous estate near Asheville, North Carolina, on which Olmsted spent the last years of his career, was an exception.) These estates had other drawbacks, argued Frank J. Scott, one of the most forceful advocates of suburbia in the mid and late nineteenth century. With "extensive private grounds," he wrote, comes "isolation and loneliness," especially among the women of the house. The very wealthy can compensate for the lack of neighbors by inviting people to their homes. "But much company brings much care," he pointed out. "It is paying a high price for company when one must keep a free hotel to secure it." How long will "the 'fine mansions' and broad fields, in a lonely locality, bring peace and comfort to the owner?" A few families may enjoy a life "without neighborly society," but they are "cluster-jewels of great rarity."[10]

Another solution available to the very rich, one that avoided some of the drawbacks spelled out by Scott, was to build homes in Tuxedo Park or one of a handful of other exclusive suburban communities, among the best known of which were Llewellyn Park and Short Hills, New Jersey, and Kenilworth, Illinois. Each of these places was the brainchild of an extremely wealthy businessman—or, in the case of Tuxedo Park and Kenilworth, one of his heirs. But none were commercial enterprises. Lorillard did not become a developer to add to his already huge fortune. Neither did Llewellyn S. Haskell (of Llewellyn Park), Stewart Hartshorn (of Short Hills), or Joseph Sears (of Kenilworth). (For Hartshorn, it was just as well. He did not make a profit from Short Hills until the mid-1930s, by which time he was well into his nineties.) Rather these men used their huge fortunes to build utopian communities for people like themselves. They spared no expense in acquiring and subdividing the sites. And to ensure that the communities retained their high quality, they carefully screened prospective residents (and also tightly restricted what they could do with their property). To give a couple of examples, Hartshorn ran character checks. If he was not sure the buyers would fit into the community, he would insist they rent first. If they passed muster, he would hold the closing at his Short Hills mansion, where they would be served tea and, writes historian Mary Corbin Sies, "judged according to their command of contemporary social niceties." Sears met prospective residents at a downtown Chicago office building, where, one later recalled, "I had to give an account of myself, my family, occupation and, in the language of the Constitution, my 'age, race, color and previous condition of servitude.'"[11]

These exclusive communities embodied the ideal suburb, providing, in Scott's words, "half-country, half-town life" and the company of "congenial gentlemen."[12] But as a solution to the general problem of suburbia that greatly troubled Olmsted and others, they left much to be desired. Although a home in Short Hills was much less expensive than an estate on Long Island's North Shore, it was still way beyond the reach of all but a few Americans. And of the few who could afford to buy property there, even fewer met Hartshorn's stringent standards. Moreover, very few Americans had the resources of a Lorillard, Haskell,

Hartshorn, or Sears. And of those who did, very few were inclined to follow their lead. Most were too busy making money. If they felt an obligation to give away part of their fortune, they made a gift to a college, museum, or symphony orchestra. Whereas a few idiosyncratic millionaires could open suburbia to the very rich, it would take thousands of ordinary subdividers to open it to the middle and upper middle classes. But these people would not move to the suburbs unless they felt confident their house would not soon have a dram shop on its right or a beer garden on its left. This meant that the subdividers would have to keep out those "undesirable" people and activities that were widely blamed for the deterioration of so many once delightful residential neighborhoods.

In the absence of zoning, a form of systematic land-use regulation that had not yet been adopted anywhere in the country, the subdividers had three options, none of which looked promising. One was to resort to nuisance law, a field, wrote a commentator in the mid-1880s, that "escapes all rule and definition." According to H. G. Wood, an authority on the subject, nuisance law was based on the principle that property rights were not absolute. "It is," he wrote, "a part of the great social compact to which every person is a party, a fundamental and essential principle in every civilized community, that every person yields a portion of his right of absolute dominion and use of his own property [so that] others may also enjoy their property without unreasonable hurt or hindrance." As Wood explained, there were two types of nuisances —public nuisances, whose suppression was the responsibility of local officials, and private nuisances, over which these officials had little authority. Private nuisances, a source of great concern to Olmsted, Sr., fell into two categories. Some—a slaughterhouse or a tannery, for example—were nuisances per se, noxious by their very nature, producing intolerable noise, smells, or fumes. Others, which were not inherently noxious—a livery stable, for instance—were nuisances because they were located or operated so as to work, in Wood's words, "material inconvenience, annoyance, discomfort, injury and damage" on nearby property owners. Under nuisance law, a subdivider (or, for that matter, any nearby property owner) could ask the courts to issue an injunction—and, if the injury was irreparable, to award damages.[13]

But the subdividers had little reason to believe that nuisance law could do much to prevent residential deterioration. Although Richard M. Hurd and other real estate economists argued that in a fashionable residential district "the erection of almost any building other than a residence" was a nuisance, most judges did not agree. A "row of mean and unsightly tenements" was not a nuisance, one ruled, even if located next to "a costly house, upon a fashionable street." Nor was a building a nuisance, Wood pointed out, because it was "offensive to the eye or cultivated tastes of people" or because it blocked a neighbor's "unobstructed prospect." A "well-kept butcher's shop" was not a nuisance, another judge held; nor was "a green grocery near a costly dwelling house." A business would be a nuisance if it covered the nearby houses with "smoke and vapor, or offensive odors, or dust and dirt," but not, a New Jersey judge wrote, if it attracted "crowds of orderly people, and numbers of carts and carriages" whose presence reduced property values and rent rolls. As Wood put it, "the law will not declare a thing a nuisance because it is unpleasant to the eye, because all the rules of propriety and good taste have been violated in its construction, nor because the property of another is rendered less valuable, nor because its exis-

tence is a constant source of irritation and annoyance to others."
It would declare something a nuisance only if it "produces a tan-
gible and appreciable injury to the [nearby] property." Given that
the bar was set so high and, said Wood, that the burden of proof
was "always cast upon the plaintiff," it is little wonder the courts
were very reluctant to issue an injunction against an alleged nuisance.[14]

The courts were even more reluctant to issue an injunction
against a prospective nuisance—one, said a New York judge, that
was only "threatened or anticipated." In such a case the complain-
ant had to establish the prospective nuisance with "reasonable
certainty"; the danger had to be "imminent" and "clearly impend-
ing," and the injuries "irreparable." Just how hard it was to meet
these criteria was revealed when a group of Chicago homeowners
asked the courts to issue an injunction against the construction
of a nearby icehouse. The courts refused, pointing out that no
one could say with certainty how much damage it would do.
Would the wagons make too much noise? It depends, said Judge
Edmund W. Burke, on "the kind of pavements on the streets
and the character of the wagons used." Would the horses give
off "offensive odors"? It depends, he wrote, on how many were
used, where they were kept, and how they were cared for. But
as Olmsted, Sr., pointed out, nothing was more offensive to "the
better class" of residential suburbs than manufacturing establishments. Even if the courts were willing to issue an injunction after
one was up and running—which, in view of the capital already
invested, was highly unlikely—the damage would already have
been done. The factory would have set in motion the forces that
would lead inevitably to the deterioration of the residential environment. The nearby property owners could sue for damages,

but no amount of money could restore those qualities that had drawn them to the community in the first place.[15]

This deep-seated reluctance to issue an injunction stemmed largely from the widespread belief that what the complainants viewed as nuisances were part of the price of urban life. Explaining an Illinois appellate court's decision to deny an injunction against an eight-story hotel that spewed dense smoke, dust, and soot into the nearby homes, Judge Joseph E. Gary wrote, "Those who seek and enjoy the advantages of life in a great city must take them with all the inevitable drawbacks." "The air of open fields cannot be hoped for in the streets of a commercial and manufacturing metropolis," he said. Gary applied the same logic when the court refused to issue an injunction against a noisy bowling alley. By "choosing to live in a great city," he wrote, the plaintiff must bear up with "the inevitable concomitant of the city amusements." (Another Illinois judge put it more bluntly, saying, "I can not regulate the noise of a city by injunction.") A Pennsylvania justice showed a similar solicitude for the city's business interests. A court, he wrote, "whose arm may fall with crushing force upon the every day business of man, destroying lawful means of support and diverting property from legitimate uses," cannot approach an application for an injunction "with too much caution." H. G. Wood nicely summed up the conventional wisdom of the bench. "People living in cities and large towns must submit to some inconvenience, to some annoyance, to some discomforts, to some injury and damage; must even yield a portion of their rights to the necessities of business, which, from the very nature of things, must often be carried on in populous localities and in compact communities."[16]

Another thing the subdividers could do was to adopt new design guidelines, an approach favored by Olmsted, Sr., and other landscape architects. According to Olmsted, most subdivisions were laid out in a way that left them vulnerable to pernicious changes. Much like city streets, the roads were arranged in a grid, one about as wide as the other, most running to the business district and connecting with many other roads. Thus laid out, said Olmsted, they served not to preserve the "conditions of rural attractiveness" but rather to facilitate the conversion of single-family houses into stores and shops. They created prime sites for "butchers and bakers and tinkers and dramsellers and the followers of other bustling callings." Along with the "mechanics & laborers" who followed in their wake, and the "cheap tenement & boarding houses" in which they lived, the shopkeepers and tradesmen soon turned "quiet & secluded neighborhood[s]" into "noisy, dusty, smoking, shouting, rattling and stinking one[s]." Making matters worse, the lots were often so small that if some property owners did something distasteful—if, said Olmsted, they built "ill-proportioned, vile-colored, shabby-genteel dwelling houses, pushing their gables or eaveboards impertinently over the sidewalk," or erected "high dead-walls, as of a series of private mad houses, as is done in some English suburbs"—many others would be affected. Also, few subdividers set aside land for parks and open spaces, which might have served as a buffer between property owners within the subdivision or between the subdivision and its surroundings.[17]

To lay out suburbs in a way that preserved, in Olmsted's words, their "tranquility and seclusion"—and thereby to offer some assurance to prospective purchasers "that these districts shall not be bye and bye invaded by the desolation which thus far has invariably advanced before the progress of the town"—Olmsted and other landscape architects came up with a set of guidelines that was widely accepted by the end of the nineteenth century. Instead of straight, most roads should be curvilinear, designed not to run through the natural surroundings but to fit into them — and to enhance the views where possible. A handful should be wide enough to handle through traffic, the rest only wide enough to provide access to local residents. With very few exceptions, the roads should not lead, as Olmsted put it, "with special directness," to the business district or connect with many other roads. Nor should they be too steep, he wrote, "as anyone knows who has been to Boston, Liverpool or Edinburgh." The roads should be well planted too, full of grass and trees, without which they would differ from town streets "chiefly in the quality of desolation and dreariness." The roads should be good—well-paved, well-drained, and "frost-proof, rain-proof," wrote Olmsted, "let them cost what they will." And they should be convenient. But they should not be too good and too convenient. They should be good enough and convenient enough to attract residents, but not so good and so convenient that they attracted businesses (and drove out residents).[18]

As well as good roads, the guidelines called for good sidewalks, "pleasant to the eye," said Olmsted, conveying a sense of "refined domestic life." No less important were large, well-planted spaces between the sidewalk and the homes. "We cannot judiciously attempt to control the form of the houses which men shall build," he wrote, "[but we can] take care that if they build very ugly and inappropriate houses, they shall not be allowed to force them disagreeably upon our attention when we desire to pass along the road upon which they stand." Large lots, much larger than customary suburban lots, would also help stabilize the community. Shopkeepers and tradesmen would be put off by their size, working people by their cost. Plenty of open spaces —what Olmsted Brothers called "generous provision for parks and recreation areas"—were highly recommended too. "There is probably no custom which so manifestly displays the advantages of a Christian, civilized and democratic community," Olmsted wrote, than the tendency of people "of all classes" to assemble "on equal terms" on "common property." (One of the best known of these places was the Ramble, a fifty-acre common in the middle of Llewellyn Park.) Perhaps also worth considering were stone lodges or wooden gates at the entrances to the property. Among other things, said Olmsted, they could "exclude from the lanes whatever it may be thought undesirable to admit."[19] If subdividers followed these guidelines, Olmsted believed, they stood a good chance to slow down, and perhaps even head off, residential deterioration in suburbia.

But it was far from clear that the subdividers would follow the guidelines. Although Olmsted downplayed the point, they would have raised costs and, unless there was a strong demand for large and expensive lots, lowered revenues. A few subdividers were ready to run the risk. A case in point was J. C. Nichols, the developer of Kansas City's Country Club District, who was determined to do whatever was necessary "to prevent business encroachment" on the "quiet, residential streets" in his subdivision.[20] But few subdividers had the long-term vision that Nichols had. Most were running a small business, operating on a narrow margin, and eager to get rid of their lots and start over again elsewhere. It was also far from clear that the guidelines would work as well as Olmsted and others hoped. An aesthetic tour de force, they had serious limitations. As Olmsted conceded, they could not prevent someone of poor taste from building a "very ugly and inappropriate" house or from building it to the very edge of the property. Nor could they prevent someone who had bought a lot as a short-term investment from selling to someone who wanted it as a site for a store, boardinghouse, or, worse still, a dram shop or a beer garden. By the late nineteenth century, even Olmsted realized that the guidelines by themselves were not enough to bring about a high degree of permanence in suburbia.

Yet another thing the subdividers could do was to impose restrictive covenants, a measure that meshed nicely with the landscape architects' design guidelines. These covenants had been used in England as early as the mid-eighteenth century by members of the nobility who wanted to add to their fortunes by subdividing parts of their huge estates in and around the rapidly growing cities. But since they preferred to lease the lots rather than to sell them, they wanted to retain control over how the lots were used in the years ahead. As well as to generate income, their aim was to preserve what historian Donald J. Olsen calls "the reversionary value of the property," to make sure that when the lease expired, in, say, ninety-nine years, and the property reverted to them, it could be profitably re-leased or redeveloped by their heirs. The best way to preserve the reversionary value, it was widely assumed, was to prevent the lessee from using the property in undesirable ways, and especially from converting houses into shops and stores. Hence the strong appeal of restrictive covenants. Typically, they provided that the property could only be used, in Olsen's words, as "gentlemen's private residences." It could not be occupied by butchers, bakers, brewers, pubs, bone-boilers, cheesemongers, and, in the commonly used phrase, "any noisy, noisome or offensive trade or business whatever." Also barred were schools, colleges, police stations, and public offices "of any kind," as well as brothels, hospitals, infirmaries, and dispensaries. Some covenants prescribed how far the houses had to be set back, how high they could rise, and what sorts of materials had to be used in construction.[21]

Restrictive covenants soon made their way from England to America. During the second half of the eighteenth century and the first half of the nineteenth, some property owners used them to preserve their fashionable neighborhoods as "quiet and desirable places of abode," in the Massachusetts Supreme Judicial Court's words. Boston's Lewisburg Square was one example, New York's Gramercy Park another. A few subdividers also used them, said Judge William T. McCoun of New York, "to form a respectable neighborhood," if not necessarily a fashionable one, and to make sure "that the sale of one or more [lots] should not impair the value or prejudice the sales of the rest." With one or two exceptions, restrictive covenants were used to keep out "undesirable" activities more than "undesirable" people. A New Yorker who subdivided thirty-nine lots in Greenwich Village in the 1820s banned a long list of noxious industries—as well as "any other manufactory, trade or business whatsoever which should or might be *in anywise offensive to the neighboring inhabitants*." And a Cambridge lawyer who subdivided a small parcel east of Harvard Square in the 1840s prohibited any activity "which shall tend to disturb the quiet or comfort of the neighborhood." (The lawyer was Richard Henry Dana, Jr., best known today as author of *Two Years Before the Mast* and counsel to Anthony Burns, the most famous fugitive slave in U.S. history.) Included in many covenants were provisions that barred the owners from building more than one house per lot, building it too close to the property line, or building it of anything but brick or stone. A few covenants specified that the house had to be built no later than one year after the sale of the lot, a provision designed to discourage speculation.[22]

By the mid-nineteenth century restrictive covenants had been imposed on a number of properties, especially in New York and other big cities. A noteworthy, if somewhat idiosyncratic, case in point was Boston's Back Bay. Early in the 1850s, after almost half a century of discussion, the state decided to fill nearly six hundred often foul and noxious acres along the banks of the Charles River and turn the reclaimed land into the city's premier upper-middle-class neighborhood. In an effort to attract what the Boston Public Land Commissioners called "industrious, enterprising, intelligent and order-loving citizens," many of whom would otherwise have moved to the suburbs, the authorities not only created a magnificent system of streets, squares, and boulevards. They also imposed a host of restrictive covenants. Besides banning "any business which shall be offensive to the neighborhood for dwelling-houses," the covenants stipulated that the houses "shall be of a good class, not less than three stories in height, and built of no other materials than brick, stone, or iron." On Commonwealth Avenue they also had to be set back at least twenty feet from the property line. In the event of a violation, the city was empowered to act after giving sixty days' notice. Underlying these restrictions was the belief, wrote the Land Commissioners, that "useful and respectable" Bostonians were more likely to move to Back Bay if they felt secure "that their own places are not to be rendered less desirable by the uses to which other lands in their neighborhood are to be appropriated." As the state's Supreme Judicial Court later said, Bostonians would not have built fine homes in Back Bay unless assured that the neighbors were bound by "the same restrictions by which they themselves were bound."[23]

But as late as the 1880s, the imposition of restrictive covenants was very much the exception. Most city lots were not restricted. And except in a few places—among the best known of which was Llewellyn Park, whose developers took the unusual step of creating a homeowners association to enforce the rules—neither were most suburban lots. Of the others, most were restricted in minor ways—a provision for setbacks, say, or a ban on saloons—and for short periods. As historian Michael Holleran has pointed out, the early restrictions "did not withdraw land from potential change indefinitely to protect purchasers, but only long enough to protect the developer while selling off the lots in a subdivision."[24] Few covenants included effective enforcement mechanisms either. Thus, as a solution to the problem of rapid residential deterioration in suburbia, restrictive covenants looked no more promising than nuisance law or design guidelines. But in this case looks were deceiving. For several momentous changes were—or would soon be—under way that would weaken the legal and other constraints that had thus far discouraged most subdividers from employing restrictive covenants.

Legal and Market Constraints

Some subdividers were reluctant to impose restrictive covenants out of fear that the courts would not enforce them. Under common law, it had been settled that the courts would not enforce a covenant that restricted an owner's right to "alienate" his property—or, in lay terms, to sell or otherwise transfer ownership of it. One anonymous legal commentator nicely spelled out the logic of this position. "To say that one shall have an estate in fee simple in land [or, in other words, to own it outright]," he wrote, "and yet that he shall not alienate it, is to say that he shall have such an estate, and at the same time that he shall not have it." To impose restrictions on alienation was therefore to create "an inalienable estate," which was "an absurd impossibility." Chancellor James Kent, the eminent American legal theorist, agreed. "[I]n a country like ours, where lands are as much an article of sale and traffic as personal property, and the policy of the state has been to encourage both the acquisition and easy and free alienation of lands, such restrictions ought not to be encouraged by the courts." Although the U.S. Supreme Court ruled in 1879 that prohibitions aimed at "particular persons" or imposed for "a limited period" were not necessarily invalid, most state courts refused to enforce restrictions on alienation. The Michigan Supreme Court held in the mid-1870s that even a partial restriction—even one that "would suspend all powers of alienation for a single day"—was "unreasonable and void." Decades later the Maryland Court of Appeals struck down a covenant that prohibited the buyer from selling or renting without the written consent of the subdivider—who, in order to maintain the neighborhood as "a desirable high class residential section," had retained the right "to pass upon the character[,] desirability and other qualifications of the proposed purchaser or occupant."[25]

But as early as the late 1820s the Massachusetts courts began to draw a distinction between restrictions on alienation and restrictions on use. During the next few decades other courts followed suit. By the middle of the century the validity of restrictions on use was no longer in doubt, said the Massachusetts Supreme Judicial Court. Explaining the court's decision to uphold a ban on taverns or "any mechanical or manufacturing, or any nauseous or offensive business whatever," Justice George T. Bigelow declared that a subdivider had the right to impose restrictions to prevent the lots from being used in ways that might reduce the value of the rest of the subdivision or "impair its eligibility" as sites for private residences. "That such a purpose is a legitimate one, and may be carried out, consistently with the rules of law, by reasonable and proper covenants, conditions or restrictions, cannot be doubted." The only qualifications were that the restrictions "be exercised reasonably, with a due regard to public policy, and without creating any unlawful restraint of trade." If doubts remained about the validity of restrictions on use, they were dispelled by the U.S. Supreme Court in 1879. In *Cowell v. Springs Company* it upheld a restriction banning the manufacture or sale of intoxicating liquor on a parcel in Colorado Springs. Counsel for the defendant, the proprietor of a "billiard saloon," insisted that his client had "absolute ownership" of the property, "with liberty to use it in any lawful manner which he might choose." Rejecting this argument, Justice Stephen Field wrote that nothing in the Constitution precluded the state from imposing "a limited restriction" on the use of property, "however much the restriction may affect the value or the nature of the estate." Noting that many courts had upheld similar restrictions, he said that to rule against them would "defeat numerous arrangements in our large cities for the health and comfort of whole neighborhoods."[26]

By drawing a distinction between restrictions on alienation and restrictions on use, the courts removed one of the legal obstacles to the use of restrictive covenants. But others remained. If a covenant was a form of contract, a Maryland judge wrote, it was binding on the original seller and buyer. But suppose the buyer sold the property to someone else. Was the covenant binding on the new owner, who had not been a party to the original contract? It was not, some lawyers argued. The covenant, one said, "is merely personal," an agreement between the grantor and grantee that does not "run with the land." If so, there was little the courts could do if the new owner violated the restrictions. Nor was that all. Under contract law, the seller could ask the courts to enforce the restrictions. But suppose he had sold all or most of the lots and no longer had a stake in making sure the restrictions were enforced. Could the people who had bought the lots file suit if one of the neighbors was violating the restrictions? They could not, some lawyers contended. The new owners, they said, had no contract with one another—only with the original seller. Even if the restrictions were imposed for their benefit, they could not ask the courts to enforce a contract that did not exist.[27] If restrictive covenants were binding only on the original buyer and could be enforced only at the request of the original seller, it was hard to see how they could protect residential neighborhoods from unwanted change for long.

But the situation was not as bleak as it seemed. During the second third of the century the New York and Massachusetts courts removed the remaining legal obstacles to the use of restrictive covenants. In landmark decisions they ruled that restrictive covenants were binding on others besides the original seller. In *Brouwer v. Jones,* which was decided in 1856, the New York Supreme Court upheld a trial court's decision to enjoin the defendant, who had bought two lots in a Greenwich Village subdivision that prohibited dangerous, noxious, or offensive trades, from operating a sawmill that spewed smoke, dust, and soot on the adjoining lots. Speaking for the court, Judge James Emott rejected the argument that the defendant could not be sued for violating the restrictions because he had not purchased the property from the original seller and thus was not a party to the original agreement. Since the objective of the covenant was "to protect the whole tract and every lot belonging to it," Emott said, it was binding on everyone, from "the original owners" to "any subsequent grantees." The Massachusetts Supreme Judicial Court took much the same position. In *Whitney v. Union Railway Company,* which was decided in 1858, it barred the defendant from building stables, constructing a turntable, and laying down rails on a lot in a Cambridge tract that banned mechanical and manufacturing activities. Writing for the court, Justice Bigelow dismissed the defendant's argument that since he had not bought the lot from the plaintiff there was no "privity of contract" between them. So long as the defendant had notice of the covenant, he was bound to abide by it. "It is not essential that it should run with the land," Bigelow declared. "A personal covenant or agreement will be held valid and binding in equity on a purchaser taking the estate with notice."[28]

In other landmark decisions the courts ruled that these covenants could be enforced at the request of others besides the original seller—an issue that did not arise in *Brouwer* and *Whitney* because in both cases the plaintiff was the original seller. In *Barrow v. Richard,* which was handed down in 1840, the New York Court of Chancery issued an injunction preventing the defendant from operating a coal yard on two lots in Greenwich Village (and spewing coal dust over the nearby houses) in spite of a covenant that prohibited any business offensive to the neighbors. Writing for the court, Judge William T. McCoun declared that the object of the covenant was to protect not the seller, who no longer had an interest in the property, but the buyer, who was entitled to relief in the event of a breach by another buyer. The defendant appealed, arguing that the plaintiffs were not parties to his contract with the seller, but Judge Reuben H. Walworth upheld the decision. The Massachusetts Supreme Judicial Court came to much the same conclusion. In *Parker v. Nightingale,* which was handed down in 1862, it ordered the defendant to stop running a restaurant on one of several lots in Boston's Hayward Place that could be used for "a dwelling-house only." Noting that the restaurant's "noisy and boisterous" patrons made Hayward Place "almost unfit for quiet and comfortable residences," Bigelow, now chief justice, declared that "there can be no room for doubt that the plaintiffs are entitled to equitable relief." Every Hayward Place property owner who was subject to the restrictions had the right to ask the courts to enforce them. There was no need for the original seller, who had no "present interest" in the property, to be a party to the proceedings.[29]

Although one legal scholar observed late in the nineteenth century that the subject was "still in its infancy," a consensus was rapidly emerging in favor of restrictive covenants. In what one commentator called the leading case on the subject, the New Jersey Court of Chancery followed the lead of the New York and Massachusetts courts in the early 1890s. The Maryland courts joined the fold soon after, as did the West Virginia and Wisconsin courts. The Illinois Supreme Court bucked the trend for a time. (Stressing that "real estate is an article of commerce" and "the uses to which it should be devoted are constantly changing as the business of the country increases," Justice Alfred M. Craig declared that it was contrary to public policy "to tie up real estate" with restrictions. Quoting Judge Murray F. Tuley, the Cook County judge who had tried the case, he went on to say, "All doubts should, as a general rule, be resolved in favor of the free use of property, and against restrictions [thereon].") But eventually it came around. Two decades later the West Virginia Supreme Court said that in the case of a breach of a covenant the courts now grant an injunction almost "as a matter of course."[30]

The West Virginia court's statement was a slight exaggeration. In the course of crafting a new consensus, the courts spelled out several conditions under which they would not enforce restrictions on the use of property. It had long been settled that they would not enforce ones that were contrary to public policy or in restraint of trade. Nor would they enforce ones about which the buyers had no notice. Now it was also settled that the courts would not enforce a covenant unless it was designed for the benefit of the buyers—and, in many states, unless it was part of what the New Jersey Court of Chancery called "some general scheme or plan for the improvement or development of the property." No less important, the courts would not issue an injunction where, in one legal scholar's words, the plaintiffs had "acquiesced in a breach [of a covenant] for an unreasonable time." As Justice Bigelow wrote, "It would be contrary to equity and good conscience to suffer a party to lie by and see acts done involving risk and expenses by others, and then permit him to enforce his rights and thereby inflict loss and damage on parties acting in good faith." Nor would the courts issue an injunction where the surroundings had already changed so much that, as the New York Court of Appeals wrote, "neither their better improvement nor permanent value can be promoted by enforcing its [the covenant's] observance." If a covenant's objective could not be achieved, its enforcement "would work oppression, and not equity." It would "harass and injure the defendant," said the Massachusetts Supreme Judicial Court, without helping the plaintiff.[31]

But in the absence of any of these conditions—in a case where the restrictions were part of a general plan, the plaintiffs were seeking relief in a timely manner, and the surroundings were as yet largely unchanged—the courts would enforce the covenant. Provided the restrictions had not yet expired, they would enforce it even if the defendant was not the original buyer nor the plaintiff the original seller. Some courts stressed that covenants would be "strictly construed," that restrictions would be taken to mean what they said, not what they implied, and that doubts about their meaning would be resolved in favor of the defendant. Refusing to stop a Chicago property owner from building an apartment house on a lot that could be used for "only a single dwelling," the Illinois Supreme Court wrote that if the subdivider had intended "to prohibit the erection of a flat" or any other dwelling to be occupied by more than one family, he should have said so in the deed. But as long as the meaning was clear, even these courts would enforce the covenants. Writing in 1925, by which time the employment of restrictive covenants had become commonplace, Justice William C. Walsh of the Maryland Court of Appeals said what most of his colleagues had long come to believe: "Whether this tendency is wise or unwise, it is not our province to determine." So long as the restrictions are reasonable (and the intentions clear), the courts would uphold them.[32]

Most subdividers, however, were reluctant to impose restrictive covenants less out of fear that they would not hold up in court than that they would drive away prospective purchasers. As J. C. Nichols recalled, "When I began selling lots at the tag-end outskirts of the city [at the turn of the century], I was afraid to suggest my present broad building restrictions. I thought nobody would buy rigidly restricted lots." It was, Nichols pointed out, "hard enough to sell them anyhow!" And selling lots was how subdividers made their living. As King Thompson, a Columbus, Ohio, subdivider, said, "I did not enter the land business some years ago because I had any theories of city building to work out, but merely because I thought I could make a living at it." To make a living, the subdividers had to do more than just cover the costs of buying the land, putting in the streets, installing the utilities, and laying out the lots. They also had to pay property taxes and interest charges. Unless we sell the lots, and sell them quickly, "the carrying charge will eat us up," Nichols warned his fellow subdividers. But as E. H. Bouton, head of the Roland Park Company, pointed out, most people were in no rush to buy suburban lots. They were loath to sell their homes in the city and leave their friends and neighbors behind. They were also reluctant to move into even well-designed subdivisions before the schools and churches were built and the saplings provided much in the way of shade.[33]

As hard as it was to sell ordinary suburban lots, it was even harder to sell highly restricted ones. When the Roland Park Company began selling "restricted land" just outside Baltimore in the mid-1890s, one of its executives later recalled, it ran into a good deal of resistance. "Salesmen, in describing the advantages of these restrictions, were met with the comment, 'When I have bought and paid for a lot, I do not understand why you retain such control that I cannot make use of it as I see fit.'" A representative of another real estate company reported that many prospective purchasers refused to buy restricted lots on the grounds that "they did not care to hold property in their name unless they could build what they wanted and dispose of their lot to anybody they saw fit. In other words, they did not care to buy property with any restrictions whatsoever upon it." To the extent that his observation implied that prospective purchasers found all restrictions equally objectionable, it was misleading. But as a reflection of a widespread sentiment, it was on the mark. As Thomas Adams, a prominent English town planner who was visiting the United States, remarked, "It ha[s] been stated to me over and over again that you could not get an owner of land in this country to submit to any restriction of his claim to use his land as he chooses."[34]

Restrictive covenants were objectionable because they ran counter to deep-seated beliefs about property rights, home-ownership, and suburbia. Although some Americans were starting to think that some form of land-use control was necessary, most were still wedded to the traditional view of private property. No one had the right to tell anyone else how "to use, enjoy and dispose of" their property, wrote a New Jersey judge, unless it was being used in a way that created a nuisance or otherwise infringed upon the property rights of others. Yet in addition to banning slaughterhouses and other noxious businesses, the customary restrictions barred all sorts of other activities that were by no means a nuisance or an infringement of property rights. Most Americans also believed in the virtues of homeownership. A home of his own, they held, gave a man not only a stake in the community, a commitment to its long-term well-being, but also what one real estate promoter called "a certain independence, a force of character that is obtained in no other way." If a home-owner was his "own man" and his home was "his castle," why should he put up with so many restrictions on what he could do with it? Such restrictions might be appropriate in cities, it was conceded, but not in suburbs. Suburbia encourages "individualism," one suburbanite wrote. There "you may wear what you please," she said, and do other things "you would never dare in the City." There "you may, if you wish, paint your house orange and purple and put a pink roof on."[35]

Restrictive covenants were also objectionable because they put a damper on speculation in suburban property. Given that the United States was, in the words of two real estate experts, "a nation of speculators," it is small wonder many Americans viewed a suburban lot as an investment as much as a homesite. They knew that a good deal of money could be made from a lot that underwent a change in land use, but they also knew that restrictive covenants made such a change highly unlikely, if not impossible. For the many people who saw real estate speculation as, next to poker, the "great American game," it made no sense to play by such strict rules. Also underlying their reluctance to play by these rules was a strong belief that change was not only desirable but also inevitable, that it was, said the *Detroit Free Press,* a "universal law," a law that applied to people, to cities, and, above all, to real estate. As Richard M. Hurd wrote, land would always go to "the highest bidder," the one who could earn "the highest amount" from it. It would always be changing because its owner would always be looking for its "highest and best use."[36] From this perspective restrictive covenants were a shortsighted and ultimately fruitless attempt to interfere with the natural laws of the real estate market, if not the universe itself.

But during the late nineteenth century, a time of widespread civil disorder, many well-to-do Americans began to question the conventional wisdom that change was desirable and inevitable. Unlike their fathers and grandfathers, they were dismayed as old landmarks and elegant houses were torn down to make way for stores and offices and tall buildings were demolished to make way for even taller ones. Like Olmsted, Sr., they were appalled as once fashionable neighborhoods—what a Dallas subdivider later called "the very best part of town," the part that housed "the better class of people"—were taken over by apartment and boarding houses.

Why was it, many Americans asked, that "every good development around every growing city should have a life of only ten or fifteen years and then give way to something less desirable and perhaps hideous"? Why was it not possible that a good development could withstand the forces of change? Why was it not possible that with "the softening influences of time" it might become even more attractive? Prompting these questions was a growing longing for permanence, the lack of which was now lamented by many well-to-do Americans other than Olmsted. As John F. W. Ware, a Unitarian minister from Cambridge, said, "The want of permanence is one of the crying sins of the age. It prevents that local attachment which is one of the strongest and purest sentiments of the human breast." Americans, he added, "are always getting ready to live in a new place, never living."[37]

As many Americans voiced their growing concern about "the want of permanence," some subdividers began to have second thoughts that restrictive covenants would drive away prospective purchasers. Could it be that their longing for permanence might outweigh their devotion to property rights? Could it be that their fear of the market might overcome their opposition to land-use regulation? Might they be willing to bear up with restrictions in order to exclude those "undesirable" people and "undesirable" activities that inevitably led to unwanted change? Might they be willing to forgo the chance of a short-term windfall for the sake of long-term stability? Was it possible, some subdividers wondered, that there was a large market of what Olmsted, Jr., called "the most discriminating and intelligent and enterprising among the people of means" that could be tapped by imposing restrictive covenants? At a time when few suburban tracts were highly restricted, and many not restricted at all, was it possible that these covenants would give them an edge over their competitors? Provided the restrictions imposed on one lot were imposed on all the others—provided, as a Baltimore attorney put it, "they apply equally and uniformly to all other lots similarly situated"—some subdividers came to the conclusion it might be easier to sell lots with restrictive covenants than without.[38]

Some subdividers also came to the conclusion that restrictive covenants might help solve the problem of what J. C. Nichols called "the tag ends." As early as the mid-nineteenth century, subdividers had realized that once a tract of more than a few acres was laid out it would take a while before all the lots were sold. Even if a subdivider could afford to hold on to the unsold lots, there was always a chance that in the meantime one of the buyers might use a lot in a way that, in Judge McCoun's words, might "prejudice the sales of the rest." This problem grew even more serious in the late nineteenth and early twentieth centuries, by which time it was commonly believed that a subdivider had to sell two-thirds or perhaps even three-quarters of the lots to break even; the profits would come from the sale of the last third or quarter. If some of the initial buyers used their lots in an offensive way, if they built houses up to the property line or if, as Charles H. Cheney wrote, they built houses that were ugly or tacky, even "of bad design or off-color," the subdivider might have trouble selling the remaining lots.[39] If a subdivider could not sell them—or could sell them only at a deep discount—so much for the profits. Other than by imposing restrictive covenants, subdividers were hard pressed to think of a way to deal with this problem.

By the early 1890s it seemed that restrictive covenants were an idea whose time had come. Some Americans had already bought restricted lots; and if a subdivision appealed to them, others were inclined to buy them. Some Americans who had once been skeptical about restrictive covenants had changed their minds too. Even Olmsted, Sr., who in the late 1860s had expressed reservations about anything but the least onerous restrictions, was now urging his clients to impose stringent restrictions for a long period. Writing in 1889 to Brookline subdivider Henry M. Whitney, he recommended banning trade and manufacturing, barring more than one house per lot and, among other things, requiring that the house cost at least ten to fifteen thousand dollars, a huge sum at the time. No revisions should be allowed for sixty years—and, after sixty years, only with the unanimous consent of the lot owners.[40] But whether subdividers were ready to impose such tough restrictions for so long a time remained to be seen. With the conspicuous exception of Llewellyn Haskell and a few other idiosyncratic millionaires, none of them had done so yet, at least not on a subdivision of more than a few acres. For the time being it seemed that they were all waiting for someone else to take the lead, to test the market for restricted suburban property, to do on a large scale what had hitherto been done, when done at all, on a small one.

A Breakthrough in Baltimore

They did not have to wait long. During the late 1880s Charles Grasty, editor of the *Kansas City Times* and part-time real estate speculator, formed a working relationship with Jarvis and

Conklin, a Chicago investment house that acted as a conduit for British investors looking for opportunities in America's growing cities. Although he moved to Baltimore in 1890 to become editor of the *Baltimore News,* Grasty continued to keep an eye out for property that might interest Jarvis and Conklin and its British clients. He soon learned that William H. Edmunds, publisher of a trade paper called the *Manufacturers' Record,* was willing to sell a one-hundred-acre parcel about five miles north of downtown Baltimore, not far from Lake Roland, that was well suited for development as a fashionable residential suburb. Grasty told Jarvis and Conklin about it. He also urged Edward H. Bouton, another Kansas City real estate man, to join the venture. Bouton, who was having troubles with his creditors, decided it was a good time to seek his fortune elsewhere. After Grasty, Bouton, and a representative of the British investors visited the site in the spring of 1891, Jarvis and Conklin bought not only Edmunds's one hundred acres but nearly four hundred additional acres next door. To develop the property, it formed the Roland Park Company, which was capitalized at $1 million, the bulk of it in inflated real estate, and named Bouton, who had worked for Jarvis and Conklin in Kansas City in the 1880s, general manager.[41]

The timing could hardly have been worse. Within two years the Panic of 1893 left the nation reeling. In its wake, Jarvis and Conklin went under, and Stewart and Young, another Chicago investment house, took over Roland Park. The capital markets dried up, leaving the company in a precarious position. Worst of all, the demand for suburban property in and around Baltimore, which had not been strong before the Panic, grew even weaker. Still, Bouton and his associates pressed ahead with their plan to turn Roland Park into a fashionable residential suburb. To lay

out the first tract, the company hired George E. Kessler, who had
worked under Olmsted, Sr., on Central Park before moving to
Kansas City in the 1880s. For the next tract, which was started
several years later, it retained Olmsted Brothers. At a cost of more
than one hundred thousand dollars, the company laid out and
graded the streets and put in the sidewalks, gutters, utilities, and
storm drains. It also brought in George E. Waring, Jr., the country's leading sanitary engineer, to help with the sewage system. In
an effort to make the community more accessible to downtown
Baltimore, the company built the Lake Roland Elevated Electric
Railroad. And in an effort to stimulate lagging sales, it erected a
few houses, a measure designed to give prospective purchasers
a sense of things to come. After looking into Tuxedo Park, Llewellyn Park, and Sudbrook, Maryland, a subdivision laid out by
Olmsted, Sr., in the late 1880s, Bouton and his associates made
perhaps their most far-reaching decision. They imposed restrictive covenants on all the lots.[42]

It was a calculated risk, akin, J. C. Nichols later said, to setting out onto "an uncharted sea." And in the aftermath of the
Panic, it was anything but smooth sailing. The restrictions drove
away some prospective purchasers. In a few cases, Edmunds informed Bouton in 1894, they drove them to other subdivisions.
Anticipating resistance from prospective purchasers, Bouton and
his associates shied away from imposing highly onerous restrictions. They banned privies and other nuisances as well as stores,
saloons, and businesses of any kind; and they forbade more than
one house per lot. But under the restrictions an owner could build
a house for as little as two thousand to three thousand dollars, a
sum well within the reach of Baltimore's upper middle class; and
at the start it was possible to build without first submitting the

plans to the company for approval. The restrictions prevented an owner from building a house up to the property line, but not from putting up a fence around it. They barred raising hogs, but not keeping chickens and rabbits. Bouton and his associates thought about imposing a restriction that no lot could be sold to or occupied by "negroes or persons of African descent." But on the advice of their lawyers, who held that such a restriction was an illegal restraint on alienation, they shelved the idea. The company did not impose restrictions against other racial and ethnic minorities either—though in one case it bought back a lot to prevent "a jew named Walters" from buying it.[43]

Bouton and his associates also downplayed the restrictions. Some of the company's ads did not even mention them. Instead they highlighted Roland Park's hilly site and healthy surroundings and compared its "pure air" to the "smells, dust and decaying filth of the city." The ads that did refer to the restrictions did so in a cautious, even defensive way. "We hear," said one, "of erroneous impressions as to the restrictions on Roland Park lots," especially impressions that they were sweeping and stringent. To the contrary, they are "few and simple," "proper" and "reasonable." They were designed, on the basis of "careful thought and mature experience," to protect Roland Park from "unhealthful surroundings and undesirable neighbors." Homeowners could rely on them to ensure "a satisfactory class of residents," to "maintain the beauty of the place, its healthfulness, the value of the property and [the] purity and cleanliness of the air and its soil," and to ensure "the permanence of its [Roland Park's] advantages and attractions." What the company said in its ads, it repeated to prospective purchasers. "We have thrown around our property a number of well chosen and reasonable restrictions," Richard W.

Marchant, Jr., told William R. Abbott, for no purposes other than
to prevent nuisances and maintain property values. Nothing in
the restrictions, said a member of the sales department, would
deprive an owner of "the full use and enjoyment of his property
at all times."[44]

During the 1890s the Roland Park Company weathered a financial panic, a chronic dearth of capital, and a sluggish real
estate market. Although it did not earn much of a profit until
later, long after the British investors sold out to Bouton and a
local syndicate in 1903, the company stayed afloat. It sold some
lots, opened a second tract, and achieved a degree of stability that
had once seemed unattainable. During the 1900s the company
sold more lots. And as the owners built houses and planted trees,
bushes, and lawns, Roland Park gained a reputation as one of
the country's outstanding residential suburbs. Duncan McDuffie, developer of St. Francis Wood and other wealthy suburbs in
and around San Francisco, called it "by far the most successful residence subdivision in the United States." The "secret of
the success," he said, was that the Roland Park Company put a
higher value on creating "an ideal residence district" than on producing "large dividends for its stockholders." Olmsted, Jr., urged
other subdividers to visit Roland Park and held it up as a model
to students at Harvard's Graduate School of Design, where he
taught the next generation of landscape architects. After a trip
east in 1912, J. C. Nichols, who was rapidly emerging as the chief
spokesman for the leading subdividers, paid Roland Park the ulti-
mate tribute. "When people ask me how I enjoyed my trip and
what I saw," he wrote Bouton, "I tell them I saw Roland Park;
and I feel there is not much need of describing anything I saw
elsewhere."[45]

According to Thomas Adams, Bouton and his associates believed that Roland Park's success was due largely to its restrictions. So did others. The *Baltimore American* attributed Roland Park's "phenomenal growth" to its "wise restrictions." And journalist Arthur Tomalin held that these restrictions, "rightly adhered to, have been the making of Roland Park." Even more important, the residents of Roland Park, some of whom had once viewed the restrictions "as a curtailment of their personal rights," now saw them, wrote the *Roland Park Review*, as "vital to the future well-being of our suburb"—"as not only desirable but as necessary," a former president of the company later recalled. The residents, wrote the *American*, "would be loath to see them abolished." If anything, said another journalist, "the demand of the community has not been for fewer restrictions, but for more detailed, comprehensive ones." Over the years residents occasionally violated one or another of the restrictions. But down through 1911 none filed suit to stop the company from enforcing them. A few objected to the requirement, imposed on the second tract, that they submit their plans to the company for approval before building. But most—even those, Adams wrote, who had paid four to five thousand dollars for a lot and now wanted to build a house for ten to twenty thousand dollars—were willing to put up with this and what he called other "arbitrary" restrictions to make sure, as one ad said, that "no undesirable house will be built near [their homes], and that nothing will be done to render the neighborhood unhealthful and objectionable."[46]

After reorganizing the company in 1903 and taking over as its president, Bouton began to look for other opportunities in suburban Baltimore. Eight years later he and his associates joined forces with the Guilford Park Land Company, which owned roughly three hundred acres not far from Roland Park. The result was a stronger Roland Park Company. With Bouton at the helm, the company brought in the Olmsteds to lay out a new subdivision called Guilford. Although a replica of Roland Park in many ways, Guilford was far more sweepingly and stringently restricted. Fully convinced of the value of restrictions, Bouton and his associates incorporated them into a twenty-three-page declaration that covered the whole subdivision. Besides banning nuisances on all the lots and businesses and multifamily houses on all but a few, the restrictions called for setbacks not only at the front but at the rear and sides. They barred not only hogs and livestock but "any live poultry." They forbade the emission of "dark smoke or thick gray smoke" too. Although they dropped the minimum cost requirements, about the value of which Bouton had grown skeptical, they strengthened the design review process, giving the company the right to reject plans "for aesthetic or other reasons," and to take into account whether the proposed house was in "harmony" with its surroundings. A property owner could still build a fence, but only after the company approved the plans. Unlike the Roland Park restrictions, the Guilford restrictions included a provision that no house or lot could be occupied "by any negro or person of negro extraction"—by then "a very common provision in Baltimore," said Bouton, one found "even in subdivisions that almost have no other restrictions at all." This provision did not apply to other racial or ethnic minorities, but as Bouton told his fellow subdividers, the Roland Park Company did not sell to Jews "of any character whatever."[47]

Far from downplaying the restrictions at Guilford, as they had at Roland Park, Bouton and his associates built their marketing campaign around them. The company's ads boasted of "1000

Acres of Restricted Land." "NONE of the many desirable features of GUILFORD," said one, "appeals more to the careful home investor than do its protective restrictions." More than anything else, the ads stressed that the restrictions guaranteed permanence. "Regardless of changes that may take place in other parts of the city," read one, "property owners in this district [meaning Roland Park and Guilford] have full control for all time over the uses to which the land may be put." Given "a degree of protection" found nowhere else, said another, the residents could be confident that nothing would encroach upon their property and reduce its value. To those who had doubts about the benefits of restrictions, the company suggested, "'Ask the man who lives there'—the longer he has lived there the better." To reinforce the point, the company took half-page ads in the major Baltimore newspapers in which more than thirty residents, most of them well-off businessmen and professionals, gave testimonials to the value of restrictions. One after another they said that the restrictions were the best thing about Roland Park. Without them it would have lost the admirable qualities that set it apart from other residential suburbs. Some added that they would not live in Roland Park without restrictions—and even that they would not live anywhere but in a highly restricted community.[48]

"The Rule, Rather than the Exception"

Where Bouton led, others followed—albeit with some trepidation. By far the most famous was J. C. Nichols, whose Country Club District, which consisted of two dozen tracts on more than three thousand acres by the mid-1920s, stood "head and shoulders above all other subdivisions in America," said Samuel S. Thorpe, a Minneapolis subdivider and former president of the National Association of Real Estate Boards. At the turn of the century, Nichols later recalled, he had been afraid to impose restrictions on his property. But over the objections of his associates, he decided to give them a try. And "now," he told a national conference of real estate men in the early 1910s, "I cannot sell a lot without them." At first the restrictions were simple and far from onerous. But inspired by Bouton's success at Roland Park, Nichols later imposed more sweeping and stringent ones. In spite of strong opposition from prospective purchasers, he even required owners to submit their plans to his company before construction. By the late 1910s the Country Club District was one of the nation's most highly restricted communities. And Nichols was one of the chief advocates of restrictive covenants. It pays to impose restrictions, he said at a conference in the early 1920s. It pays because prospective purchasers are more likely to buy lots with restrictions than without. "Our protective restrictions largely are responsible for the extensive demand for homesites and homes in [the] Country Club District," said the Nichols Company in the mid-1920s. "They are our most valuable asset."[49]

Nichols's story was a familiar one. At the start "I was very much opposed to placing any restrictions upon the property," said a Baltimore real estate man, referring to a seventeen-acre plot close to Roland Park and Guilford that he had been asked to subdivide in the mid-1910s. But he soon found that buyers were so worried about what their neighbors might do that it was impossible to sell the lots at a good price without them. A decade later a Minneapolis subdivider remarked that he and his associates had initially been "a little apprehensive" about imposing restrictions, having not yet "learned our lesson," he wrote. But learn it they did. So did other subdividers. By the mid-1910s so many sub-dividers were employing restrictive covenants that, Nichols wrote with some exaggeration, "Practically every city has its restricted and highly protected residence section for the better homes." By the 1920s, Olmsted, Jr., pointed out, the use of restrictive cove-nants was "general among developers who aimed at what they believed to be a discriminating market of lot buyers." And on the eve of the Great Depression, Charles E. Clark, a Yale Law School professor and a leading authority on restrictive covenants, wrote that "restricted residential property is now becoming the rule, rather than the exception, in or near our cities."[50]

What drove subdividers to embrace restrictive covenants was the belief, as a Cleveland real estate man put it, that restricted property was "more valuable and more desirable" than unre-stricted property. What made it more valuable and more desirable was that it was more marketable. And what made it more market-able was that many middle- and upper-middle-class Americans were afraid that the neighbors would use their property in ways that would make the community less appealing. Out of this deep-seated fear grew the widespread belief that restrictions were, as an Omaha subdivider wrote, "not only desirable, but quite neces-sary." They were, said Hugh E. Prather, subdivider of Highland Park, the most fashionable suburb in Dallas, "the life-blood of a high-class development." Provided the same restrictions were im-posed on their neighbors' property, many Americans were willing to accept them on their own. Indeed, many would not buy unre-stricted property. Writing in the mid-1920s about Colony Hills, a highly restricted suburb in Springfield, Massachusetts, one jour-nalist said, "Springfield property twenty years ago was difficult to sell if heavily laden with restrictions. The prospective buyer felt that he was being imposed upon if he could not do exactly as he pleased with his own property. But to-day the home-seeker demands the highest and most detailed restrictions as part of his right."[51]

Nothing revealed the new attitude toward restrictive covenants more clearly than an article in *Suburban Life*, a magazine devoted to promoting the well-being of suburbia. Written in 1911 by journalist Charles K. Farrington and titled "When You Buy Your Building-lot," it offered advice to prospective homeowners. What was striking about the piece was that it was devoted almost entirely to restrictive covenants. "Look carefully into the restrictions before you buy your lot," Farrington wrote. "Also, which is about as important, find out if the vacant property around you (even on nearby streets) is also fully protected." In addition to checking that shops and factories are banned, make sure that "only *one* house can be placed on a lot." Also be sure that "double houses, two-family houses, and flats" are prohibited. Bear in mind the impact of inflation. Twenty years earlier a minimum cost requirement of, say, five thousand dollars would have ensured the erection of "a good, substantial house." But "you will undoubtedly be astonished at the small dwellings that can be built now" for that amount. Above all, check the duration of the restrictions. If they were set to run for thirty years, which was fairly common, and twenty-five have already passed, "you will be protected for only five years."[52]

In an attempt to tap the growing market of so-called discriminating buyers, many subdividers did more than just impose restrictions. Like Bouton, they also built their marketing campaigns around them. Following Nichols's lead, Bouton and, among others, Mike and William C. Hogg, developers with Hugh

Potter of River Oaks, Houston's most fashionable suburb, they ran ads offering "1,000 Acres Restricted," a phrase that was usually put in boldface and capital letters. Other subdividers pointed out that their tracts, most of which did not have a hundred, much less a thousand, acres, were "highly restricted," "fully restricted," and "carefully restricted." Some also insisted that their tracts were more carefully (or highly or fully) restricted than their competitors' were. Besides emphasizing the restrictions in ads, the subdividers urged their salesmen to use them as what Olmsted, Jr., called a "talking point" or "selling point." And it worked. According to Samuel Thorpe, restrictions "proved to be our best sales argument." Henry Clarke, general manager of a Washington, D.C., real estate firm (and former director of sales at Palos Verdes Estates), agreed. Looking back at the history of hundreds of successful residential suburbs developed in the past twenty-five years, he said in 1932, "In practically every case the developer based his sales appeal in the protection he offered the purchasers of his property."[53]

As historian Michael Holleran has pointed out, the subdividers were selling permanence. Or to put it another way, they were exploiting the growing fear of unwanted change, especially of the encroachment of "undesirable" people and "undesirable" activities. A good example of their approach was a promotional brochure for Brendonwood, a 350-acre subdivision northeast of Indianapolis that was developed by Charles E. Lewis and laid out by George E. Kessler. The brochure showed a "Silver Flash" gas station and, under it, issued the following warning:

> You know you don't like a thing like this against or over the way from your home. You know how it grates on you. . . . Possibly it hasn't reached YOUR home yet—but how can you keep it away

once it lifts its peace-destroying, price-destroying head at your door? How can you tell when it will reach your home? One day we see in the paper that Meridian St. at Maple Road is in danger. Next we learn that Delaware at 16th St. is threatened. Look around you! See the havoc that has been and is being wrought. What street, what neighborhood is safe?

The subdividers of Raymond Village, a tract not far from Pasadena, asked prospective purchasers a similar question. "When you buy a lot for a home, what assurance do you have, ordinarily, that an unsightly shanty, a chicken ranch, or other objectionable structure will not be placed next door?" It has happened before, the subdividers warned, and it could happen again. If it was not a gas station or an unsightly shanty, it would be a saloon, a factory, a laundry, or a funeral parlor. Time and again families buy a lot in an attractive subdivision, said an ad for Hollywood Hills, a tract northwest of downtown Los Angeles. "Years later, when they have invested heavily in a handsome house, they find that restrictions are lapsing around them, values depreciating and their best neighbors leaving:—they learn, in short, that their location is becoming UNDESIRABLE for a first-class residence."[54]

Americans had a choice, the subdividers claimed. They could buy a lot in an unrestricted tract, build a house, wait for the neighborhood to decline, sell the property, more often than not for less than they paid, and buy another lot in another unrestricted tract. Or they could "GO TO BRENDONWOOD"—or one of the many other highly restricted subdivisions that had solved the problem of permanence. There, declared the Nichols Company, residents are "PROTECTED by thorough restrictions AGAINST EVERY POSSIBLE DANGER." There, said a River Oaks pamphlet, you will have a home "for all time," a home in a community of nothing but homes, all "carefully planned, substantially built, in keeping with River Oaks standards." There, another Brendonwood brochure pointed out, you can live in your home all your life and "hand it down" to your children. How nice, it said, to be able to live "in the homes of our fathers." Other subdividers hammered away at the same points. St. Francis Wood will remain unspoiled, claimed the Mason-McDuffie Company. Its restrictions "are a shield permanently protecting its homes and stabilizing and increasing its land values. They ward off the blighting effect of stores, flats and apartments; they prevent crowding together of houses and cutting off of view[s]; they deny entrance to undesirable neighbors and ugly and inharmonious houses." Shaker Village will never change, said the Van Sweringen Company of one of its many subdivisions in Shaker Heights. "No matter what changes time may bring around it, no matter what waves of commercialism may beat upon its borders, Shaker Village is secure, its homes and gardens . . . serene and protected for all time."[55]

In an attempt to gain an edge over their competitors, a few subdividers decided to offer prospective purchasers something in addition to permanence. That something was exclusivity. The subdividers had long known that there was a small market for exclusive suburbs like Llewellyn Park and Tuxedo Park. But now they had reason to believe that the market was rapidly growing, that the same well-to-do Americans who were joining exclusive country clubs, spending summers at exclusive oceanside communities, and sending children to exclusive prep schools might also want to live in exclusive residential suburbs. And exclusive residential suburbs meant highly restricted suburbs. In Lawrence Park, a subdivision in Bronxville, New York, prospective purchasers could be confident that the residents would be "of the very best material," said developer William Van Duzer Lawrence; all others would be "rigidly excluded." Brendonwood residents, read a brochure, could be sure that "your neighbors will be men and women of similar tastes who, like yourself, will cherish Brendonwood and treasure all it gives them." And the owners of Beverly Crest, a subdivision in the foothills of Los Angeles, advertised it as a "Permanently RESTRICTED DISTRICT for PARTICULAR PEOPLE." In some affluent subdivisions exclusivity was even more of a "talking point." Hancock Park, which boasted of "its stringent restrictions," called itself "the most exclusive residential district" in Los Angeles. Not to be outdone, Bel-Air, which said it was to suburbia what Tiffany was to gold and silver, claimed it was "The Exclusive Residential Park of the West." Short Hills described itself as "New Jersey's Most Exclusive Residence Section." And nearby Montclair said it was "The Handsomest and Most Exclusive of New York's Suburbs."[56]

By the late 1920s it seemed that the subdividers had solved the problem Olmsted had identified more than half a century earlier. By virtue of their efforts, most cities had at least one or two highly restricted suburbs for the well-to-do. Many big cities had dozens. As well as Roland Park and Guilford, Baltimore had Homeland, the Roland Park Company's third big venture. It now advertised "1,500 acres of *restricted* land." Washington, D.C., had several restricted suburbs, among the most famous of which was Chevy Chase, Maryland, a huge parcel that was subdivided by Francis G. Newlands, a U.S. senator from Nevada who had made a fortune in the West before moving to the nation's capital. Affluent Philadelphians had a host of restricted subdivisions to choose from, most of them located along the "Main Line." With dozens of restricted subdivisions spread over Westchester County, southern

Connecticut, northern New Jersey, and Nassau County, well-off New Yorkers had an even greater choice. Among the best known of these subdivisions were Lawrence Park, Great Neck Hills, in Nassau County, and Forest Hills Gardens, a highly restricted sub-division in Queens that was sponsored by the Russell Sage Foundation (and, at the start, managed by Bouton). Boston, home of the Olmsted firm, had its share of highly restricted suburbs too. One of the most noteworthy was Oak Hills Village. Located in Newton, about seven miles from the State House, it was developed by Arnold Hartmann, who not only imposed the customary restrictions but also required every prospective purchaser to submit three social and three business references, all of which were "carefully investigated." No resident, no matter how highly recommended, could let anyone lease or occupy his home without Hartmann's written permission.[57]

The Midwest had many highly restricted suburbs too. In a class by itself was Kansas City's Country Club District, which was hailed by the Nichols Company as "the largest high-class, restricted residential development under one management in the world" and praised by Raymond Unwin, a leading British town planner, as "America's best example of residential planning." (After Palos Verdes Estates was developed, the Country Club District was no longer the largest such development in the United States, but along with Roland Park it was still the most influential.) Almost as well known as the Country Club District was the Van Sweringen brothers' Shaker Heights, some of whose tracts were restricted into the twenty-first century. What the Country Club District was to Kansas City and Shaker Heights to Cleveland, Brendonwood was to Indianapolis and Ottawa Hills to Toledo. Covering more than twelve hundred acres just west of the city, Ottawa Hills was developed by John North Willys, a wealthy automaker, and managed by Paul A. Harsch, a local real estate man. It is *"The* Greatest Suburban Development Ever Undertaken," wrote landscape architect William Pitkin, Jr. Detroit, Milwaukee, Minneapolis, and Columbus had several highly restricted suburbs too—though none dominated its market in the way that the Country Club District did. Chicago, the metropolis of the Midwest, had even more, the most famous of which were spread along the North Shore.[58]

The West also had its share of highly restricted suburbs. Among the earliest was The Uplands, which was located in Victoria, capital of British Columbia. Covering nearly five hundred acres of oceanfront property, it was developed in the early 1900s by Oldfield, Kirby & Gardner, a Winnipeg firm that retained Olmsted Brothers to work on both the layout and the restrictions. Along with Montreal's Westmount, Toronto's Lawrence Park, and Calgary's Mount Royal, The Uplands became one of Canada's most fashionable suburbs—"a second Tuxedo Park," wrote Cornelius Vanderbilt, Jr., in 1921. The Bay Area lagged behind. "Except for three small tracts with a total area of less than fifty acres, there is no property in San Francisco upon which any restrictions whatever have been placed," Duncan McDuffie said in 1912. There was not much in Oakland and Berkeley either. Things changed after McDuffie's firm, Mason-McDuffie, developed St. Francis Wood, a highly restricted suburb about three miles southwest of the San Francisco Civic Center, in the mid-1910s. Inspired by the success of St. Francis Wood, which the prominent German planner Werner Hegemann called *"the most distinguished residential suburb in America,"* Walter H. Leimert and others imposed stringent restrictions on their East Bay subdivisions after World

War I. Nowhere in the West, and perhaps nowhere in the United States, did restricted subdivisions proliferate as rapidly as in Los Angeles, the country's fastest growing metropolis and its most thoroughly suburban. From the Palos Verdes Peninsula to the San Fernando Valley, from the San Gabriel Valley to the Pacific Ocean, subdividers turned tens of thousands of acres of flatlands and foothills into Oak Knoll, Beverly Hills, Huntington Palisades, and scores of other highly restricted suburbs.[59]

Even the South and the Southwest had restricted suburbs, though far fewer than the more urbanized regions. (As late as 1920, at which time a dozen American cities had more than half a million people, New Orleans, Louisville, and Atlanta were the only southern or southwestern cities with as many as two hundred thousand.) Atlanta had Druid Hills. Developed by the Kirkwood Land Company, it was another large subdivision whose manager, local entrepreneur Joel Hurt, relied heavily on the advice of the Olmsteds. Birmingham had Redmont Park and Mountain Brook Estates, both of which were subdivided by Robert Jemison, Jr., the only southerner invited to join Nichols, Bouton, and the other leading subdividers at their annual conferences. Among the other highly restricted southern subdivisions were Louisville's Bonnycastle Terrace, Greensboro's Irving Park, and Savannah's Chatham Crescent, whose promoters claimed, "Great care has been taken to protect this property with suitable building restrictions." Down through 1920 the Southwest's best known suburb was Highland Park in Dallas, which was subdivided by Hugh E. Prather, the only southwesterner invited to the developers' annual conferences. It was soon overshadowed by Houston's River Oaks, which was modeled on the Country Club District. Borrowing from the Nichols Company's ads, River Oaks billed itself as "the largest high-class residential area under one management in any Southwestern city."[60] Perhaps inspired by Highland Park and River Oaks, subdividers laid out Tucson's first restricted suburb, Colonia Solana, in the late 1920s.

Some subdividers, the best known of whom were Bouton and Nichols, appealed exclusively to the well-to-do. Others targeted other groups as well. Henry E. Huntington, the Los Angeles transit and real estate magnate who developed large parts of the San Gabriel Valley, subdivided Oneonta Park in South Pasadena for middle-class Angelenos who could only dream of living in Oak Knoll and his other posh subdivisions in Pasadena and San Marino. The Thompson brothers, King and Ben, who, along with Charles F. Johnson, were the leading subdividers in Columbus, Ohio, developed Grandview, a middle-class suburb in the mid-1910s, a few years before they followed Nichols's lead and created a Country Club District of their own for the well-to-do—a community later incorporated as the village of Upper Arlington. Still other subdividers focused exclusively on the middle-class market. And by the 1920s many middle-class subdivisions were restricted. But since the subdividers were aware that the middle class was somewhat ambivalent about restricted property, these tracts were less sweepingly and stringently restricted than the upper-middle- and upper-class tracts on which they were modeled, and as a rule their restrictions expired sooner. The subdividers employed restrictions as a marketing tool in middle-class tracts too but, except in the case of racial covenants, in a gingerly way. Instead of describing the restrictions as sweeping and stringent, the ads referred to them as sensible, reasonable, suitable, adequate, and "wise but not prohibitive." An ad for City Terrace, a lower-middle-class subdivision a few miles east of downtown Los Angeles whose "homesites" cost only $650, was typical. "Strict race restrictions and moderate building restrictions," it read.[61]

Some subdividers held that even working-class suburbs should have restrictions. Ironically, one of the most forceful spokesmen for this position was Nichols, whose Country Club District was not only very expensive, well beyond the reach of all but the well-to-do, but also very exclusive. According to a 1930 study, it was home to more than half the Kansas City elite. The working-man — "the man who earns $2 a day, or less" — needed restrictions, Nichols said. With "the help of his wife and family" and after "years of saving," he may be able "to build himself an attractive, modest, four-roomed cottage." But without restrictions, "he may soon find his little home between unpainted, one-room shacks, and the most undesirable neighbors, or he may find the adjoining lot often being used as a junk pen, or a huckster's unsanitary yard." Indeed, Nichols wrote, working people needed restrictions more than the well-to-do. They were more vulnerable to unwanted change — and, as their homes were ordinarily their major asset, less capable of coping with it. They were more likely to live in neighborhoods that were susceptible to the encroachment of stables, coal yards, factories, and other noxious activities. They were also more likely to live on very small lots, which left them at the mercy of inconsiderate neighbors. Proper restrictions, Nichols wrote, would not only safeguard the workingman's home against nuisances and give it some privacy. They would also provide space for "a little grass plot" and "a tree or two" that would protect the family from "the noise, dirt and dust" of the streets. Land-use controls "will prove just as great a benefit to the community" if applied to "neighborhoods of workmen's cottages" as they do when applied to "the residential sections of the well-to-do."[62]

A few subdividers practiced what Nichols preached. Chief among them was Jared S. Torrance, a successful New York businessman who moved in 1889 to southern California, where he made a fortune as a real estate subdivider and major stockholder in Union Oil, Union Tool, and other companies. With the backing of Lyman Stewart, president of Union Tool, which was running out of space in the southeastern industrial district, Torrance put together a syndicate that bought the Dominguez Ranch, a three-thousand-acre tract located roughly halfway between downtown Los Angeles and the Los Angeles harbor, in 1911. The aim of the syndicate, known as the Dominguez Land Company, was to turn the old ranch into a model industrial town that would serve as home to firms that were looking for more spacious quarters and, in the words of historian Robert Phelps, "a haven from a volatile labor situation" in Los Angeles proper. To draw the plan for this bastion of the open shop, the company hired the Olmsted brothers. On their advice, it adopted a set of restrictions that, to quote Torrance, after whom the town was named, treaded "pretty hard on the toes of the Constitution of the United States." Although much less sweeping and stringent than the restrictions at Guilford, which was subdivided at about the same time, they banned slaughterhouses, glue factories, and other nuisances. They prohibited saloons and the sale of alcohol. They limited many lots to single-family homes. They mandated modest setbacks and design review. And following the then conventional practice, the company excluded "Blacks" as well as "Hindoos and other Asiatics"—though it set up a separate "foreign quarter" in which non-whites were allowed to live.[63]

Although praised by one observer as "America's first great industrial garden city," Torrance languished, writes historian Becky M. Nicolaides. The company had so much trouble selling residential property that it lowered prices 40 to 80 percent. But even with lots as low as a hundred dollars, working people were not interested. Much as they favored racial covenants, they opposed building and land-use restrictions. So instead of Torrance, they headed to Home Gardens and other nearby tracts that imposed few restrictions other than a ban on non-Caucasians. What was true in Los Angeles was true in other cities. From the viewpoint of working people, factories might be a source of noise, dirt, and dust, but they were also a source of jobs. Far from a nuisance, saloons were a convivial place to relax after work. And gas stations, reviled at Brendonwood, were more a convenience than an annoyance. Many working people saw nothing wrong with building their homes without architects and contractors, copying the plans from books, doing the work themselves, using the cheapest materials, and adding rooms when they had the money. Nor did many working people see anything wrong with raising chickens and rabbits, or goats and cows for that matter, all of which served as valuable sources of food and income and helped insulate their families from the vagaries of the market. Above all, most working people did not value permanence as much as the well-to-do did. They did not intend to spend their lives in a Torrance or Home Gardens; nor did they expect their children to live there after they died. These suburbs were not so much the last stop, as, say, Roland Park or the Country Club District was, but a way station—a place that announced not that its residents had arrived, but that they were on the way.[64] Thus by the late 1920s what was the rule, in Professor Clark's words, for the well-to-do (and, to a lesser degree, the middle class) was still the exception for the workingman.

"The More Restrictions the More Buyers"

At the same time restrictive covenants were spreading over much of suburbia, they were changing in a number of important and highly revealing ways. Perhaps the most striking was in the length of the restrictions. When Bouton subdivided Roland Park, he followed the customary practice of including the restrictions in the deed—one or two sides of a long sheet of paper that gave the names of the seller and the buyer, a description of the parcel, and the price and terms of payment, if any. By the time his company developed Guilford, the restrictions were so long that it had to publish them as a separate document that ran more than twenty pages. Things were much the same in other large-scale subdivisions. Lakeshore Highlands had more than ten pages of restrictions, Ottawa Hills more than twenty, and Palos Verdes Estates more than thirty. (The Palos Verdes Estates Protective Restrictions seemed even longer because they were published in the same booklet as the articles of incorporation and by-laws of the Homes Association.) Robert Jemison, Arnold Hartmann, and a few other large-scale subdividers bucked the trend and included the restrictions in the deeds, but most went along. An interesting case in point is the Knight-Menard Company, developer of Devonshire Downs, a tract of more than five hundred acres in the affluent Bloomfield Hills district north of Detroit. Worried that if the restrictions were too long they would annoy prospective purchasers, Knight-Menard favored keeping them as short as possible. Yet its general restrictions, which applied to the entire tract, ran seventeen pages. And the general restrictions did not deal with the setback regulations, minimum cost requirements, and other items that were included in the supplementary restrictions, which were imposed on each part of the tract as it was put on the market.[65]

As well as longer, the restrictions became more wordy. The subdividers were driven to make this change largely by concerns about how the courts would respond if asked to enjoin a property owner from violating one or another of the restrictions. These concerns were so strong that subdividers began to hire lawyers to draft the restrictions—or, at the very least, to review and revise them. (Perhaps one reason the restrictions were so wordy was that lawyers were trained to anticipate every possibility, no matter how remote.) These concerns were far from groundless. At the same time the courts said that they would enforce restrictive covenants under certain conditions, they stressed that the restrictions would be "strictly construed." By this the judges meant that they would read the restrictions as they were written, that they would take them to mean exactly what they said, no more and no less. They would not infer anything from them; nor would they take into account anything they implied. Given that the law "favors the free and untrammeled use of real property," as the Missouri Supreme Court put it, the judges would not only put the burden of proof upon the subdividers (and other property owners applying for an injunction), but would also resolve all doubts against them.[66]

Just how strictly the restrictions would be construed was revealed by a Massachusetts trial court in 1881. Although restrictive covenants were by then enforceable in the Bay State, the court refused to restrain the defendant from opening a grocery store in a Cambridge tract whose subdivider had banned "any nauseous or offensive trade whatsoever" and any trade that threatened "the quiet and comfort of the neighborhood." A grocery, said the court, was not one of the trades "enumerated in the deed"; nor was it "nauseous or offensive" or a threat to "the quiet and comfort of the neighborhood." A Missouri appellate court came to the same conclusion in 1910, when it declined to issue an injunction against a property owner who was planning to build a hotel in a St. Louis tract whose developer had banned livery stables, manufacturing establishments, and, among other things, saloons and grocery stores. Upholding the trial court's decision, the court wrote that nowhere in the restrictions was there a reference to hotels. In the absence of such a reference, or a restriction against any place of business, it had no alternative but to rule that the proposed hotel was "a proper use of the property." The Illinois Supreme Court construed restrictive covenants even more strictly in 1893, when it ruled against a group of plaintiffs who had applied for an injunction against a Chicago property owner who was building flats (or apartment houses) in a tract whose restrictions allowed "only a single dwelling." Despite the plaintiff's argument that "a single dwelling" meant a "dwelling house to be occupied by a single family," which was almost surely what the subdivider intended, the court held that it meant "one dwelling house, which may be used by one family or more." If they intended "to prohibit the erection of a flat on the property, why did not the parties say so in the deed," it asked, "or if they intended that only a building such as is usually built for a private residence of a family, should be erected, why not say that in the deed?"[67]

The subdividers got the message. Instead of a short statement that the lots could be used only for "residence purposes" (or only for "a single dwelling"), they now included a carefully worded provision that excluded anything but a single-family house. "No building of any kind whatsoever shall be erected or maintained [on the tract] except private dwellings, each dwelling being designed for occupation by a single family," read the Guilford restrictions. At Devonshire Downs only "one private detached dwelling" could be built on each lot, and "no such private dwelling shall be designed for or occupied by more than one family together with the domestic employees thereof." At the Fairway Section, part of Samuel S. Thorpe's Country Club District, no lot could "be improved, used or occupied for other than private one-family residence purposes"—and, to leave no room for doubt, "flats, duplexes, [and] apartments" were expressly prohibited. Instead of saying that the lots could not be used for a handful of nuisances and any noxious, offensive, and dangerous trade, the restrictions now enumerated scores of proscribed trades, everything from oil refineries to quarries, breweries to canneries, brickyards to crematories. Palos Verdes Estates even excluded slaughterhouses—though it was inconceivable that anyone would build a slaughterhouse in a place that had no cattle and no railroads to carry them there. In 1915—a decade before Munsey Park, a highly restricted subdivision in Nassau County, listed one hundred different types of proscribed businesses—one observer noted that subdividers were already specifically banning "practically every known kind of manufactory or trade."[68]

As well as more wordy, the restrictions became more stringent. When subdividers used restrictive covenants in the early and mid nineteenth century, they routinely included a provision banning noxious, offensive, and dangerous trades, by which they meant trades most Americans regarded as nuisances. A slaughterhouse fell into this category, as did a foundry, a tannery, and a brewery, a blacksmith's forge, a livery stable, an iron factory, and, in the words of an 1825 deed, "any manufactory for the making of glue, varnish, vitriol, ink or turpentine." No fashionable residential neighborhood, it was believed, could survive the encroachment of these smelly, noisy, and dirty businesses. But things changed in the late nineteenth and early twentieth centuries, when the subdividers realized there was a large market for tightly restricted property. To tap this market, they not only added to the list of proscribed trades. They also banned trades that were far from noxious, offensive, and dangerous—a hardware store, for example, or a stationery store. Instead of enumerating all the proscribed businesses, which would have taken pages, The Uplands banned "any trade or business whatsoever." So did other large-scale subdivisions. In line with the conventional wisdom of the real estate economists, subdividers even expanded the concept of nuisance to include anything other than single-family homes. A case in point was the Mason-McDuffie Company, subdivider of St. Francis Wood, which banned "flats, double houses, apartment houses, tenement houses, hotels, and public boarding or lodging houses" as well as a "store, grocery or mercantile business of any kind."[69]

Some subdividers were worried that such restrictions, however well intended, might be too stringent. How, they wondered, would doctors and other professionals who were in the market for suburban property react when they found out that they would not be allowed to keep offices in their homes? How would other prospective purchasers respond when they learned that they would not be able to shop for groceries and stationery anywhere in the neighborhood? What was the point of such restrictions when there were many well-to-do Americans who had raised their children and grown tired of running a house and now were in the market for an apartment in the same neighborhood? And, said Nichols, what was the point of such restrictions when there were many nearby property owners who stood ready to build shops and stores to capitalize on the buying power of the Country Club District and other affluent communities? Some subdividers were so worried that they allowed doctors and other professionals to work out of their homes—though, in one case, only with the approval of 50 percent of the owners of the nearby lots. Some also set aside a few small parts of the tract for shops and stores, which had restrictions of their own, and other small parts for low-rise apartment houses, which were often located at the edge of the tracts, where they served as a buffer between the small business centers and the large single-family neighborhoods. A few even built large shopping centers, the best known of which was Nichols's Country Club Plaza. (Nichols also rented some lots for use as gas stations—which, he told his fellow subdividers in 1919, were generating a good deal of much needed revenue.)[70]

During the early and mid nineteenth century a few subdividers used restrictive covenants to bar owners from building too close to the street. A typical restriction, imposed on a tract in West Roxbury, one of Boston's "streetcar suburbs," defined too close as less than twenty feet. Once again things changed in the late nineteenth and early twentieth centuries, when restrictive covenants grew much more common. Not only did many subdividers impose what were known as setbacks, but they also imposed them at the rear and the sides as well as the front, where they ordinarily ran from fifteen to fifty feet. Garages and other outbuildings were subject to setbacks too. So, on occasion, were covered porches, bay windows, and other projections. In some cases the setbacks were uniform, in others they varied from one section to another. Often the owners were forbidden to subdivide their property. And sometimes they were barred from building on much of it. Perhaps the most stringent such restriction was imposed at Hycliff, a very expensive subdivision that was laid out in Stamford, Connecticut, in the late 1920s. No house could cover more than 22 percent of the lot. Nor could the width of the house (or, to be precise, of the "main part" thereof) exceed 60 percent of the width of the lot.[71] Except on lots of at least one or two acres, these restrictions very much limited what an owner had to say about the siting and size of his home.

Less common than setback regulations, though more common than area requirements, were height restrictions. These restrictions had a curious history. During the mid-nineteenth century some subdividers found themselves in a bind. They had to sell lots. But if they sold one to someone who built a small and flimsy house, one out of place in a fashionable residential neighborhood, they might have trouble selling the remaining lots. Hence some subdividers imposed a minimum height limit, a restriction that no house could be built that was less than two or three stories high, exclusive of the basement and attic. By the turn of the century, however, many subdividers found themselves in a different bind. By imposing minimum height limits, they could block the erection of small and flimsy houses, but such a restriction would not prevent a lot owner from building a house that obstructed a neighbor's view or detracted from the natural setting. So instead of a minimum height limit, many subdividers imposed a maximum height limit, which was usually two or three stories, again exclusive of the basement and attic. As a rule subdividers set a uniform limit in the whole tract, though sometimes they set different limits in different sections.[72]

As well as more stringent, the restrictions became more sweeping. As late as the 1890s subdividers seldom imposed more than a handful of restrictions—if they imposed any at all. A typical deed included little more than a ban on nuisances, saloons, livery stables, and offensive trades as well as a setback regulation and a height limit. "Our first restrictions," one associate of Nichols later recalled, "were all contained in one paragraph." But in response to what one observer called "the constantly increasing demand . . . for homes in restricted residential districts," subdividers now competed with one another to offer even more highly restricted tracts. That meant, said Nichols, they had to impose more restrictions. And impose them they did. In Wilmington, Delaware, for example, the number of restrictions per deed increased from an average of four in the early 1900s to an average of thirteen in the late 1920s. In general, large subdivisions, most of which were laid out by professionals, had more restrictions than small ones, most of which were laid out by amateurs. Some of the new restrictions followed in the path of the old ones, but many went off in what Bouton called "other directions."[73] Some had never been considered. Others had been considered, only to be rejected because the subdividers feared that the market was not ready for them or, even if it was, that the courts were not likely to enforce them.

Among the new restrictions were the minimum cost requirements. Starting in the 1880s, a few subdividers adopted a novel strategy to prevent the erection of houses that might lower the value of the remaining lots. Instead of imposing a minimum height limit, they banned houses that cost less than a specific sum —two thousand dollars in an Everett, Massachusetts, tract, for example, and four thousand dollars in a Brookline subdivision. A major break with past practice, this restriction caught on quickly. Over the next three decades most of the dozens of subdivisions the Olmsteds worked on imposed this requirement. So did most of the hundreds of others whose subdividers managed without the Olmsteds. In Columbus, Ohio, for example, nearly three of every four subdivisions laid out between 1900 and 1930, many by Charles F. Johnson and the Thompson brothers, had a minimum cost requirement. This restriction was found not only in very expensive subdivisions but also in moderately priced ones—even in a few where the minimum cost was as low as five hundred to a thousand dollars. From 1900 to 1930 the minimum cost rose steadily, if unevenly, the result in large part of the rising cost of living. By the 1920s many subdivisions had restrictions of five to ten thousand dollars, several of ten to fifteen thousand, and a few, including one in Scarsdale named Berkley and another in suburban Detroit named Chelmsleigh, of twenty to thirty thousand dollars.[74] (It is interesting to note that in the wake of the great wartime inflation some subdividers began to think it might be time to replace a minimum cost requirement with a minimum square footage requirement, which would not be affected by the rising cost of living.)

But as the subdividers knew, an expensive house was not necessarily an attractive one—or, for that matter, one that contributed to the architectural harmony of the community. And if they forgot, the architects were there to remind them. "A $5,000 cottage, tastefully designed, adds greatly to the charm of its environment," said Oswald C. Herring of New York in 1913, "where a $50,000 house of commonplace or freakish design becomes an indelible blot upon the landscape." Money and taste were not

the same, he pointed out: "Many families of cultivation and refinement lack a well-filled purse and could not afford to invest
more than $10,000 or $15,000 in a suburban home. Why should
persons of this highly desirable class be barred from settling in
a convenient and attractive locality that allows an ill-mannered,
uneducated boor to build a huge costly edifice awkwardly proportioned, vulgar in outline and glaring in color, an eyesore to
the neighborhood?" If minimum cost requirements did nothing
to prevent the erection of architectural eyesores—if, as Frank L.
Meline, a Los Angeles real estate man, put it, they did nothing
to discourage the unsightly mix of "pseudo-Italian villa[s]" next
to Colonial cottages and "within a stone's throw" of Spanish-style
dwellings—perhaps more drastic measures were needed. Instead
of permitting "each owner to build without regard to what his
neighbor has done or is likely to do," wrote John Charles Olmsted in 1914, perhaps it made sense to impose restrictions that
allowed only "a single style of architecture" and "a limited choice
of exterior building materials." Perhaps it also made sense to include in the deeds a provision that gave subdividers the right
to review building plans before construction. These restrictions
would drive away some customers, Olmsted conceded, but in the
long run they would boost sales.[75]

By the mid-1910s the idea of design review had been floating
around for nearly half a century. It had been tried as early as 1870,
when the Peabody Heights Company laid out Lilliendale, Baltimore's "ideal dwelling house neighborhood," and included in the
deeds a provision that the design of the houses had to be approved
by the company's directors, a provision upheld by the Maryland
courts. But the idea did not catch on as quickly as minimum cost
requirements, and through the 1890s design review was uncom-

mon. It was one thing to prevent a lot owner from operating an offensive business or building a house up to the property line, but as even Olmsted, Sr., admitted, it was quite another to sit in judgment on the design of someone's home. Subdividers, wrote one well-informed observer, were reluctant to evaluate architecture, about which they had no special expertise, and "to criticize the taste of a prospective buyer and his architect." Buyers "fancied the idea as little" as subdividers. "It seemed like over-stepping the legitimate bounds of real estate restrictions and impertinently to interfere with a man's private opinion." Even Nichols, a strong supporter of restrictive covenants, was hesitant to impose design review. "I am trying to get my nerves up to requiring purchasers to submit their plans to me for approval," he wrote to Bouton, one of the first subdividers to adopt this restriction, in 1913. "I have talked to a great many of my purchasers about it, and almost invariably they say at first that they would not buy the ground under that regulation, because it has never been done in any way in this part of the country, and it will take time for me to work it out."[76]

It did not take long. Nichols soon followed Bouton's lead, as did other subdividers who had come to believe their customers were more likely to buy if they felt confident the neighbors could not build houses that were poorly designed (or, even if well designed, unsuitable for the site or the neighborhood). By the mid-1920s design review was fairly common. (Some subdividers went over the plans themselves; others turned the job over to an independent art or architectural jury, a step taken to insulate them from irate property owners.) Besides requiring good design and architectural harmony, a few subdividers also imposed restrictions on style, color, and materials. Outside of Palos Verdes Estates, nowhere were these restrictions as tough as in Shaker Village. No artificial stone was allowed, no buff or colored brick, and no black or dark-colored mortar either. No tar or composition sheet roofing was permitted ("because it has neither character nor beauty"), no asphalt shingles ("for a similar reason"), and no tile roofs on Colonial houses. On "the side elevations in the principal rooms," only full-length windows would do. Once seen as an obstacle to sales, Olmsted, Jr., wrote, architectural control turned into a strong "selling point." Of all the restrictions, it was "one of the most important, certainly the most broadly inclusive, and when skillfully employed the most effective." Although troublesome, it was necessary, said Bouton, who added that in a subdivision with architectural control minimum cost requirements were "wholly unnecessary." Despite his misgivings, Nichols was pleased to report in the mid-1920s that he had not lost more than a dozen sales because of his decision to require lot owners to submit their plans to him.[77]

Other restrictions went in still other directions. Late in the 1880s Olmsted, Sr., persuaded the owners of Sudbrook, a tract outside Baltimore, to include in the deeds a provision that barred fences (and hedges) more than four feet high. Another major break with past practice, this restriction was soon adopted by many other subdividers. During the next three decades they regulated the type and location of fences as well. In some subdivisions fences were even subject to design review. In one they had to be screened by hedges or other plants. In many they could not be put up without the subdivider's permission. In one, fences could not be built "except for the purpose of protecting growing hedges." In a posh subdivision in Erie County, Pennsylvania, they could not be built at all. Starting in the early twentieth century, many subdividers also imposed restrictions on billboards and

other signs. They prevented property owners from posting anything but a doctor's or dentist's doorplate and "For Sale" and "For
Rent" signs. Even these signs were strictly regulated—nowhere
more so than in Great Neck Hills, where they had to be "lettered
in gilt with a black back-ground" and could not exceed "one foot
in height by three feet in length." Along with Great Neck Hills,
St. Francis Wood was one of many highly restricted subdivisions
in which no sign could be posted without prior approval. To be
on the safe side, its subdividers reserved the right to "summarily
remove and destroy all unauthorized signs."[78]

Olmsted, Sr., also included in the Sudbrook restrictions a provision banning pigs and putting a limit on the number of horses
and cows. Although one Boston subdivider had barred swine as
early as the mid-1860s, this restriction was yet another major
break with past practice, one that was widely adopted after the
turn of the century, and especially after World War I. In Wilmington, for example, 70 percent of the restricted subdivisions
filed in the 1920s prohibited domestic animals. As this restriction grew more common, it also became more sweeping. Starting with pigs, many subdividers soon banned horses, cows and
cattle, goats and sheep, and, in some places, chickens (and other
fowl) and rabbits. A typical subdivision, Thorpe's Country Club
District, for example, banned domestic animals "of any kind, except dogs and cats"—though it allowed riding horses with the
written permission of the subdivider. Hycliff also allowed "household pets"—though it drew the line at vicious dogs and "raucous"
parrots. Even the subdivisions that did not prohibit domestic animals carefully regulated them. The Uplands permitted cattle, but
only on a lot of at least five acres, a very large lot indeed, and only
if "well screened." Brendonwood allowed chickens, but only with

the permission of the property owners' association. Other sub-divisions permitted some domestic animals, but not, as at Devon-shire Downs, if they were "offensive or obnoxious to neighbors or to the community."[79]

After the turn of the century subdividers imposed other novel restrictions, most of which were less common than the restric-tions on fences, signs, and domestic animals. In some tracts no one could operate a quarry (or a gravel or sand pit), and in a few— many of them in southern California, the site of vast petroleum deposits—no one could drill for oil, natural gas, or other hydro-carbons. A handful of subdividers required that an owner start or finish building a house within two or three years after buying the lot, a provision favored by Olmsted and his sons as a way to curb speculation. More common were restrictions that prevented the owner from occupying the house before it was completed or putting up a garage or other outbuilding before the house. Re-strictions were also imposed on what the owners could do once they moved in. Some forbade them to burn bituminous (or soft) coal or any fuel that gave off heavy black smoke. Some barred them from leaving garbage and ash cans in the open or burning refuse without the permission of the homeowners' association. A few even regulated clotheslines. In Great Neck Hills, for ex-ample, owners were required to screen "articles of a conspicuous nature," in order to avoid marring "the general appearance of the premises as high-class residence property." And in Colony Hills, wrote a journalist, garages—which were allowed only as "part of, or closely attached to, the house"—could not open to the street. "There is," he pointed out, "no special pleasure to be gained from peering into your neighbor's garage and seeing his storm doors, oil cans, and his very utilitarian but dirty overalls in which he putters over his gasoline slave."[80]

Caucasians Only

Many subdividers also employed restrictions to exclude "undesirable" people as well as "undesirable" activities. By far the most common of these provisions were racial covenants. Under a typical covenant, an owner was forbidden to sell or lease the property to a member of any of a number of allegedly undesirable racial, ethnic, or religious groups. He or she was also forbidden to allow a member of these groups, other than chauffeurs, gardeners, or domestic servants, to use or occupy the property. A few subdividers had employed racial covenants in the mid-nineteenth century. In Brookline, for example, one forbade "any negro or native of Ireland" to occupy a dwelling, and in Baltimore another barred the sale or lease of a house to "a negro or person of African or Mongolian [that is, Asian] descent." But such restrictions were very much the exception before the 1890s. Indeed, not even the most racist subdividers imposed racial covenants. A case in point was Francis G. Newlands, the mining magnate and U.S. senator who laid out Chevy Chase in the early 1890s. Newlands saw the United States as "the home of the white race." To him, "race tolerance" meant "race amalgamation," and "race intolerance" meant "race war." Fusing the racism of the South with the racism of the West, he called for repealing the Fifteenth Amendment, thereby denying African-Americans, "an inferior race," the right to vote, and restricting immigration to "the white race," thereby excluding Chinese, Japanese, and other Asians. Despite his outspoken racism, Newlands did not include racial covenants among the minimum cost requirements and other restrictions he imposed on the first subdivisions at Chevy Chase.[81]

At a time of widespread racism, not to mention nativism and anti-Semitism, why did Newlands and other large-scale subdividers refrain from imposing racial covenants? The answer is two-fold. Most subdividers had reason to believe that racial covenants were unnecessary. Very few African-Americans lived in their communities. Even fewer earned enough to buy a lot, much less to build a house that met the minimum cost requirement. What was true for African-Americans was true for Asian-Americans, though not necessarily for Jewish Americans. In the unlikely event that, say, an African-American wanted to buy a lot, a subdivider could always refuse to sell, even in the absence of a racial covenant. If a black person wanted to buy a house in a white neighborhood, most real estate agents would not show it to him. And if he somehow managed to find a place, said Hugh E. Prather of Dallas, "the next morning he would be hanging to a flag pole." Many subdividers also had reason to believe that racial covenants were illegal. Asked by Bouton in 1893 for an opinion on his company's plan to impose a covenant aimed at "negroes or persons of African descent," a Baltimore law firm replied that it would be invalid. What it called "the weight of authority" was against restrictions on alienation, especially ones that excluded "not a limited number of persons, but a whole race of people," a race whose civil rights were protected by the Fourteenth Amendment. Hence for the time being Bouton refrained from imposing a racial covenant. So did other subdividers, at least some of whom were afraid that if the courts held one restriction invalid they might feel obliged to invalidate the others.[82]

After the turn of the century, and especially after World War I, a few developments drove the subdividers to rethink their position. By far the most momentous was the exodus of African-Americans from the rural South that began in the late nineteenth century and picked up momentum in the early twentieth. In its wake the number of African-Americans rose sharply in cities all over the country. Between 1910 and 1920 it more than doubled in Chicago, more than quadrupled in Cleveland, and went up more than sixfold in Detroit. By 1920 African-Americans made up 10 percent of the population in Indianapolis, 15 percent in Baltimore, 25 percent in Washington, D.C., and more than 30 percent in Richmond and Birmingham. The number of African-Americans also went up in Los Angeles, though not as much as the number of Japanese-Americans. Most of the newcomers settled in crowded and squalid neighborhoods in the center of the city. But before long a few attempted to move into the surrounding residential communities, most of them home to working- and middle-class whites, many the children and grandchildren of European immigrants. Fears of what was known as encroachment soon surfaced in the cities—where they fueled the race riots that erupted after World War I—and then spread to the suburbs. For the first time subdividers grew frightened that African-Americans might "invade" their communities as they had "invaded" LeDroit Park. A suburb of Washington, D.C., that was laid out in the 1870s and called as "exclusive a settlement as one might want or imagine," it was taken over by African-Americans a few decades later. Subscribing to what one scholar has called "an exclusionary real estate ideology that associated the presence of blacks [and other non-whites] with declining property values and neighborhood instability," subdividers (and other white property owners) came to believe that racial covenants were needed to ensure racial homogeneity.[83]

To subdividers, the need for racial covenants grew especially pressing after 1917, when the U.S. Supreme Court ruled that racial zoning was unconstitutional. An idea that had been around since 1890, racial zoning made no headway until 1910. That year, over the strong objections of many African-Americans (and some white property owners and real estate brokers), Baltimore adopted the first of four ordinances that excluded blacks from any block on which more than half the residents were white (and vice versa). Richmond followed suit, as did Birmingham, St. Louis, and other cities. Given that the courts had already upheld segregation in public schools and on railway cars, legal experts assumed that racial zoning was constitutional. But when the laws were challenged, the results were mixed. They were upheld in some states, struck down in others. The issue came to a head when the U.S. Supreme Court agreed to hear *Buchanan v. Warley*, a 1915 case in which the Kentucky Supreme Court had upheld racial zoning in Louisville. Speaking for the defendant, Louisville city attorneys Stuart Chevalier and Pendleton Buckley argued that the ordinance was a valid exercise of police power, one that would prevent racial conflict and protect property values. (It would, they said, stop "a few of each race from overstepping the racial barriers which Providence and not human law has erected.") Representing the plaintiff, Clayton Blakey and Moorfield Storey, president of the NAACP, countered that the ordinance violated the Fourteenth Amendment, which barred the states from depriving anyone of property without due process of law. Writing for a unanimous court, Justice William R. Day conceded that it was important to prevent racial conflict and promote "public peace." But it had to be done without violating constitutional rights. And the Louisville ordinance deprived whites of the right to dispose of property and blacks of the right to acquire it. After *Buchanan v. Warley*, it was clear that if subdividers wanted to ensure racial homogeneity they would have to use racial covenants.[84]

But would the courts enforce them? As late as the early 1910s most legal experts would have agreed with Bouton's lawyers that the answer was no. Some courts held that racial covenants were an unlawful restraint on alienation, and in a highly influential decision one ruled in 1892 that they were a violation of the Fourteenth Amendment. Rejecting the argument that the state was not party to the covenant, Judge Erskine M. Ross of the circuit court for California's Southern District wrote, "Any result inhibited by the constitution can no more be accomplished by contract of individual citizens than by legislation, and the courts should no more enforce the one than the other." But starting in the mid-1910s, by which time subdividers were routinely employing racial covenants, many courts came around. These covenants, said the Louisiana Supreme Court, do not violate the Fourteenth Amendment, which "applies only to state legislation, not to the contracts of individuals." As long as restraints on alienation are not "total and perpetual," they do not run counter to public policy. As the Missouri Supreme Court wrote, a seller has the right to impose a restraint on alienation "in certain cases to certain persons, or for a certain time, or for certain purposes." The Washington, D.C., Court of Appeals upheld racial covenants too, and it was on an appeal of its decision in *Corrigan v. Buckley* that the issue reached the U.S. Supreme Court in 1925. The plaintiff's attorneys, who included not only Storey but Louis Marshall, a pillar of the New

York bar, argued that the covenant, which barred "any person of the negro race or blood," violated the Fifth, Thirteenth, and Fourteenth amendments. (They also warned that it would not be long before the same covenants that were applied to Negroes and Jews were extended to Catholics.) Writing for a unanimous court, Justice Edward T. Sanford dismissed the appeal, declaring, "It is obvious that none of these Amendments prohibited private individuals from entering into contracts respecting the control and disposition of their own property." After *Corrigan v. Buckley,* one legal scholar has written, many courts "disposed of the constitutional issue on grounds that the Supreme Court had settled the matter once and for all."[85]

Some courts did not come around, at least not all the way. In a landmark decision handed down in 1919, a California appellate court held that racial covenants did not violate the Fourteenth Amendment. But taking issue with the Louisiana and Missouri courts, it ruled that they did violate the common law restraint on alienation. Delivering the court's opinion, Judge Frank G. Finlayson declared that "any restraint on alienation, either as to persons or time, is invalid." (If one could be barred from selling or leasing property to persons of African, Chinese, or Japanese descent, one could also be barred from selling or leasing "to any but Albinos from the heart of Africa, or blond Eskimos.") In other words, racial covenants were invalid not because they violated the civil rights of blacks (and other racial minorities), but because they violated the property rights of whites. A few months later, however, the California Supreme Court issued a decision that left the appellate court's ruling standing, but more or less eviscerated it. Racial covenants could not be imposed to prevent whites from selling or leasing property, wrote the court, but they could be imposed to prevent blacks (and other racial minorities) from occupying or otherwise using it. Despite counsel's argument that these covenants place "the negro and people of other sects and creeds in the same category as slaughter houses, livery stables, tanneries, garages, etc.," the Michigan Supreme Court took the same position as the California courts. So did the West Virginia Supreme Court. "It may be an anomalous situation where a colored man may own property which he cannot occupy," the Maryland Supreme Court wrote, but so long as his procedural rights were protected these restrictions would be enforced.[86] And so long as they were enforced, African-Americans were highly unlikely to buy or rent in a restricted subdivision.

As the courts were aware, racial covenants were an idea whose time had come. Nichols employed them for the first time in 1908, and in an attempt to keep up with the competition Bouton followed suit not long after. Duncan McDuffie also imposed racial covenants, as did the Thompson brothers and the Hogg brothers. By the late 1920s, a decade after Newlands died, the Chevy Chase Land Company excluded "any person of negro blood" as well as "any person of the Semetic [sic] race." The exception in the early 1900s, racial covenants were the rule two decades later. Worried about how the courts would respond, a few subdividers refrained from imposing restraints on alienation. A case in point was the Knight-Menard Company, developer of Devonshire Downs. In an attempt to abide by the Michigan Supreme Court's rulings, it provided only that none of the lots "shall be used or occupied . . . by any persons not of the pure, unmixed, white, Caucasian, Gentile race." But Knight-Menard was in a small minority. Most subdividers, even California subdividers who had reason to be worried about how the courts would respond, included a ban on alienation as well as on use and occupancy. By the 1920s these covenants were commonplace not only in middle- and upper-middle-class subdivisions, but also in working-class ones. Eastmont No. 2 Tract, a tract east of downtown Los Angeles designed expressly for "the working man," advertised "Permanent Race Restrictions." City Terrace, another East Los Angeles tract that offered lots for as little as $400–650, boasted "strict race restrictions and moderate building restrictions." And Petroleum Gardens, a subdivision near Santa Fe Springs whose promoters were peddling mineral rights more than homesites, assured prospective purchasers that lots would be sold only to members of "the Caucasian or White Race." As Bouton told his colleagues in the mid-1920s, even subdivisions that imposed few or no other restrictions imposed racial covenants.[87]

Some subdividers excluded anyone who was not "white." But as scientists were not sure who belonged to the "white race," indeed were not even sure whether there were four or five (or even fifteen, twenty-nine, or sixty-three) races, many subdividers preferred to use the term "Caucasian." To be Caucasian, historian Matthew Frye Jacobson has pointed out, was by the 1920s "to be *conclusively, certifiably, scientifically* white." Leaving nothing to chance, some subdividers explicitly barred Africans (who were also referred to as Negroes and Ethiopians) and Asians (who were also referred to as Mongolians, Chinese, and Japanese). Olmsted Brothers even urged Walter H. Leimert to include East Indians in his racial covenants—and to add the phrase "or any other races in the discretion of the Lakeshore Homes Association." Some subdividers also excluded Semites, which, said a Washington, D.C., developer, included "Armenians, Jews, Hebrews, Persians, and Syrians." (How Jews differed from Hebrews was not spelled out.) Others barred Mexicans, Hawaiians, Puerto Ricans, Filipinos, and American Indians. One even excluded "foreigners of the Dago class." Except for Westdale, a subdivision in Ontario, Canada, which barred a host of racial and ethnic groups, including "Armenians, whether British subjects or not," and "foreign-born Italians, Greeks or Jews," no subdivision excluded so many types as the Lake Shore Club District, which was located in Erie County, Pennsylvania. As well as anyone "of Negro or Mongolian birth or parentage," the subdivider, the Hardscrabble Farm Real Estate Trust, barred "any person of Hungarian, Mexican, Greek, Armenian, Austrian, Italian, Russian [which may have meant Jewish], Polish, Slavish, or Roumanian birth."[88]

Issues of Enforcement and Duration

As J. C. Nichols pointed out, it was one thing to impose restrictions and quite another to enforce them. But if subdividers imposed them, they had to enforce them; if they were not prepared to enforce them, they should not have imposed them in the first place. Subdividers might be well advised to overlook trivial infractions, remarked one associate of Nichols, but they had to keep a keen eye out for serious violations, even unintentional ones, the accumulation of which, said Nichols, "may lead to the downfall of the whole character of the property." Given what one well-informed observer called "proper machinery," subdividers believed it was possible to enforce the restrictions in a way that not only protected the community from undesirable people and undesirable activities but also, as a Roland Park homeowner put it, preserved "pleasant relations among the residents." Hence at the outset many subdividers expended a good deal of time and

energy enforcing the restrictions. Nichols instructed his salesmen and groundsmen to keep an eye out for violations. And if he
spotted one, he jotted down the address of the house in a small
black leather notebook and then asked one of his employees to
call it to the owner's attention. Bouton routinely reviewed building plans and on occasion had the unpleasant task of informing
a lot owner that the proposed structure violated one or another
of the Roland Park (or Guilford) restrictions.[89]

Before long subdividers realized that enforcing the restrictions
was a thankless task. It took time, energy, and money they would
rather have spent on other things. It put them in an adversarial
relationship with the residents, the very people who, they hoped,
would help sell the subdivision to others. And sometimes it left
them caught between those residents who favored a lenient in-
terpretation of the restrictions and those who favored a strict one.
No matter which side the subdividers took, they were bound to
offend someone. Although serious, these problems were dwarfed
by another one. If all went well, the subdividers expected to dispose of most of the lots in a few years and the rest not long after.
Once they did, they would move on—sometimes to a tract nearby,
sometimes to one elsewhere in the city, and sometimes, as in
the case of Walter H. Leimert, who left Oakland for Los Angeles,
to one in another city. Why, the subdividers asked, should they
enforce the restrictions in a tract in which they no longer had a
stake? Often they declined to do so—with the result, the *Palos
Verdes Bulletin* lamented, that many fine tracts in and around Los
Angeles have been allowed "to go to seed."[90]

The subdividers could have turned the matter over to the residents, who, as the beneficiaries of the restrictions, had a right to
enforce them. But this approach had serious drawbacks. It was

not just that, as Nichols said, what is "everybody's business is nobody's business." It was also that most residents were reluctant to take a neighbor to court. As a resident of Roland Park pointed out, people were highly unlikely to sue unless the infraction was "of such a nature as to be an unbearable nuisance." Even if residents were willing to risk antagonizing their neighbor, they had reason to think hard before proceeding. As a prominent midwesterner pointed out, they would have to be ready to "pay the cost of starting the litigation, employing attorneys, and assuming the incidental trouble and expense." In states where the courts held that the burden of proof should be placed on the plaintiff and all doubts resolved in favor of the defendant, a resident would have to demonstrate conclusively not only that the restrictions had been violated but also that they were "valid and proper." Making matters worse, wrote Charles S. Ascher, an expert on the administration of restrictive covenants, judges did not always look kindly on what they viewed as squabbles between neighbors, especially when their calendars where "clogged with commercial disputes, condemnation proceedings, divorces, and affairs of state." Even if the suit was upheld, it would engender ill feelings that would long "survive the litigation." "After all," Ascher added, "the home owners will have to live next door to each other for many years after."[91]

If a resident could not file suit without what one called "great cost and trouble," who would enforce the restrictions after the subdivider, as Nichols put it, "sold out"? The Olmsted brothers began wrestling with this issue shortly after the turn of the century. Writing to a Boston lawyer about a subdivision in nearby Winchester, Olmsted, Jr., proposed that the deeds include a provision authorizing the formation of a property owners' association, to which everyone who held land in the subdivision would belong, and empowering it to enforce the restrictions. Such a broad-based organization would do more than shift the financial burden of litigation from a handful of residents to the whole community. As John Charles Olmsted observed, it would also relieve individual residents of "the often disagreeable task of enforcing their rights upon neighbors." In a country where homeowners' associations, taxpayers' associations, and voluntary associations of all sorts were well established, this proposal struck a responsive chord. Bouton created a property owners' association, called the Roland Park Roads and Maintenance Association, in 1909 and later advised other subdividers to delegate the enforcement of the restrictions "to the property owners themselves as quickly as possible." Nichols followed Bouton's lead. So did the subdividers of St. Francis Wood, Brendonwood, River Oaks, and Palos Verdes Estates, where the Homes Association was designed expressly "to pick [up]" where the developers "left off." By the time Palos Verdes Estates came on the market, property owners' associations of one sort or another were widespread—especially in subdivisions for the well-to-do, where they were regarded as the most effective mechanism for enforcing restrictive covenants.[92]

Once the subdividers decided to impose restrictions, they faced another knotty problem. They had to figure out for how long to impose them. Through the late nineteenth century most subdividers imposed restrictions, in the words of the Olmsteds, "for a very short period." Fifteen or twenty years was typical, and ten years was not unheard of. Opposition to long terms came from lawyers, real estate agents, and prospective purchasers, for many of whom, wrote Joel Hurt, subdivider of Atlanta's Druid Hills, "the longer [the restrictions], the more abhorrent." But soon after the turn of the century a few subdividers realized that ten or even twenty years was too short. Prospective purchasers, aware that the restrictions would expire in the near future, were hesitant to buy—or, if they bought, to build. In theory, it was possible to re-impose the restrictions after they expired. But in practice, Nichols pointed out, "it was impossible to get all owners [to go along]." Especially likely to object were the owners of strategically placed corner lots, who hoped to benefit from their conversion from residential to commercial use. To Hurt, fifty years seemed about right. But the Olmsteds recommended "at least sixty years," they wrote Hurt. A prospective purchaser would soon realize that the restrictions were "not intended so much to hamper his free use of his land as to ensure him the benefits of a first-class neighbor-hood." Warning that tenement houses and other objectionable structures might well be erected after the restrictions expired, the Olmsteds urged that they "be kept in force for much longer periods than have been customary."[93]

But how much longer? Should they run for fifty or sixty years, or even a hundred years, as they did at Shaker Village? Or in the interest of permanence, should they be made perpetual, as they were in the first plat at Roland Park? By the 1910s, if not earlier, the subdividers had come to believe that perpetual restrictions were inadvisable. As Nichols said, it was far from clear the courts would enforce them—a view shared by John Charles Olmsted, who told J. H. Oldfield, one of the developers of The Uplands, that judges regarded such restrictions as contrary to public policy. Even if the courts would enforce them—and, it turned out, a few would—it was not a good idea to impose them, said Bouton. Ex-plaining his decision to abandon perpetual restrictions in favor of ones lasting twenty-five years, he told his fellow subdividers that no one should presume to be "wise enough for all eternity." By the 1910s the subdividers had also come to believe that very long restrictions were inadvisable. As Nichols pointed out, things change over time, sometimes driven by technology, sometimes by fashion. A good example was the advent of the automobile. Suppose he had imposed a restriction against garages a few years ago, he said in 1916. Now that all his prospective purchasers wanted a place to store their motorcars, "we would be up against it to-day." Given how hard it was to predict the future, Nichols suggested that subdividers should build "a certain amount of elasticity" into the restrictions.[94]

In an effort to come up with a term that was, in Nichols's words, "long enough to give reasonable assurance [of permanence] and yet short enough to permit readjustment . . . to changing modes of life," the subdividers were at sea. Some favored twenty-five or thirty years, others fifty or sixty, and still others somewhere in between. (In general, one expert found, "the more highly developed the subdivision, the longer the term of the restrictions.") But no term had more to recommend it than any other. In 1909, however, Nichols made a breakthrough. In the restrictions for Rockhill Place, a tract located at the eastern edge of the Country Club District, he did more than extend the term from twenty to twenty-five years, which was something he had recently done for the first time at Sunset Hill, his most exclusive subdivision to date. Following a plan he credited to Bouton, Nichols also included in the deeds a provision whereby Rockhill Place property owners could extend the restrictions for another twenty-five years ad infinitum. All it would take was the approval of the owners of a majority of the front footage. A novel idea, an early reference to which is found in a letter from John Charles Olmsted to J. H. Oldfield in

1907, it caught on quickly, not least because it offered prospective purchasers a high degree of permanence without tying up their property for a very long time.[95]

But as Nichols soon found out, it was "a Herculean task" to get hundreds of property owners to agree to extend the restrictions. Hoping to capitalize on a change in land use, some wanted to see them expire. Others who might have approved an extension were hard, if not impossible, to find. Some had moved out of the subdivision, even, said Nichols, out of the country. To make matters worse, some lots had been left to heirs. Others were in the hands of trustees or guardians. Still others were subject to a mortgage. To persuade many heirs, lawyers, and bankers who had little interest in the subdivision to approve the extension was a time-consuming and often futile effort. To overcome these obstacles, Nichols came up with another innovative idea, one for which he took full credit. It worked as follows. Five years before the expiration date, the homeowners' association would notify the property owners that they had the right to modify or eliminate the restrictions. If they took no action—if, to be more precise, the owners of a majority of the front footage did not approve a change—the restrictions would be automatically renewed for another twenty-five years. Adopted for the first time at Mission Hills, a tract in the Country Club District that was subdivided in 1914, this scheme had several advantages. It shifted the burden from those property owners who wanted to retain the restrictions to those who wanted to modify or eliminate them. It also ensured that the owners could not let the restrictions lapse inadvertently. By doing so, it made the restrictions pretty much self-perpetuating. Nichols later adopted this scheme at his other tracts, and other subdividers followed his lead.[96]

"Hand and Hand" with Zoning

Late in 1928 Richard T. Ely, one of the nation's foremost economists, announced that the Institute for Research in Land Economics and Public Utilities intended to publish two series of monographs, one in Land Economics and the other in Public Utility Economics. Founded by Ely in 1920 at the University of Wisconsin and later moved to Northwestern University's campus in downtown Chicago, the institute was the most influential organization of its kind in the country. Although the institute's reputation was based largely on pioneering work in finance and marketing, Ely chose to inaugurate the Land Economics series with a monograph titled *The Use of Deed Restrictions in Subdivision Development*. Written by economist Helen C. Monchow, it was the first systematic study of the subject. If it did nothing else, it highlighted the vital role these restrictions played in suburbia. Found everywhere in the United States, especially in subdivisions for the well-to-do, deed restrictions were as integral to the suburbs as the single-family houses whose setting, design, and cost they regulated, as integral as the narrow streets (with, wrote Olmsted Brothers, "gentle curves and comfortable grades") and the well-tended lawns, ornamental bushes, and shade trees.[97]

By the late 1920s restrictive covenants were so widespread that it was easy to forget they were a relatively new phenomenon, albeit one whose origins went back to the late eighteenth and early nineteenth centuries. At the time Monchow wrote her monograph, Roland Park was less than forty years old, Guilford less than twenty. The first tracts of what became the Country Club District were subdivided shortly after the turn of the century. St. Francis Wood was put on the market in the early 1910s, Great

Neck Hills a decade later. Restrictive covenants were such a new phenomenon that many of the subdividers and the advisers who had drafted them were still around—and could remember the time when it was all but impossible to sell a lot with restrictions. Bouton was still going strong. So were Nichols and McDuffie. Although his father had been gone for more than twenty years and his brother for nearly ten, Olmsted, Jr., was still in practice, well established as the nation's leading landscape architect and urban designer. And Charles H. Cheney was living in Palos Verdes Estates, where he spent much of the last two decades of his life as secretary of the Art Jury, secretary of the Homes Association, and, if that were not enough, editor of the *Palos Verdes Bulletin*—the closest thing to the community newspaper.[98] Less fortunate was E. G. Lewis, who was serving five years in a federal penitentiary for mail fraud.

By the late 1920s most subdividers had come to believe that restrictive covenants were indispensable—that more than anything else, more than the huge sums spent on improvements and amenities and more than the careful attention paid to design guidelines, the imposition of stringent restrictions had solved the problem of unwanted change that Olmsted, Sr., had spelled out in the 1860s and 1870s. With restrictions in place, said an employee of the Van Sweringens, Americans no longer need fear that an attractive subdivision would soon "give way to something less desirable and perhaps hideous." Restrictions, the subdividers believed, also stabilized property values and encouraged homeownership. Above all, they paid. They attracted prospective purchasers, many of whom demanded the most stringent and sweeping restrictions possible.[99] Restrictions paid so well that suburban subdivisions made Bouton, Nichols, McDuffie, and Jemison among the wealthiest businessmen in their communities. And they greatly increased the Van Sweringens' already huge fortune.

Several other groups also favored restrictive covenants. Speaking for many city planners, Harland Bartholomew stressed that property values soared in suburbs with stringent restrictions, but not in ones that allowed "promiscuous development," ones that allowed a mix of homes, tenements, factories, stores, and stables. Voicing the conventional wisdom of the real estate economists, two experts insisted that restrictions "enhance the desirability of the neighborhood as a location for high grade homes."

> Home builders seeking to invest substantial sums of money in fine houses desire to know that a neighborhood will be maintained as a district of homes for a sufficient length of time so they will be undisturbed in the enjoyment of property. Few wish to invest large sums of money in homes in locations where business blocks may soon be built with accompanying heavy street traffic and where, perhaps, next door may be constructed a cheap apartment house, or a building with small stores.

Realtors and builders supported restrictions on the grounds that they enhanced stability. Lenders, many of whom had hitherto worried that restrictions would cloud titles, were beginning to look favorably on them. And taking their cue from the experts, journalists "underscored the desirability of restrictions," writes historian Susan M. Chase.[100]

Although most middle- and upper-middle-class Americans were in favor of restrictive covenants, some had reservations. They stemmed not from a notion that restrictions were an infringement of property rights, but from a belief that they were an ineffective way to regulate land use. As Lawrence Veiller, the country's leading tenement-house reformer, told a conference of city planners in 1916, it was unreasonable to expect to maintain the long-term integrity of residential districts with "what is at best merely a private contract or agreement between two parties." It made as little sense to regulate the use of land by private agreements as it did to regulate the purity of milk or the safety of pedestrians by them. Restrictions, critics pointed out, could be imposed in new subdivisions, but not as a rule in built-up communities, where it was ordinarily very hard to get homeowners to agree to anything. (Interestingly, the one exception to the rule occurred when white homeowners felt so threatened by an influx of African-Americans that they joined forces to impose racial covenants.) Even in new subdivisions, critics claimed, things often went wrong. In an otherwise highly restricted Cleveland subdivision, several lots were sold without restrictions against apartment houses because of a foreclosure proceeding. Their omission resulted in "very great injury [to] the nearby restricted property," wrote Robert H. Whitten, advisor to the Cleveland City Plan Commission.[101]

Restrictive covenants had two other serious defects, critics charged. One was that they were very hard to enforce. Few residents had the stomach for a lawsuit. And as Charles E. Merriam, a Chicago alderman and one of the city's leading reformers, pointed out, even fewer had the wherewithal. Litigation, he wrote, is so expensive that only the wealthy can afford it. Even if the residents filed suit, the odds of success were not good. Once the restrictions expired, Veiller observed, the courts would not enforce them. Nor would they enforce them if the plaintiff had ignored the violations for an unreasonably long time or if the neighborhood had changed so much that an injunction would do damage to the defendant without giving relief to the plaintiff. According to the Advisory Council of Real Estate Interests, a New York City trade organization, the courts were extremely inconsistent as well. In spite of restrictions that banned anything but private homes, they permitted landowners to construct an apartment house in Manhattan but not a three-family house in the Bronx. Despite other restrictions, they allowed businessmen to operate a livery stable on East 193rd Street but not a bakery on Southern Boulevard, a service station on Broadway but not a garage in Flatbush. No less puzzling, said the council, were other rulings by which "a private house may be altered into an undertaking establishment on Madison Avenue and Forty-first Street; into a dressmaking shop on West Twenty-fourth Street; but not into a business building on West Fortieth Street."[102]

The other serious defect was that the restrictions were enforceable only within the subdivision. Even if a subdivider imposed stringent restrictions on a tract, Merriam pointed out, he had no control over what took place "on the other side of the street from his property." No one could prevent another subdivider from imposing lenient restrictions on the adjacent property—or even from leaving it completely unrestricted. Nor could anyone stop the new owners from using the lots in a way that rendered the restrictions ineffective. Even if you buy a lot in a tract of thirty, forty, or a hundred acres, Nichols wrote, "you never can be assured that the holders of the adjoining property will not do something to depreciate the value of your own." There was no easy solution to what he called the problem of "the Border." Subdividers could adopt "a common covenant" that extended from one tract to another. But the real estate business was so competitive that they were not likely to do so. They could also set aside land for parks and open spaces that would serve, Nichols said, "as a barrier to injurious encroachment of unrestricted or lowly restricted property." But these buffers did not come cheap. Nor did they produce revenue. Finally, subdividers could acquire very large tracts, "large enough," said Paul A. Harsch, "to be self contained."[103] But unless they were bounded by a river or, as in the case of Palos Verdes Estates, the ocean, even very large tracts had borders.

In light of the many defects of restrictive covenants, Veiller, Merriam, and other reformers called on the local authorities to adopt a new form of land-use regulation known as zoning (or districting). Zoning, said Edward M. Bassett, a lawyer and planner who played a pivotal role in the passage of New York City's pioneering ordinance of 1916, had many advantages over private restrictions. It was enforced by public officials, it was enforceable all over the city, and it was "more permanent and more elastic" than private restrictions. But not even zoning's strongest advocates thought it would ever replace restrictive covenants. Noting that zoning could not be used to set a minimum cost for a house or specify the style of its architecture, Veiller conceded that much would still have to be done through private restrictions. Bassett agreed. "Zoning and private restrictions do not interfere with each other," he wrote; "both may exist hand in hand. Prudent developers will still use private restrictions to supplement the zoning regulations." After thoroughly documenting the proliferation of restrictive covenants and evenhandedly analyzing their advantages and drawbacks, Monchow concluded that they "seem likely to continue for some time to be an important force in controlling the development of urban land."[104]

two

Bourgeois Nightmares:

Fears of Almost Everyone and Everything

...u know you don't like a thing like ...s against or over the way from ...r home. You know how it grates ...ou and how you swear (possibly in ...-like words or under your breath ...ut swear, just the same) about it. ...sibly it hasn't reached YOUR ...ne yet—but how can you keep ...way once it lifts its peace-destroy-price-destroying head at your door? How can you tell when it will reach your home? One day we see in the paper that Meridian St. at Maple Road is in danger. Next we learn that Delaware at 16th. St. is threatened. Look around you! See the havoc that has been and is being wrought. What street, what neighborhood is safe? You know you can't buy all the land "jinin' onto yourn." You know when the ugly thing comes, whether as a public garage, apartment, business building, as shown above, or in any of its numerous forms, you will have to swear and bear it or get away, and your getting away may be only an adjournment of trouble, for the Ugly Thing may hunt you out wherever you go—

WHEREVER YOU GO—UNLESS YOU GO TO BRENDONWOOD

Early in 1918 a dozen of the leading developers of what was called "High Class Residence Property" held their second annual conference at the Belvedere Hotel in downtown Baltimore. Attending were J. C. Nichols, who had hosted the first annual conference in Kansas City a year earlier, E. H. Bouton, Duncan McDuffie, Robert Jemison, Jr., King G. Thompson, and, among others, John F. Demarest, vice president of the Sage Foundation Homes Company, developer of Forest Hills Gardens, and Emerson W. Chaille, head of the company that had subdivided Brendonwood. Absent were Paul A. Harsch and Hugh E. Prather. After spending several hours touring Roland Park and Guilford (and taking lunch at the Roland Park Country Club), the participants got down to business. With Nichols serving as chair, they devoted much of the first two days to sales, especially to the problems of recruiting, retaining, and supervising an effective sales force. (For the benefit of the others, Nichols read a long list of instructions he gave his salesmen. For example, "Don't sit too far from your prospect or across the table." "Don't assume a careless, lounging attitude." "Don't sigh." "Don't chew gum." "Don't enter a private office with a cigar or cigarette in your hand or mouth." "Never in any case have an odor of liquor on your breath." "Never express a strong opinion on any political, religious, war or city administration matter that might prove antagonistic to the prospect." Also, "Get plenty of sleep." "[Take a] cold bath in the morning." "Eat slowly." "Breathe deeply." "Be a 'joiner.'" "Belong to lodges, church and clubs." "Always know a great deal about your purchaser before you call on him." "Make friends [with] the secretary, stenographer or telephone operator in [his] office.")[1]

On the third day, the last and by far the longest of the conference, the developers turned to a number of subjects other than
sales. At Nichols's request, Bouton presented a paper on the ten
best reasons for living in places like Roland Park and the Country
Club District. The topic was of much interest to the subdividers,
some of whose projects were laboring not only because of the
wartime downturn in the real estate market but also because
of strong competition from apartment houses. Rehashing long-
standing anti-urban arguments, Bouton pointed out that these
subdivisions satisfied what he called *"the universal desire for space,
light, air and sunshine."* Instead of the "dirt-laden, smoke-laden
and evil-smelling" air of the city, they provided the "clean, sweet-
smelling air" of the country, instead of the "nerve-racking, sleep-
destroying noises of the city, the restful quiet of the country."
Bouton also emphasized the beauty of the suburbs—a sharp con-
trast to "the ugliness of the city," with its lack of order, harmony,
and "green spaces." And he stressed that the suburbs provided a
pleasant place to raise a family, even assuring "desirable companions" for the children. Not least of all, Bouton highlighted "protective restrictions," which relieve the resident "from many an-
noyances to which he is subjected [in communities] where such
protection is not afforded," which help maintain property values,
and which foster "a spirit of neighborliness" that is not found
elsewhere.[2]

So far as his remarks about restrictions went, Bouton was
preaching to the converted; it would have been hard to find a
dozen leading real estate men who were more favorably disposed
to them. All the subdividers at the conference had used stringent restrictions and found them an effective marketing tool.
They could no more have imagined opening up a new subdivi-

sion without restrictions than one without roads, lots, and utilities. But one thing about restrictions troubled them, and that was
the word itself. As Demarest, who had worked as a Brooklyn real
estate man before taking over as manager of Forest Hills Gardens, pointed out, developers thought of restrictions as a benefit. But prospective purchasers often thought of them as an imposition, which, he noted, is what the word "implies ordinarily."
Demarest made the point more sharply at the third annual conference, which was held in Birmingham, Jemison's hometown,
in 1919. "Restrictions, in the minds of the average purchasers,
mean restraint," he said. "The word 'restriction' is an ugly word."
At the very least, Demarest suggested, subdividers should in-
struct salesmen to explain the benefits of restrictions to prospective purchasers. They should also discourage them from "rattling
off," in Demarest's words, "'We restrict against this and we restrict against that.'"[3]

Demarest's remarks struck a responsive chord. There was
something offensive about the word "restrictions," even "something quite unAmerican," as the German city planner Werner
Hegemann told a group of American city planners in 1916. Mc-
Duffie said his company was "endeavoring, as far as possible, to
eliminate the use of the 'restrictions' and refer to restrictions as
'Protective agreement[s].'" Chaille remarked, "We speak not of
restrictions, but of 'Brendonwood protections.'" When the subject came up at the third annual conference, Jemison asked, "Isn't
there some other word that could be used?" Harsch, who had
made it to Birmingham, replied, "Why not say protections, instead of restrictions?" Why not indeed, said Prather, who was also
on hand this time: "I think it is a fine word." Bouton was skeptical. Restrictions "is a hard word to get away from," he said, and

protections "is vague."[4] Despite Bouton's skepticism, the Roland Park Company used the term "protective covenants." The Knight-Menard Company, developer of Devonshire Downs, preferred "protective restrictions." So did the subdividers of Palos Verdes Estates. Indeed, well before Palos Verdes Estates came on the market, subdividers everywhere were insisting that restrictions were above all a form of protection.

But who were they supposed to protect? And against what were they supposed to protect them? To Nichols and the other subdividers—and also to Frederick Law Olmsted, Jr., who was held in such high esteem that he was invited to attend the first annual conference—the answers were obvious. The restrictions were supposed to protect the subdividers, who were worried that one of the first buyers might do something that would make it very hard, if not impossible, to sell the remaining lots. They also were supposed to protect the purchasers, lot owners and homeowners alike, who were afraid that the neighbors might use their lots in a way that would undermine the community's long-term well-being. A solution to the problem that Olmsted, Sr., had spelled out half a century before, the restrictions were supposed to protect subdividers and purchasers against unwanted change that might destroy the sylvan setting that had drawn people to the subdivision in the first place. Such changes, in Demarest's words, had "ruined" one high-class residential district after another, often in less than fifteen years, forcing the residents to sell their homes at a loss and start up again elsewhere. The restrictions were supposed to prevent unwanted change by keeping "undesirable" people and activities, commonly referred to as "undesirable encroachments," out of the community.[5]

What made otherwise respectable and law-abiding people undesirable? Was it race, religion, or ethnicity? Or was it class—a lack of money or the absence of what one real estate ad called "good-taste and refinement"? Or was it something else entirely? An incident that occurred in Los Angeles in 1948 nicely illuminated the problem. It began when Nat King Cole, an African-American and one of the most successful entertainers of the day, bought a twelve-room house in Hancock Park for eighty-five thousand dollars, a huge sum at the time. Located a few miles west of downtown Los Angeles, Hancock Park had been subdivided in the early 1920s and marketed as one of the city's most exclusive and highly restricted communities. The residents, most of them lawyers, doctors, and wealthy businessmen, mobilized to keep Cole out. But they soon learned that the U.S. Supreme Court had recently ruled that racial covenants were unenforceable. Through the Hancock Park Property Owners Association, the residents therefore offered to buy Cole out. When he refused to sell, they asked for a meeting. As Maria Cole recalled, "There it was patiently explained to my husband that the good people of Hancock Park simply did not want any undesirables moving in." "Neither do I," the singer replied. "And if I see anybody undesirable coming in here, I'll be the first to complain."[6]

Nor was it clear why otherwise ordinary activities were deemed undesirable, especially those that were not immoral, illegal, or criminal—or which, in the words of Olmsted Brothers, were not "obviously noxious or offensive and liable to become nuisances actionable at law."[7] Why was it undesirable to operate not just a slaughterhouse but also a bakery, a grocery, a stable, or a stationery store? And why was it undesirable to run a saloon, an institution widely regarded even by many who did not patronize it as "the workingman's club"? Why was it undesirable to erect an apartment house (or even a two- or three-family house)? And why was it undesirable to build a single-family house that extended to the property line, covered more than a third of the lot, stood more than two or three stories high, cost less than, say, seven thousand dollars, and had not been approved by an art or architectural jury? Why was it undesirable not only to drill for oil but also to put up a billboard, a large "For Sale" or "For Rent" sign, or a fence more than four or six feet tall? And why was it undesirable to raise domestic animals, even ones as small as chickens and rabbits?

There is a fairly simple answer to these questions. What made some people and some activities "undesirable" was that they were the subjects of the restrictions. That is, they were undesirable because the subdividers branded them undesirable. That was how they saw them, and that was how they thought their customers saw them. But what was it about these "undesirable" people and activities that would set in motion the unwanted changes that sounded the death knell of even the most fashionable suburbs? What was it about them that required the imposition of "protective restrictions"? To answer these questions, it is necessary to look beyond the restrictions to the deep-seated fears that were embodied in them—fear of others, even of others with whom the subdividers and prospective purchasers had, in the words of Olmsted, Sr., "much in common," fear of change, and fear of the market.[8] A look at these fears reveals much not only about suburbia but also about American society in the late nineteenth and early twentieth centuries.

Fear of Others

Like J. C. Nichols, H. S. Kissell believed that it could well be ruinous to sell to "undesirable" people. A leading subdivider in Springfield, Ohio, and one of the select few invited to the annual conferences in Kansas City, Baltimore, and Birmingham, Kissell told a group of developers in 1923 that "we must have the courage to lose sales rather than sell the property to undesirable neighbors." We must have the courage not only when the tract goes on the market and the subdivider has "a great deal at stake," but also when most of the lots have been sold and "the temptation to clean up becomes very strong." Assuming their prospective purchasers were just as concerned, Kissell and other subdividers assured them that by dint of well-crafted restrictions they need have no fear of "undesirable neighbors." Hence one subdivider promised "good neighbors," another "EXCELLENT NEIGHBORS," and still another "residents of the best material." Others promised congenial people, "substantial people," "PARTICULAR PEOPLE," even "the most desirable people." Residents would be of the "HIGHEST CHARACTER" in the Country Club District and of the "highest grade" in Delafield Estates, a subdivision in the northern Bronx. Whitley Park, a San Fernando Valley subdivision, was for Americans who adhered to the Eighteenth Amendment, which prohibited the sale of alcoholic beverages. And Hancock Park was for the "leaders of the community"—and only for those of "good taste and refinement." Nearby Bel-Air, which required references from prospective purchasers, assured the public that "the object will be not to sell this acreage as rapidly as possible," but rather to sell it "to the highest class of homeseekers."[9]

When Kissell spoke of "undesirable" people, he meant something quite different from what Olmsted, Sr., meant when he spoke of them more than half a century earlier. To Olmsted, people were undesirable because of what they did, because of how they used (or, more precisely, misused) the land—how, through "ignorance, incompetence, bad taste, or knavery," they allowed

rural buildings and fences to decay, cut down tall trees and polluted sparkling streams, defaced the countryside with shops, factories, stables, brickyards, beer gardens, and dram shops and
otherwise destroyed the bucolic setting that had drawn them to
suburbia in the first place. But to Kissell, people were undesirable because of who they were. And who they were was defined
not by how well they dressed or how nicely they sipped their tea,
but rather by which racial (and, to a lesser degree, religious and
ethnic) group and social class they belonged to. In other words,
it was not what they did, no matter how appropriate, or how they
behaved, no matter how respectable, that made them undesirable. It was just who they were. Their presence in the community
was deemed so offensive, threatening, and unsettling that it invariably set off what a Chicago real estate man called "a stampede
among the others to get out."[10]

Among the many "undesirable" groups, none was more undesirable than blacks, who were also referred to in racial covenants
as Africans, Negroes, and Ethiopians—which, in light of the long
history of Ethiopian civilization and culture, is "in no wise to the
discredit of the negro," wrote Justice Hammond Maxwell of the
West Virginia Supreme Court. To most whites—who no more
wanted to live in the same neighborhood as blacks than to ride in
the same railroad car, dine in the same restaurant, or be buried in
the same cemetery—it was so self-evident that blacks were highly
undesirable that they rarely bothered to explain why. But on the
few occasions they did—as, for example, when they attempted to
justify racial zoning—they stressed that blacks would drive out
whites in the same way that "bad dollars drive out good ones."
Their presence would also depress property values, by as much as
25 to 30 percent, according to a Louisville real estate agent, and

provoke conflict and violence. Although one lawyer thought it outrageous, most whites viewed blacks as "a nuisance, loathsome and undesirable in [good] neighborhoods." The Olmsted brothers found Negroes so undesirable that they suggested to one subdivider that if it were practical he should not even allow them to live on the property as servants, a common practice even in highly restricted tracts. "The raising of negro children, even those of gardeners, coachman and others often provided for," they wrote, "is almost certain to result in disagreeable conditions," notably excessive noise and even "trespassing, pilfering and other criminal acts."[11]

Almost as undesirable as African-Americans—and, in Los Angeles and other West Coast cities, as much so—were Asian-Americans, who were referred to in racial covenants as Chinese, Japanese, Asiatics, and Mongolians, one of the five major racial groups, wrote the U.S. Immigration Commission in 1911, that "school geographies have made most familiar to Americans." To most whites, Asian-Americans were undesirable for much the same reason as African-Americans. Although the Japanese keep their homes up as well as whites, a Hollywood realtor pointed out, their presence depresses property values. "They are alright in their places," he insisted, "but they should be segregated." He was especially troubled by the way they "worm their way into the best residential districts." In response to the "invasion" of Japanese-Americans, a phenomenon one California real estate man called "the Jap menace," Los Angeles property owners not only drafted racial covenants but also attempted to drive the newcomers out, even on one occasion resorting to arson. According to historian John Modell, one Los Angeles suburb even "refused to accept new subdivisions" without racial covenants, a practice that was probably unconstitutional under *Buchanan v. Warley*. Also undesirable were Malays and American Indians (a group that included Mexican-Americans), the brown and red, as opposed to the white, black, and yellow, races. But few racial covenants singled out these groups. Most dealt with them by excluding anyone of other than "the white or Caucasian race."[12]

Racial covenants were only one of the many manifestations of the racism that permeated American society in the late nineteenth and early twentieth centuries—as shameful as the spread of Jim Crow legislation, if not as horrific as the epidemic of lynchings in the South, the outbreak of race riots in the North, and the resurgence of the Ku Klux Klan, especially in the Midwest. This widespread racism gave rise to the deep-seated fear of African- and Asian-Americans that was held by both the subdividers and their prospective purchasers. This fear led most real estate men to believe that the presence of even one or two African- or Asian-American families in an otherwise stable residential neighborhood would drive out the whites—and seal its fate. This belief, more than anything else, drove many subdividers to impose racial covenants even in cities with very few African- and Asian-Americans (and hardly any who could afford to buy a lot, much less build a house, in suburbia). To give two examples, the Mason-McDuffie Company, subdividers of St. Francis Wood, banned any person of African descent even though only 1,600 of San Francisco's 417,000 residents (or less than four-tenths of one percent) were African-American. And the Ottawa Hills Company excluded "any Chinaman or person of the Mongolian race" even though fewer than one hundred of Toledo's roughly two hundred thousand residents (or less than one-tenth of one percent) were Asian-American.[13]

The subdividers had no qualms about using racial covenants to keep out African-Americans, Asian-Americans, and other "undesirable" people, and as a rule that included Jews. During the late nineteenth and early twentieth centuries, a time of rampant anti-Semitism, some subdividers expressly banned Jews, Hebrews, "any person of the Semitic race," or anyone of other than the "Gentile race." At a time when American Jews were at the midpoint of what historian Matthew Frye Jacobson calls their "racial odyssey" from "white persons" to "Hebrews" to "Caucasians," other subdividers attempted to exclude Jews simply by banning anyone other than a Caucasian. Still others kept out Jews by honoring the "gentlemen's agreement" whereby developers and real estate agents refused to show property to Jews and other "undesirables," a practice that was endorsed by the National Association of Real Estate Boards. On occasion subdividers took more drastic steps. E. H. Bouton bought back a lot in the mid-1890s to prevent a Jew from buying it. And afraid that a Jew would "hurt the property badly," as he later put it, Hugh Potter, one of the developers of River Oaks, took much the same tack in the mid-1920s. When he learned that an owner had sold his property to a Jew, Potter tried to get the new owner to sell it back to the company, but the man refused. "Perhaps," Potter wrote, "he resents our attitude." Whatever the reason, the Jew later sold the property to a non-Jew, and a relieved Potter informed his associates, "we have gotten rid of him."[14]

By the late 1910s, however, some subdividers who had hitherto refused to sell to Jews were having second thoughts. As Nichols explained, a delegation of prominent Jews had complained that he was keeping them out of many of the best residential neighborhoods, "making Kansas City a poor place for a Jew to live." The meeting left him uncomfortable. Kansas City had some "fine Jew-ish families," he said. Some Jews were "good friends," with whom he sat on the boards of the city's charitable organizations. One headed the largest such organization in the city. No group had "served the country more loyally" in the recent war. The matter "is getting very much under my skin, by George," he declared; "it is so un-American, and undemocratic, and so unfair to exclude a man on account of his nationality." Hence he had decided that if "a very exceptional" Jew, one "very satisfactory and acceptable in every [other] way," wanted to buy, "we would not hesitate to sell [to] him." A few subdividers agreed with Nichols. Elmer A. Rowell of Berkeley, California, said that he had sold to two "very choice Jews." And Hugh Prather of Dallas added that he too had sold to two of "the best Jews in town," whom he referred to as "pet Jews." "I would just as soon have them as anybody else." A case in point, he said, was "old man Sanger," the head of Sanger Brothers, a Dallas department store, who was thinking about buy-ing property in Highland Park. "Everybody loves Mr. Sanger; he goes with the very best Gentiles in town," Prather said, "and the people in Highland Park will be glad to have Mr. Sanger or that kind of Jew [as a neighbor]."[15]

Other subdividers thought Nichols was making, in Bouton's words, "a perfectly ghastly mistake." We would not sell to "a Jew of any character whatever," he said. E. W. Chaille would not sell to Jews either, not "even to the best Jews in our city." Nor would King Thompson, who conceded that "some of the nicest busi-ness men in town are Jews," and H. S. Kissell, who acknowledged that he had been under strong pressure to sell to Jews. "We had some very narrow escapes," he said. John Demarest, whose For-est Hills Gardens was located a few miles east of the largest Jewish community in the country, if not the world, would not sell to Jews either. "We have sold to two or three choice Jews" and ever since had been wondering why. "We will never do it again," he said, "because they are absolutely objectionable." Bouton and other subdividers found Jews, even Jews like "old man Sanger," objectionable not because they let their property run down or because they depressed property values, as African-Americans allegedly did, but rather because they wanted to live together. Once one Jew moved in, others followed. Before long, said Bouton, a "stampede" got under way that drove out the Christians. Faced with a similar problem, worried that the rising number of Jewish students would discourage Christians from applying, Columbia and other Ivy League schools imposed quotas and otherwise revised the admissions process. But in the absence of such an option, Bouton and many other subdividers chose to exclude Jews completely.[16]

Racial covenants and other exclusionary measures were far from foolproof. Other Americans had no doubt that African- and Asian-Americans were not white. Nor were they Caucasian, a term that even Madison Grant, one of the country's most outspoken racists, called "at best, a cumbersome and archaic designation." But what about Indians, Burmese, and Filipinos? Or Syrians, Armenians, Mexicans, and southern Italians, whose racial identity was a source of considerable uncertainty? Were they "undesirable" too? It was hard to say. Also, some unquestionably undesirable people found ways to circumvent the exclusionary measures. A Providence subdivider sold a lot to "an Irishman or a Native," unaware that he was acting on behalf of a "Hebrew." (The Hebrews, he reported, built some of the nicest houses and "kept [them] up the best of any," but his competitors exploited "the presence of Hebrews" on his tract to boost sales on theirs.) And a light-skinned African-American real estate agent acquired the house in Hancock Park for Nat King Cole. Most subdividers would not knowingly sell to anyone undesirable. But what about the new owners? As Bouton and Potter found out, a few would sell to anyone if the price was right. Demarest ran into the same problem. Upon learning that one homeowner had a purchaser who was Jewish, he "tried to prevail upon him not to sell." "I couldn't do it," he said. Whereupon the next-door neighbor warned the homeowner "if he sold his house to a Jew that he would put a negro in his house as a tenant," a warning he passed on to the prospective purchaser.[17]

Although far from foolproof, racial covenants were relatively clear-cut. Under ordinary circumstances, African- and Asian-Americans (and, to a lesser degree, Jews) were easily identifiable. And since all were undesirable, the covenants did not have to draw distinctions between members of these groups—between, say, "pet Jews" and typical Jews. But to the subdividers (and their prospective purchasers), people were undesirable by virtue of class as well as race. And to exclude people by class was much more problematic. Since subdividers aimed at different markets, what was undesirable to one was not necessarily undesirable to another. All would agree that the lower class was undesirable, and most felt the same way about the working class. But only the developers of the most exclusive tracts regarded the middle class as undesirable. The only rule was that a class was undesirable if it stood below the one at which the subdivision was aimed. Even if a subdivider knew which class was undesirable, how could he tell whether a prospective purchaser belonged to it? Was it a matter of wealth? Or income? Of occupation? Or education?

Or was it a function of "good taste and refinement"? Short of holding personal interviews, requiring references, or conducting background checks, which was done in a few very exclusive sub-divisions (as well as many very exclusive cooperative apartment houses), the subdividers were much harder pressed to find a way to exclude undesirable people by class than by race.[18]

But find a way they did. While paying lip service to "good taste and refinement," they defined class as a function of money. It was a crude definition, though perhaps the only one possible in so fluid a society. The subdividers attempted to exclude unde-sirable people by making it too expensive for them to buy and build on the property. One approach was to set a price for the lots well above what these people could afford. (A closely related ap-proach was to divide the property into large lots. Although there was always a chance that "a poor man" might use a large lot "in such a manner as to make it offensive to neighbors," the Olm-steds advised Joel Hurt, the subdivider of Druid Hills, in 1902, it was more likely that the land would be misused if the lots were small.) This approach had a drawback. As Edward A. Loveley, a Detroit real estate man, pointed out in 1925, the higher the price, the smaller the market. "It is always well to bear in mind," he said, "that the highest priced property with the highest restric-tions necessarily limits the number of available buyers." There were five to ten times as many people who could afford to buy a lot for five thousand dollars as there were who could afford to buy one for ten thousand.[19] Despite the drawback, this approach was an effective way to exclude some people without driving away others, many of whom would have been reluctant to solicit refer-ences, much less to undergo personal interviews and background checks.

Another approach was to set minimum cost requirements that were out of the reach of "undesirable" people. These requirements were originally designed to prevent property owners from erecting cheap and flimsy houses. During the mid and late nineteenth century subdividers imposed them for the same reason they imposed restrictions that banned the construction of houses of fewer than two or three stories or of materials other than stone and brick. This practice continued well into the early twentieth century. Writing to the subdividers of The Uplands in 1907, John Charles Olmsted recommended that instead of banning one-story houses they set a minimum cost requirement of five thousand dollars. "It seems to us," he explained, "that the price limit would sufficiently protect the property from the erection of a poor class of dwellings, and that there is not likely to be anything essentially objectionable about a 1-story cottage if it be as costly as $5000." But in time it became clear that a minimum cost requirement would also help exclude undesirable people. As the Olmsted brothers informed Hurt, "The higher the minimum limit [that] can be placed [on the cost of a house,] the more certainty there will be of establishing a desirable neighborhood." Hurt should not consider a limit of less than three thousand dollars, the Olmsteds insisted, and in the long run a limit of five to six thousand dollars was advisable.[20]

This approach had drawbacks too. It was not just that minimum cost requirements did nothing to prevent what New York City architect Oswald Herring called "an ill-mannered, uneducated boor" from building an "eyesore." It was also that, along with many undesirable people, they excluded some otherwise desirable "families of cultivation and refinement," families who, as John Charles Olmsted noted, would make "charming and delightful neighbors" but, as Herring put it, "lack a well-filled purse." The problem of attracting these families concerned Bouton, who imposed minimum cost requirements at Roland Park but dropped them at Guilford. His solution, he told a Philadelphia banker, was to build "a group of ten small houses, which we rented at a very low rate to ten young married couples, all of whom belong to prominent Baltimore families." Even if the houses made no profit, they would reflect well on the community. Despite the drawbacks, most subdividers remained wedded to minimum cost requirements. When Bouton said at the third annual conference that these requirements were "wholly unnecessary" in communities that required design review, none of the other subdividers sided with him. Even if no longer necessary to prevent the construction of ugly or tacky houses, minimum cost requirements were still useful as a way to exclude undesirable people. As Olmsted Brothers put it, they still served as a "rough indication" of social class.[21]

For Americans living in the early twenty-first century, when it costs at least $20–30,000 to build a modest two-car garage, it is very hard to appreciate the significance of the Olmsteds' recommendation that Hurt set a minimum cost requirement of $5–6,000 for an entire house. But $5–6,000 was a great deal of money in 1902. Despite the sharp rise in wages and prices during and immediately after World War I, it was still a substantial sum as late as 1929, at which time the American family earned on average only $2,335 a year. (The lowest two-fifths earned a mere $725, the third fifth roughly $1,600, the fourth fifth just over $2,250, and the highest fifth around $6,300.) Given the widely accepted guideline that a family should spend no more than two and a half times its annual income on a home, most American families could not go above $5–6,000. But as historian Margaret Marsh has pointed out, it was hard to find even a small suburban house at that price. The minimum cost requirements ran $5–10,000 in some subdivisions and as high as $15–20,000 in others. Added to the price of the lots, many of which went for $3–5,000 (and much more in the most exclusive subdivisions), they brought the total cost of a pleasant but not luxurious house to $8–15,000, within reach of the top 5 percent of American families, who earned on average about $14,000 a year, but very few others. To make things even harder, aspiring homeowners were normally required to make a large down payment and if they were able to obtain a mortgage, which was much more difficult then than it is now, to amortize it in five or ten years.[22]

When Olmsted, Jr., wrote that Palos Verdes Estates was "predominantly for fairly prosperous people," he could just as well have been writing about Roland Park, St. Francis Wood, the Country Club District, and other highly restricted subdivisions. These communities were designed for well-to-do merchants and manufacturers as well as for well-off lawyers and doctors. They might have been within the reach of the planners and landscape architects who laid out the subdivisions, but not the laborers who cleared the woods, paved the roads, and installed the pipes or the truck drivers who delivered the materials and carted away the trash. They might also have been within the reach of the architects who designed the houses, but not the carpenters, plasterers, painters, masons, electricians, and plumbers who built them. Most of these tradesmen earned only about a dollar an hour. Even if they worked forty-four hours a week for fifty-two weeks, which was extremely rare, they were lucky to make $2,000 a year. A survey made in Los Angeles in 1925, near the end of a great real estate boom, revealed that plumbers, the best paid tradesmen, earned only $1,900. These communities might have been within the reach of the fire and police chief and the superintendent of the schools, but not of the firefighters and police officers who protected the residents or the teachers who educated their children.[23]

The subdividers laid out less exclusive and less expensive tracts, some for the middle class (as opposed to the upper middle class) and even a few for the working class. But most of these tracts had racial covenants too. And many had minimum cost requirements, albeit much lower ones. These restrictions were imposed on middle- and working-class tracts for much the same reason they were imposed on upper-middle-class ones—to exclude "undesirable" people and, by so doing, to create a strictly homogeneous community. No one spelled this out better than Charles H. Cheney. Speaking about his efforts at Palos Verdes Estates, he wrote in 1928:

> The type of protective restrictions and the high scheme of layout which we have provided tends to guide and automatically regulate the class of citizens who are settling here. The [racial] restrictions prohibit occupation of land by Negroes or Asiatics. The minimum cost of house restrictions tends to group the people of more or less like income together as far as it is reasonable and advisable to do so.

At the heart of this objective was the assumption that heterogeneity was incompatible with permanence, that a mix of races and classes was incompatible with a "bourgeois utopia." And underlying this assumption was a deep-seated fear of others. (To the extent there were differences among subdivisions, it was largely over who the others were. Were they only African- and Asian-

Americans? Or were they also the lower class? Or perhaps the working class? Or, in places like Hycliff and Hancock Park, even the middle class?) More than anything else, more than the difference between public space and private space, this fear accounts for the sea change from Olmsted, Sr.'s, inclusive view of America's parks to Olmsted, Jr.'s, exclusive view of America's suburbs.[24]

Fear of One Another

The racial covenants, minimum cost requirements, and other exclusionary measures were highly effective. Most residential suburbs had very few African- or Asian-Americans (or other people of color). To give a couple of examples, Beverly Hills, an affluent community west of downtown Los Angeles (where the median value of a home was about $18,000), had almost 5,000 families in 1930, of whom 1 was African-American and 8 were of "other" races. And South Gate, a working-class community south of downtown L.A. (where the median value of a home was less than $4,300), had about 5,600 families, of whom 1 was African-American and 41 were of "other" races. Of the few suburbs for which information is available, most had only a handful of Jews or none at all. As late as 1919 Dallas's Highland Park had two; Houston's River Oaks, which was laid out in the mid-1920s, had none. Since Bouton refused to sell to "a Jew of any character whatever"—and most Baltimore real estate agents honored the "gentlemen's agreement"—only a few Jews managed to acquire property in the Roland Park Company's four large subdivisions. And in 1928 a mere 13 of the more than 2,250 families who lived in Roland Park, Guilford, Homeland, and Northwood were Jewish, less than 1 percent of Baltimore's large Jewish population. Although information is sparse, there is reason to believe that the exclusionary measures segregated the suburbs by class as well as by race, though not as rigorously, and that journalist Carey McWilliams's description of Los Angeles as "an archipelago of ethnic, cultural, racial, and socio-economic islands" applied as well to other American cities.[25]

But if racial covenants, minimum cost requirements, and other exclusionary measures were so effective, why did subdividers impose so many other restrictions on their tracts? And why did they impose the most stringent restrictions on the most exclusive tracts? If the subdividers could "automatically regulate" the racial and class makeup of a tract—if they could ensure that it would consist entirely of well-to-do whites, even well-to-do Christians—why was it necessary to impose so many onerous restrictions on how the residents could use their property? Perhaps no subdivision illustrated this paradox better than Pacific Palisades. Set in the hills of Los Angeles, high above the Pacific, it was developed in the mid-1920s under the auspices of the Southern California Conference of the Methodist Episcopal Church (and, like so many other subdivisions, laid out by Olmsted Brothers). Although the conference envisioned the Palisades as a God-fearing Christian community—a community that would be home to none but "Christian people and institutions of all denominations"—it nonetheless felt obliged to impose the customary restrictions.[26] These restrictions were aimed at people other than African-Americans, Asian-Americans, Jews, and the lower, working, and, in a few cases, middle classes for the obvious reason that these "undesirables" could not buy or build in most restricted subdivisions.

Who were these other people? According to the subdividers, the restrictions were aimed not so much at the residents as at their neighbors. They were designed to protect residents against what an employee of the Van Sweringen brothers called "acts of others." As an ad for the Country Club District said, "The restrictions applying to your own lot mean little to you. It is the restrictions on your neighbor's lot which count." The residents had no reason to be afraid of all the neighbors or even most of them. But they had good reason to be afraid of the few who, in the words of Olmsted, Jr., "through carelessness, ignorance, neglect," or sheer numbers, "destroy or seriously impair . . . the very qualities which drew them [to the community in the first place]." Of the few, Olmsted said, who would put up an apartment house on a lot designed for a single-family home, who would build right up to the property line, or who would open a store or a saloon in a residential neighborhood. Of the few, as Cheney put it, who would erect a house "that is ugly, ungainly, or in such bad taste as to make living near by most uncomfortable and undesirable." And of the few, said Bouton, who would lead the other residents astray. "People may not want to burn the soft coal to start with in your subdivision," he pointed out, "but if one of the neighbors does decide to burn it then the other neighbors will say that as long as they are getting the black smoke in their houses anyway they might as well take advantage of the economy of burning soft coal."[27]

But why did the residents have reason to be afraid of any of their neighbors when all of them were white and well-to-do and virtually all were Christian? What was there to be afraid of in Cahuenga Park, a tract in the San Fernando Valley, where, its subdividers assured prospective purchasers, "You know . . . what type of man [your neighbor] will be"? In River Oaks, where the residents would live in "a neighborhood," said the developers, "in which the people you like, like to live"? Or in Brendonwood, home of "the very best representatives of Indianapolis citizenship," where, said the subdividers, "your neighbors will be men and women of similar taste who, like yourself, will love Brendonwood and treasure all that it gives them"? In other words, why were the subdividers and their prospective purchasers afraid of people like themselves—and not just of people of racial groups other than white and social classes other than middle and upper middle? What did they know—or, if know is too strong, sense—that led them to expect the worst of others? If the "bourgeois utopia" was, as J. C. Nichols said of Sunset Hill, one of the most exclusive tracts in the Country Club District, "the result of our supreme faith in human nature," why was it covered with so many restrictions besides racial covenants and minimum cost requirements? Were there no informal mechanisms—no measures less oppressive than restrictive covenants—to prevent the neighbors from using their property in ways that would have undermined the community's long-term well-being?[28]

In an attempt to answer these questions a good starting point is an often-quoted entry from the diary of Philip Hone. A successful New York businessman and onetime mayor of the city, Hone lived on lower Broadway in the 1830s, at which time what a special New York State Senate commission called "the inexorable demands of business" were transforming Lower Manhattan from residences into stores, offices, workshops, and warehouses. By 1836 Hone was afraid he would soon be forced to move uptown. "Almost everybody downtown is in the same predicament," he wrote, "for all the dwelling houses are to be converted into stores." Hone moved; so did many other well-to-do New Yorkers. But no one forced them to. No public agency condemned their property to make way for a school, a park, or a street. Why then did they move? One reason was that they were unwilling to live amid stores and offices and the traffic, noise, and dirt that followed in their wake. Another was that they were aware that once their property was reassessed on the basis of its potential for commercial use their taxes would rise. But above all they moved because, as Hone put it, "We are tempted with prices so exorbitantly high that none can resist."[29] What they could not resist was the prospect of a windfall, the chance to capitalize on an anticipated change in land use, the opportunity to sell their property for much more than they paid for it—often so much more that they could build a new house uptown and still pocket a great deal of money.

In a country pervaded by what Alexis de Tocqueville, perhaps the most astute observer of antebellum America, called "commercial habits and money-conscious spirit," the prospect of a windfall was irresistible to many others besides Hone and his neighbors. For all the momentous changes in the late nineteenth and early twentieth centuries, it was no less irresistible in the 1920s than in the 1830s. Small wonder, as Thorstein Veblen wrote in 1923, that wheeling and dealing in real estate was, next to poker, the "great American game." It was also the source of many of America's great fortunes, one of the greatest of which was made by John Jacob Astor, who once said, "Could I begin life again, knowing what I now know, and had money to invest, I would buy every foot of land on the island of Manhattan." For every Astor, there were thousands of others who dabbled in real estate, often with success. As one journalist wrote about Los

Angeles in the 1920s, "Time and again people have bought land at prices that were highway robbery at the time, only to sell at an advance in a few years." Even those who ignored the advice of reputable bankers and real estate dealers and bought overpriced lots in subdivisions for speculative purposes "have in a few years sold at a large profit." The profit came from rising land values, which were driven by population growth, economic development, improvements in transportation, and changes in land use, especially changes from rural to urban and residential to commercial.[30]

To many Americans, a lot was as much an investment as a homesite. And to some it was exclusively an investment. Even a home was more than a residence. Visiting Los Angeles in the mid-1920s, journalist Albert W. Atwood "was struck, not altogether pleasantly, by the great number of people who had sold, or expect to sell their homes at a profit." The subdividers were well aware of this "money-conscious spirit." And in all but a few highly exclusive developments like Hancock Park, they tailored their ads accordingly. Beverly Wood was "Doubly Profitable," said its promoters; it was both a splendid setting for a suburban home and "the most promising investment today in Los Angeles foothill property." Brentwood Terrace was not only for home seekers but also for "hard headed investors." Lots were "a top-notch investment" in Belle Mead, "a splendid investment" in Altadena Country Club Park, and an investment that "cannot be duplicated" in Hollywood Crescent Rose Tract No. 2. Other Los Angeles subdivisions promised "BIG PROFITS," "tremendous profits," and "QUICK PROFITS." Still others assured prospective purchasers that property values would rise by 100 to 200 percent. The message was the same in other cities. Make sure your home is "an investment as well as a dwelling place," said an ad for Scarsdale Estates in

Westchester County. "Build your home today in a spot where, if necessity [or presumably opportunity] should arise, you can sell it quickly at a good profit."[31]

The suburbanites were confident that most people would refuse to sell to an African- or Asian-American or other "undesirable" person even if offered a very high price. (So were the subdividers. Time and again, Nichols said, residents of the Country Club District told him, "I could get more money for my property from so and so but I certainly would not do it after everything your company has done to create such fine surroundings.")[32] But the suburbanites were far from confident that most people would turn down a good offer from a desirable person, a well-to-do white Christian like themselves, who intended to use the property for an undesirable purpose. They were afraid that most people who owned a large corner lot would sell to a builder who wanted to erect an apartment house (or, even worse, open a store, saloon, or gas station) and was ready to offer five or ten times what the lot was worth as the site for a single-family home. They were also afraid that if offered enough money many would give an outdoor advertising company permission to erect a billboard on their property or an oil company the right to drill for petroleum beneath it. They were afraid that if the price was right most people would move to another (perhaps more fashionable) suburb and put up another (perhaps more expensive) house. They were afraid that was what most people would do because they knew that if they found themselves in the same position that was what they would do.

That was what they would do because that was what they had always done. Most Americans moved many times—from Europe to America, from east to west, from the countryside to the city, from one city to another, from the city to the suburbs, and from one suburb to the next. Even in colonial times, a British observer wrote, "wandering about seems engrafted in their Nature." By the antebellum period, it was second nature to most Americans. As Tocqueville remarked:

> In the United States a man builds a house in which to spend his old age, and he sells it before the roof is on; he plants a garden and lets it just as the trees are coming into bearing; he brings a field into tillage and leaves other men to gather the crops; he embraces a profession and gives it up; he settles in a place, which he soon afterwards leaves to carry his changeable longings elsewhere.

"If God were suddenly to call the world to judgment," wrote another European visitor in the 1840s, "He would surprise two-thirds of the American population on the road like ants." Said novelist William Dean Howells in the 1870s, it was un-American for a man to yearn for "the homes of his ancestors, or even the scenes of his own boyhood." Writing in the 1950s, historian George William Pierson nicely summed up the restlessness of the American people. "We began as explorers, empire builders, pilgrims and refugees, and we have been moving, moving ever since." If "an impressive number of us now own our own homes," he added, "these are certainly not where our grandfathers lived, and probably not where we ourselves were born."[33]

Over the past few decades a host of studies have confirmed Pierson's observations. What two historians call a "dizzying rate of population turnover"—and two others a "remarkable impermanence"—was characteristic of virtually all cities in the nineteenth and twentieth centuries. About one of every four families, possibly as many as one of every three, moved each year. Some were uprooted when their homes were torn down to make way for stores and offices, streets and parks, bridges and railroads. Others chose to move, at times because they could not find a job that enabled them to make ends meet, at times because they found a better or cheaper place to live, and at times because they just wanted to start anew somewhere else. The result, write historians Howard P. Chudacoff and Judith E. Smith, was that, "From Boston to San Francisco, from Minneapolis to San Antonio, no more than half the families residing in a city at any one time could be found there ten years later." (Far fewer could be found in the same neighborhood, and fewer still in the same house.) Or as historians Stephan Thernstrom and Peter R. Knights point out, "The typical city-dweller of nineteenth-century America had not been born in the city in which he resided, nor was he likely to live out his entire life there." It did not matter whether he was a homeowner or tenant, rich or poor, white or black.[34]

This endemic restlessness troubled many Americans, few more than John F. W. Ware, the Unitarian minister from Cambridge who decried the "want of permanence" as "one of the crying sins of the age." As unsettled as a "wandering horse of the desert," we Americans "strike our tents, and flit at any moment," he wrote in 1864. Some, it seems, aspire just "to see how many houses" they can live in. "All this," he said, "is fatal to the home. It breaks up any thing like continuity of life. It prevents fixedness of habit, and so fixedness of purpose." Above all, it weakens "that local attachment which is one of the strongest and purest sentiments of the human breast." Woe to a people "who have ceased to regard permanency of abode as among the cardinal virtues." Ironically, J. C. Nichols, whose success depended on persuading local residents that they would be much better off moving to the suburbs than staying in the city, voiced many of the same concerns. Pointing out, with some exaggeration, that Kansas City residents seem to "move pretty nearly every month," he said in 1916 that it is deplorable that a man "will offer his home for sale" after his wife and daughter "have carefully planned it," he has built it, and his family had moved in. How sad, Nichols remarked, when "some fellow comes along and says, 'Will you sell your home?' [and the owner replies,] 'You bet your life; I will sell anything I have except my wife and children.'" How sad that he is "perfectly willing" to uproot his family "in order to get a little more money to speculate in oil and other stocks."[35]

These concerns did not keep Nichols from encouraging people to move—though once they moved to the Country Club District, he spared no effort to persuade them to stay put. Nor did these concerns stop Americans from moving, especially when a desirable person, whatever his intentions, offered to buy or rent their property for an "exorbitantly high" price. From their viewpoint, it made little difference if they moved from, say, one part of Palos Verdes Estates to another. Nor did it make much difference if they moved from Palos Verdes to Oak Knoll, Beverly Hills, Hancock Park, Bel-Air or any other highly exclusive suburb with large lots, winding roads, and expansive views. For residents who were inclined to move but could not afford a lot in these communities, there were a great many less expensive subdivisions that were well within the reach of the middle class and, in some cases, even the working class. The residents had so many subdivisions to choose from because far more land had been subdivided than was needed. By 1925, at which time the population of Los Angeles was approaching one million, enough land had been subdivided for more than seven million.[36] Residents had a great many choices in

New York, Chicago, Philadelphia, and Detroit too. And they had more than a few even in smaller places like Baltimore and Kansas City.

The result of this endemic restlessness was not only that Americans were constantly on the move and routinely settling in communities to which they had no "local attachments," but also that they invariably lived among strangers, among people who, in Pierson's words, had no "prior knowledge of each other," much less of one another's families, of their fathers and grandfathers, of their close relatives and old friends, of their past triumphs and tribulations.[37] Before Vanderlip, Cheney, Olmsted, Jr., and the other newcomers moved to Palos Verdes, no one lived there except the Bixby family and a few dozen truck farmers, many of them Japanese-Americans who were later barred from buying, renting, and occupying property there. And virtually no one lived on what later became Beverly Hills, Oak Knoll, Huntington Palisades, and the hundreds, if not thousands, of less fashionable subdivisions that were laid out in the late nineteenth and early twentieth centuries. Moreover, the people who bought lots and built houses in these subdivisions did not find themselves in a modern version of an old New England town with long-settled families and well-established norms. To put it another way, most suburbanites would have to create a community before they could join it.

What was true of the suburbs was true of the cities. A case in point, albeit an extreme one, was Los Angeles. From a town of only 11,000 in 1880, it grew into a city of more than 1.2 million (and a metropolitan area of more than 2.3 million) by 1930, a hundredfold increase in half a century. Most of the newcomers came from elsewhere in the United States, the largest contingent by far from the Midwest. As one journalist wrote, with more than a little disdain, they were "'leading citizens' from Wichita; honorary pallbearers from Emmetsburg; Good Templars from Sedalia; honest spinsters from Grundy Center—all commonplace people, many of them with small competencies made from the sale of farm lands or from the lifelong savings of small mercantile businesses." After decades of "hard labor and drudgery," wrote another journalist, some were looking for an easier life, free from the "cold winters and blistering summers of the prairies." Others, including architect Myron Hunt and publisher Harry Chandler, were attracted by the region's salubrious climate. Still others were hoping to find good jobs in the rapidly growing metropolis. At first most newcomers made the long trip by train. Later many drove—the well-to-do in comfortable sedans, the less well-off, wrote one observer, in "rattletrap automobiles, their fenders tied with string, and curtains flapping in the breeze." "As New York is the melting-pot for the peoples of Europe," said another, "so Los Angeles is the melting-pot for the peoples of the United States."[38]

What the Chamber of Commerce called a "great stream of humanity" left in its wake a metropolis in which, wrote one journalist, "nearly all are newcomers." Speaking to the Underwriting Subscribers of the Palos Verdes Project in 1922, E. G. Lewis said, "They tell me that a man who has been here six years is a native son, and if he has been here eight years he is an old inhabitant." On a trip to Los Angeles eight years later, a visitor was struck by "the singular fact" that in a city of a million and a quarter "every other person you see has been there less than five years" and more than nine of every ten less than fifteen years. A few residents arrived in the mid-nineteenth century. But for every one of them there were hundreds who arrived in the late nineteenth and early twentieth, among whom were some of the city's most influential and colorful characters. Besides Hunt, Chandler, and McWilliams, they included Henry E. Huntington, the transit and real estate magnate, Samuel Goldwyn, the flamboyant Hollywood producer, Frank Wiggins, secretary of the Los Angeles Chamber of Commerce (and the region's leading booster), and Aimee Semple McPherson and Reverend Bob Shuler, the city's most popular (and, in the case of "Sister Aimee," most notorious) evangelists. Whether the expression "I'm a stranger here myself," with which residents often greeted one another, originated in Los Angeles is not clear, McWilliams writes. What is clear is that it reflected one of the quintessential features of the metropolis.[39]

Were there communities in urban America where the residents had so strong an attachment to a place and so close a relationship with the neighbors that even if offered a very high price for their property they would have refused to sell and move elsewhere? Were there communities where the neighbors could have drawn upon family ties, old friendships, and traditional values to dissuade a resident from using property in an unacceptable way (or from selling or leasing it to someone who would so use it)? Perhaps there were, but if so, these communities were few and far between and highly unlikely to be found in the new suburbs of the big cities. There may also have been something else about these suburbs that discouraged close relationships. Writing in 1904 about Rochelle Park, a subdivision in southern Westchester County, journalist Samuel Swift noted that the developer had taken pains to "preserve proper standards" and to exclude anyone "known to be obnoxious." But he pointed out that "no close friendship is necessary because dwellings adjoin. You may, you must, be civil to the man next door, but you need not invite him to dinner even once a year unless you like him; you need not even offer to share a seat with him in the train to and from New York."[40] In such a loose-knit community the residents would have been hard pressed to find measures less oppressive than restrictive covenants to prevent the neighbors from using their property in undesirable ways.

A World of Nuisances

Of the many activities that were banned by these covenants, some were intrinsically undesirable. By this I mean that they were undesirable to virtually all Americans and by virtually any definition. They might well be necessary—and even highly profitable. They might produce goods for which there was a strong demand. And they might provide much-sought-after, if not necessarily well-paying, jobs for working people, especially recent immigrants. But so far as most people were concerned, these activities were wholly incompatible with a pleasant residential environment. Given a choice, no one would raise a family close to them. In this category were activities that were popularly (and, in some cases, even legally) deemed nuisances. Among the worst of them were slaughterhouses, tanneries, foundries, refineries, and brickyards, one of which was at issue in *Hadacheck v. Sebastian,* a case in which the U.S. Supreme Court upheld the constitutionality of the pioneering Los Angeles zoning ordinance in 1915. Also in this category were factories. As Olmsted, Jr., told Joel Hurt, "It is obvious that in a first-class residential neighborhood . . . any form of factory would be extremely objectionable"—as would "a large stable for the livery business or for a contractor's use."[41] Although they were not nuisances per se, saloons were also "extremely objectionable." Indeed, to many middle- and upper-middle-class Protestants, they were even more objectionable than factories and livery stables. What made saloons so objectionable —what made it "impossible," said the Chicago Board of Aldermen's Licensing Committee in the early 1850s, "to establish good neighborhoods in the[ir] midst"—were two things. One was that they attracted the wrong sorts of people. At its best, said its defenders, the saloon was "the poor man's club" and "the workingman's club." As a miner wrote, "It offers a common meeting place. It dispenses good cheer. It ministers to the craving for fellowship. To the exhausted, worn out body, to the strained nerves —the relaxation brings rest." For its working-class customers, the saloon served as a surrogate home, a mailing address, a labor exchange, and a place to eat, sleep, cash a check, and use the toilet. (It also served as an avenue of social mobility for the saloonkeeper.) But the middle- and upper-middle-class suburbanites did not want in their communities an institution that attracted working people. Even less did they want in their midst an institution that, in historian Jon M. Kingsdale's words, offered an alternative to "the traditional American ascetic ethic of work, frugality, self-control, discipline and sobriety," which were the very values the suburbanites hoped to preserve in their "bourgeois utopias."[42]

The other thing was that saloons led to what John Marshall Barker, a professor of sociology at Boston University's School of Theology, called "moral and social degradation." At its worst, Barker and other critics charged, the saloon fostered "poverty and thriftlessness," weakened resistance to "infectious and contagious diseases," undermined self-esteem, and promoted "an un-American spirit among the foreign born." It was "a menace to the family," a place where men spent their hard-earned wages, bringing "untold suffering and sorrow to many wives, mothers, and children." It was also "a veritable school and hotbed of crime [and immorality]," one that lured boys into theft and gambling and girls into prostitution. (It accounted for fully 90 percent of criminal activity, critics contended, and, said the Chicago Vice Commission, it did more than any institution other than the brothel to encourage "the social evil.") It was "the chief promoter of bribery and rascality in politics" too. "Wherever the saloon is most strongly entrenched," wrote Barker, "there knavery, plunder, graft, and bad government are most rampant." In a country where successive waves of temperance reform had won millions of adherents, a country where many cities, states, and in 1918 the nation itself had adopted prohibition, it is easy to see why subdividers commonly imposed restrictions banning the sale of "intoxicating liquors"—or, in the quaint phrase from an 1864 Kentucky deed, "ardent spirits."[43]

But it is not easy to see why subdividers commonly imposed restrictions banning a great many activities that were not intrinsically undesirable. It is not obvious why subdividers, many of whom permitted doctors, dentists, and lawyers to use part of their houses as offices, barred other owners from using their lots for a hardware, stationery, or drug store, a grocery, bakery, or butcher's shop, an office or small workshop for an electrician, plumber, or carpenter or a retail shop of any kind. It is easy to point out that John Charles Olmsted advised Walter H. Leimert, the Oakland developer, "against allowing stores" on his tract and that his brother Frederick recommended to Joel Hurt that "stores for ordinary household supplies . . . would much better be kept at a distance of from quarter to half a mile from your property if it can be managed." But it is not easy to explain why the Olmsted brothers took it for granted that the proximity of shops and stores disqualified a subdivision as a site for "first-class residences." Nor is it easy to account for why both Richard M. Hurd, the prominent real estate economist, and Henry Clarke, the former director of sales for Palos Verdes Estates, held that in a residential district a commercial building was a nuisance.[44]

Why did many Americans, especially middle- and upper-middle-class Americans, find stores, shops, and offices so objectionable in residential neighborhoods? One reason is that even a business that was, in Nichols's words, "a very great convenience" was incompatible with their vision of the "bourgeois utopia." As Minnesota judge Oscar Hallam put it, "The man of thrift, whether of large means or small, looks forward to a home out from the center of business activities, where he may live upon a plot of ground more or less ample in space, suitable for the bringing up of a family." One is willing to put up with a good deal of inconvenience in a quest for "better light and air, better moral surroundings, and better conditions for recreation" and in an effort to avoid the tumult and traffic that accompanied even the least noxious businesses. Residents of fashionable neighborhoods, wrote H. S. Kissell, wanted nothing that "savors of commercialism," not even a greenhouse, which, he said, filled the site not so much with flowers and bushes as with fertilizer and shipping crates. Given this antipathy to commercial activities, even the least offensive store, in Hallam's words, "annihilates the value of residences round them."[45] Doctors', dentists', and lawyers' offices savored of "commercialism" too. But for fear of driving away some of the most affluent of their prospective purchasers, a good many subdividers excluded in-home professional offices from the customary restrictions against commercial activity.

Another reason is that businesses that were far from offensive were a source of instability. As *American Architect and Building News,* a Boston periodical, observed in 1904, "it is the uneasy retail shopkeeper who forces change in our cities," who "transforms one-time agreeable residential districts into business sections. . . . He pursues his customers, and they flee from him." A blacksmith shop, store, hotel, and residence could "dwell peacefully side by side" in a village, wrote George E. Kessler, the landscape architect who laid out the first tract in Roland Park, but not in a city and not in its suburbs. There the retailers, in a misguided effort to get close to their customers, inadvertently drive out the residents. In much the same way as an African- or Asian-American family, a single store was a serious threat, said the Country Club District's Homes Association. Vigilance, it wrote in 1928, must be "exercised to snuff out an occasional business that creeps into the district, whether it be a millinery shop, musical establishment, etc., preventing the entering wedge of business outside of [the] business centers."[46] The subdividers and their prospective purchasers favored restrictions against stores, shops, and offices out of a deep-seated fear that these businesses would set in motion the forces that would undermine the permanence of the community—that, as Olmsted, Sr., warned, they would destroy the features that had drawn people to the suburbs in the first place.

Nor is it obvious why many subdividers barred owners from using their lots for residences other than single-family houses. What makes this so puzzling is that the restrictions against multi-family housing barred not only boarding and lodging houses, wooden "three-deckers," which, said a spokesman for the Massachusetts Civil League in 1911, were spreading all over eastern New England "like the cholera or yellow fever," and squalid tenement

houses, which, wrote E. R. L. Gould, a leader of the model tenement movement, in 1899, were "standing menaces to the family,
to morality, to the public health, and to civic integrity." They
also banned pleasant garden apartments and luxurious apartment houses, many of which were designed for the well-to-do or,
in some cases, the very wealthy. The subdividers were well aware
of what was commonly referred to as "flat fever" or "flat craze."
And they were troubled by the growing demand for apartments—
which they attributed largely to the cost of single-family homes,
the convenience of apartment-house living, and the shortage of
domestic servants. Some subdividers held that a well-designed
apartment house of not more than three or four stories (and not
more than two apartments a floor) was not intrinsically undesirable. But afraid that many suburbanites would strongly object
to an apartment house in their neighborhood, most subdividers
were ordinarily reluctant to sell lots to apartment-house builders—except on occasion if the lots were located on the edge of
the subdivision or the apartments served as a buffer between the
few stores and shops and the many single-family homes.[47]

The subdividers' fears were so well grounded that they raise the
following question. Why did many Americans, especially middle-
and upper-middle-class Americans, find multifamily houses of
any kind objectionable in residential neighborhoods? The answer
is that they saw apartment houses as a grave threat to American society. With their common hallways and stairways, they
spread infectious diseases. They also spewed smoke and soot
over the neighborhood. And they were very noisy. Even worse,
they were firetraps and, wrote a North Dakota judge, a major
cause of "the great increase" in crime and delinquency. They
undermined "civic spirit." And they discouraged homeowner-

ship, wrote Lawrence Veiller, the leading tenement house reformer, who declared, "A city cannot be a city of home owners
where the multiple-dwelling flourishes." "The apartment house
of to-day becomes the tenement of to-morrow," said a Minneapolis civic leader. It was just a matter of time, as few as fifteen years,
according to one observer, as many as twenty-five, according to
another. Some Americans did not agree that the apartment house
per se jeopardized public health and public safety or undermined
civic spirit. Too much noise is unhealthy, wrote Judge Florence E.
Allen of Ohio, but there was no evidence that apartment house
residents were noisier than other Americans. Nor was there any
evidence that apartment houses were more susceptible to fire
than single-family houses, especially ones with a wooden frame
and a shingle roof.[48] But among middle- and upper-middle-class
Americans, Judge Allen was in the minority.

Although Judge Allen was not convinced, many Americans
also believed that apartment houses were a threat to public morality. (As Allen wrote, they held that "the people who live in
apartment houses [are] less moral *per se* than those who live in
single[-family] dwellings.") Underlying this belief was the assumption that morality was contingent upon privacy. As Reverend
Ware pointed out, privacy was possible only in a single-family
house, a house that "stand[s] apart, neither subject to overlooking
or overhearing," a house "within an enclosure sacred to it." How,
asked Ware, could a family maintain its privacy in a building
where "through a thin partition comes the thrumming of a piano,
the scolding of a mother, the crying of the child, the entrance
and exit of every guest?" Where privacy is lost, wrote Bernard J.
Newman, director of the Pennsylvania School for Social Services,
morality declines. Men indulge in drinking, gambling, and pro-

miscuity. Families stop going to church. Couples file for divorce in alarming numbers. And the birth rate falls, a sign of what one critic of the apartment house called "race suicide." (Ironically, some of the same critics who decried the absence of privacy in apartment houses complained that by virtue of their anonymity they encouraged prostitution, providing "a shield to the lewd man and woman [seeking] to carry on their immoral practices.") As historian Gwendolyn Wright points out, the apartment house became a scapegoat for many of the most pressing social problems in the late nineteenth and early twentieth centuries.[49]

Many Americans also found apartment houses objectionable on still other grounds. Apartment houses, critics charged, were ugly, with as much appeal as factories and barracks. Instead of creating values, said city planner Harland Bartholomew, the typical apartment absorbs values, values based on the peace, quiet, and fresh air found only in neighborhoods of one- and two-family homes. Worst of all, apartment houses attracted the wrong sort of people. As Judge Francis P. Finch of the New York State Court of Appeals put it, apartments "bring together a changing and floating population under one roof, having no ownership of their own, and caring little for anything beyond their personal comfort and immediate needs." They were filled with tenants, "a class of nomads," said Harvard president Charles W. Eliot, "families that are here to-day and gone to-morrow, that have no stable footing in the town and no interest in its affairs." (From the fifteenth floor of an apartment house, a Philadelphian noted, it did not matter whether the streets and sidewalks were properly cleaned or the ashes and garbage promptly disposed of, much less whether the city was well governed.) By virtue of their nomadic quality, apartment house dwellers were unwelcome in residential neighborhoods. When they move in, said J. C. Nichols, the residents assume the neighborhood is on the way down.[50]

Many Americans "find apartment, flat, or hotel life necessary or preferable," wrote Judge Thomas J. Lennon of the California Supreme Court in 1925. Many families enjoy an "ideal home life in apartments, flats, and hotels." And many single-family homes are racked by "dissension and discord." But that being said, Lennon declared, multifamily housing has so many serious drawbacks that "a sentiment practically universal" has developed among Americans that "a single family home [is] more desirable for the promotion and perpetuation of family life than an apartment, hotel, or flat." And "few persons, if given their choice, would, we think, deliberately prefer to establish their homes and to rear their children in an apartment house neighborhood rather than in a single home neighborhood." Others made the point more sharply. "It is hard to think of a real home stored in [these] diminutive pigeon holes [where] the natural, free intercourse of the family is crowded out," wrote one. In even "the better class tenements" everyone is out all the time, said another. "There is little or no home life. The bond between the members of the family is gone." Taking this position to its logical, though far-fetched, conclusion, many Americans held that an apartment, no matter how well designed and well built, was not a home and should not be mistaken for one. A "'home'" said one, "is either a detached house or two-family house"—nothing else.[51]

The erection of even one apartment house in a residential neighborhood was a source of great concern because it was widely believed that the building of one led to the building of others. And once that happened the neighborhood was doomed. As Charles H. Cheney pointed out:

Once a block of homes is invaded by flats and apartments, few new single family dwellings ever go in afterwards. It is marked for change, and the land adjoining it is forever after held on a speculative basis in the hope that it may all become commercially remunerative, generally without thought of the great majority of adjoining owners who have invested for a home and home neighborhood only.

Judge Lennon agreed. An apartment house, he declared, might enhance the value of adjacent property for other apartment houses, but it "detracts from the value of neighboring property for home building." Olmsted Brothers agreed, too, and advised Walter H. Leimert to refrain from setting aside any lots for apartment houses on the grounds that they "would have a most deleterious effect on the value of the private residence district beyond." The firm told another client that if he set aside some of his land for apartment houses he "should make up [his] mind to develop the rest of the property in a similar manner." Summing up the conventional wisdom, the U.S. Supreme Court declared in 1926 that "apartment houses, which in a different environment would be not only entirely unobjectionable but highly desirable, come very near to being nuisances [in a community of single-family homes]."[52]

Setback Lines, Architectural Controls, and Fences

Some subdividers were content just to ban the erection of residences other than single-family houses. But many also imposed a host of other restrictions, some of them highly onerous, on the siting, design, and landscaping of these houses. These restrictions raise interesting questions, the answers to which reveal a good deal about the fears that permeated suburbia in the late nineteenth and early twentieth centuries. Why, for example, did many subdividers require that the houses be set back not only from the front line of the lot—a practice, wrote Olmsted Brothers, "which is universally recognized to be desirable in any suburb"—but from the rear and side lines as well?[53] Why did a few go so far as to put a limit on how much of the lot the house could cover? Why did many provide that no house—and, in some cases, no garage and other outbuilding—could be constructed until they (or an art or architectural jury) approved the plans? Why did some specify the style of architecture, the type of building material, the color of the exterior walls, and even the pitch of the roofs? Why, too, did many subdividers also impose restrictions on the grounds, among the most noteworthy of which were ones regulating the height, character, and design of fences—and, in a few cases, even banning fences outright?

The least onerous and least controversial of these restrictions, setback requirements, were designed to serve two closely related purposes. As a well-informed observer wrote, the "natural tendency" of the typical suburbanite was to build his home closer to the road than the neighbors', thereby commanding "a little better view up and down the street." This created an uneven (and unattractive) building line. It also left little room in front of the house for trees, shrubs, and what one authority on landscape gardening called "an unbroken ornamental lawn," a "well-manicured," if not particularly useful, front yard. Only by "keeping all buildings back a certain distance from the street"—at least twenty-five feet and preferably forty to fifty, the Olmsteds advised Joel Hurt—could the subdividers restrain the homeowners. As Duncan McDuffie, developer of St. Francis Wood, put it, setback requirements, in conjunction with wide lots, gave "the entire property the appearance of a park or private estate," no small thing in subdivisions named Lawrence Park and Highland Park as well as Scarsdale Estates and Palos Verdes Estates. As historian Robert Fishman points out, the setback requirements gave middle- and upper-middle-class residents the illusion of living in a parklike setting that was ordinarily well beyond their means.[54]

Setback requirements, McDuffie wrote, also enhanced "the sense of privacy." As Reverend Ware stressed, nothing was as vital to a wholesome domestic life as what the Olmsted brothers called "a desirable degree of privacy." The problem, as they saw it, was that left to their own devices the typical suburbanites, especially those who owned a narrow and shallow lot, were likely to build right up to the side or rear lines. (For example, a homeowner was likely to build as far north as possible in order "to have as much of the agreeable southern exposure on his own land," a practice that did "a decided injury to the neighboring lot north of it.") Without side and rear setbacks—at least five feet and preferably ten at Druid Hills, advised the Olmsteds, and even more at The Uplands and other subdivisions on which they worked—suburban houses would be built cheek-by-jowl. Before long they would have only a little more open space around them than rowhouses in Boston, New York, and Philadelphia. Living right next to their neighbors, whose windows, in the Olmsteds' words, "directly overlooked" their homes and yards, suburbanites would have as little privacy as city dwellers.[55] Small wonder most suburbanites went along with setback requirements.

Far more onerous and controversial than setback requirements were architectural controls, which did not catch on until the 1910s and 1920s, long after most other restrictions were well established. In the face of widespread opposition, what drove the sub-dividers to impose architectural controls? What led them to conclude that minimum cost requirements were not enough to ensure architectural quality and architectural harmony? One reason is that the subdividers were afraid some lot owners would build houses that were, in architect Oswald C. Herring's words, "of commonplace or freakish design"—awkwardly proportioned, vulgar in outline and glaring in color, an eyesore to the neighborhood." If even a few owners built what journalist F. A. Cushing Smith called architectural "gimcrack[s]" or "monstrosities"—or even, said J. C. Nichols, if they "unthinkingly" erected a badly designed house—the results would be disastrous. Subdividers would be hard pressed to sell the remaining lots or forced to sell them at a reduced price. And property values would fall on the nearby lots. As the *Palos Verdes Bulletin* said, ugly houses, "careless or stupid in their use of color or line," are "literally as great a menace to realty values in their neighborhoods as a firetrap or a noxious industry."[56]

Another reason is that the subdividers were afraid some lot owners would build houses that were well designed but out of harmony with other houses in the neighborhood. As Frank L. Meline, a prominent Los Angeles real estate man, pointed out, even a minimum cost requirement would do nothing to stop a "well-intentioned owner [from] laying the foundation for a pseudo-Italian villa," even if "on the lot right next to him and within twenty feet perhaps, another enterprising homebuilder is erecting a Colonial cottage of the Georgian period; and perhaps within a stone's-throw a deep chocolate-hued Spanish type home is nearing completion." (Or as journalist Chester S. Chase noted, "a huge palace would be as unwelcome [in Springfield's Colony

Hills] as a bungalow built of cement blocks and clapboards.")
Such an architectural hodgepodge would "spoil the entire layout"
of the best planned subdivision, wrote Richard W. Marchant, Jr.,
secretary-treasurer of the Roland Park Company. John Charles
Olmsted agreed. In the interest of the long-term well-being of the
Palos Verdes project, he advised Jay Lawyer not only to require
design review, but also to restrict all homes to "a single style of
architecture and a limited choice of exterior building materials."
"Tiresome monotony should be avoided," he explained to W. H.
Kiernan, one of Frank A. Vanderlip's right-hand men, "yet the excessive variety and especially the conspicuous lack of harmony
and absence of beauty[,] which results [sic] from the usual practice of permitting each owner to build without regard to what his
neighbor has done or is likely to do, have made our cities a shame
and reproach to all intelligent and patriotic Americans."[57]

Why were the subdividers afraid some lot owners, most of
whom were well-to-do Americans like themselves, would build
homes that were badly designed or, even if well designed, out of
harmony with the other homes? The answer, said Herring, was
that money and taste did not necessarily go together—that there
were a good many "ill-mannered, uneducated boor[s]" who had
plenty of one and little of the other. John Charles Olmsted, who
was also troubled by the poor taste of his fellow Americans, attributed the problem to a serious defect in national character.
"We regret to say," he wrote Lawyer, "that experience has shown
that Americans very generally have failed to exhibit in the choice
of architectural styles that intelligence which distinguishes them
in other directions." Meline agreed. Most Americans "are not
blessed with a keen sense of architectural discrimination," he
said at a national conference of real estate men. Compounding

the problem was what some viewed as the excessive individualism of American life, which drove people in a host of different
directions. As the editors of *Scientific American*'s Building Edition
wrote in the mid-1890s, "Where the size and style of suburban
buildings and their location are left entirely to the caprice of the
speculative builder or the individual owner, the general architectural effect is liable to be inharmonious, if not, at times, absolutely grotesque."[58]

More puzzling than the setback requirements and architectural controls were the restrictions on fences (and, in many cases,
walls and hedges as well). These restrictions were an outgrowth
of a radical change in American sensibilities. Through the first
half of the nineteenth century Americans viewed what a Boston
magazine called "good fences of durable material" as an integral
feature of the rural landscape, "unmistakably indicative of thrift
and good order." They helped to control wandering animals and
errant children, to preserve privacy and domesticity, and to de-
marcate the line between private and public space. But as early
as the 1840s Andrew Jackson Downing, the foremost authority
on landscape gardening, took strong exception to the traditional
view. The typical fence, he wrote, was an abomination. "The close
proximity of fences to the home gives the whole place a confined
and mean character." Frank J. Scott, the next generation's arbiter
of taste in suburban landscaping, held the same view. Instead of
putting up a fence, he wrote in 1870, suburbanites should trust
that their neighbors were "kindly gentlemen and women, with
well-bred families who can enjoy the views across each others'
grounds without trespassing upon them." If they put up a fence
anyway, they should bear in mind *"that kind of fence which is best is
least seen and best seen through."* Even hedges, Scott said, were "one

of the barbarisms of old gardening, as absurd and unchristian in our day as the walled courts and barred windows of a Spanish cloister." A "smooth, closely shaven surface of grass"—by which he meant a well-tended lawn free of fences, walls, and hedges— "is by far the most essential element of beauty on the grounds of a suburban home."[59]

No one spoke out against fences more forcefully than Nathaniel H. Egleston, a Connecticut native who became a Congregational minister, ardent conservationist, and leader of the village improvement movement that swept through the United States in the late nineteenth and early twentieth centuries. Writing in *The Home and Its Surroundings,* a highly influential book that was first published in 1878, Egleston argued that fences disfigure not only the home and its grounds but the whole neighborhood. "Nothing," he declared, "can be less tasteful than our common picket fence, for instance, with its stiff array of pickets set up as a barricade around the dwellings, as though every passing man or beast were accounted an enemy against whom we must entrench ourselves." At a time when cattle and swine were no longer allowed to run free, fences were also "a needless expense." Americans were accustomed to fences, Egleston conceded; and at first they feel lost without them. But once the fences are replaced by "a beautiful sweep of lawn," they realize the lot is more spacious (and more attractive). "The eye of each [resident], as he looks out from his windows, sweeps along a ground surface far beyond what he owns. He has, it may be, a legal title to a plot only fifty or a hundred feet in width. Yet he seems to be living on one of many times that extent. To look upon, his neighbor's trees and turf and flowers are as much his own as they are his neighbor's." The result, Egleston wrote, "is a practical enlargement of heart and feeling, a closer and kinder fellowship, a deepening interest in one another."[60]

"Sweep away those picket fences," Egleston urged his fellow Americans. (While they were at it, they should move the garden to another spot, put the woodpile out of sight, lay down a lawn, and plant a few trees and a flower bed.) And sweep them away they did. Everywhere in America, wrote one observer in 1903, the fence "has been done away with"—and "there is nothing about our places, large or small, that the world cannot see." (How different things were in England and other European countries, he pointed out, where visitors "can see nothing [of the houses] but stone walls.") So many fences had been removed of late, another writer said, that many now wonder "why the owners [once] clung to them so tenaciously." "It is not at all uncommon," said yet another observer, "to see whole communities without a line of any kind to denote where one property begins and another ends." The result of a nationwide campaign led by local garden clubs and village improvement societies, the removal of fences did more than create what the chair of the village improvement committee of the Massachusetts Civic League called "unobstructed stretches of attractive grounds." It also turned the front yards and adjacent streets into "a new kind of space." As one scholar wrote in 1990, "they became the open, flowing, parklike spaces we now associate with upper-middle-class suburban life."[61]

Some Americans were far from enthusiastic about what a contemporary called the "recent American craze" to get rid of fences. Fences, the skeptics held, protect the garden from chickens, dogs, and "other people's children." (To prevent the "short-legged little scamps in blue rompers" from destroying his nasturtiums, an *Atlantic Monthly* editor said, tongue-in-cheek, he was going to build "a red brick wall ten feet high all round our little plot" and on top of it put "broken bottles and a row of spikes.") Besides heading off problems between neighbors, a handsome and well-located fence "dignifies and completes" the home, much like "the little metal latchet on an old book, suggesting the preciousness of what lies within." Above all, the skeptics stressed, fences enhance privacy, which, wrote one, is "the most precious jewel of home life." And not only privacy, said another, but also the sense of seclusion, "so dear to the Anglo-Saxon heart." To preserve "the finer features of home life," the skeptics insisted, "a certain amount of privacy out-of-doors is absolutely essential." "No greater calamity could befall our national character than to become indifferent to it," they claimed.[62]

Under the circumstances, it is small wonder the subdividers were ambivalent about fences. Much like Olmsted, Sr., they objected to "useless" fences, especially ones that precluded, in John Charles Olmsted's words, "a continuous, unbroken lawn"—and sometimes, when a few property owners put up fences and others did not, created what Olmsted Brothers called an aesthetic "hodge-podge." (Olmsted, Jr., who told one subdivider that he had reservations about the "no fence" campaign, advised another that most fences, no matter how "neat and costly and well designed," are "more or less conspicuous and ugly unless masked by foliage.") But again like Olmsted, Sr., the subdividers were far from sure all fences were useless. Fences, they were aware, ensured privacy, toward which, E. H. Bouton pointed out, most suburbanites have "a very decided inclination." (By building fences or hedges, Bouton added, suburbanites could obtain a degree of privacy that would ordinarily be possible only by purchasing a lot of several acres, "the price [of which] would be prohibitive.") Fences,

Bouton noted, also helped keep the peace between neighbors by preventing "the children of one from intruding upon the property of the other." So did hedges, he added, even hedges as low as two feet, which were not objectionable even on small lots.[63]

Despite this ambivalence, some subdividers banned fences. But in an effort to reconcile the preference for open space with the passion for privacy, most opted instead to regulate them. They imposed restrictions on type, style, and location. (In a few cases the restrictions also subjected fences to design review and mandated that they be masked by foliage or covered by vines.) Even more noteworthy, the subdividers put limits on height. There was, however, one conspicuous exception to this practice. Where fences were used to conceal a clothesline, the Olmsted firm, which as a rule favored a maximum height of four feet, was willing to go as high as six or seven feet. (As it explained to the subdividers of The Uplands, "It is primitive and uncivilized to dry clothes in full view of the public or neighbors or of persons in ones [sic] own house or lawn or garden. There is an old saying giving warning of the undesirability of exhibiting ones soiled linen in public, but it applies with hardly less force to linen that has been washed.") But even these fences, the firm advised another subdivider, should be "proper lattice fences," covered with vines "or by thick evergreen hedges of adequate height."[64] To the Olmsteds—and to most subdividers—an exposed clothesline was more objectionable than a six- or seven-foot fence masked by foliage.

No Chickens, Rabbits, and Other Domestic Animals

Of all the restrictions, none gave the subdividers as much pause as the ban on domestic animals, and especially on chickens (and other fowl) and rabbits. As the Olmsteds, who were very much in favor of a ban on domestic animals, acknowledged, "many intending purchasers will strongly object to this restriction." A case in point, of which the Olmsteds were well aware, was W. S. Kies, a New York City banker who was thinking about buying a lot in Frank A. Vanderlip's subdivision in Scarborough-on-the-Hudson. After reviewing the Olmsteds' proposed restrictions, he complained that the ban on domestic animals was too stringent. "There ought not to be any objection to the keeping of poultry," he told H. J. Slaker, Vanderlip's agent, "provided it did not run at large and hen-houses were so placed as not to interfere with adjoining property." (One subdivider was reluctant to impose a ban on domestic animals not so much because of the market as because of his wife. "Poultry are especially objectionable to me and have been for fifteen or twenty years," Joel Hurt wrote the Olmsteds, "but on the other hand, Mrs. Hurt has a very decided preference for them.") Despite these concerns, most subdividers of upper-middle-class tracts, among them Duncan McDuffie, who regarded chickens as "an infernal nuisance," decided to include in the deeds a ban on domestic animals, everything from cows and pigs to goats, sheep, and even chickens and rabbits. "If we have lost any purchaser [because of] this restriction," another subdivider said, "we have gained tenfold [from it]."[65]

Their decision is more than a little puzzling. By the end of the second third of the nineteenth century there was a consensus that raising domestic animals in cities was a bad thing, if not "an almost unbearable nuisance," that should be regulated and, if need be, prohibited by the authorities. But there was also a consensus that in suburbs it was a good thing, a view that was shared by the subdividers, almost all of whom were thus far hesitant to impose restrictions on domestic animals. (In one of the rare cases where they did, the restrictions were aimed exclusively at swine.) As one observer wrote in 1867, a man who moves to the suburbs soon starts to think about acquiring a pig, a cow, and some chickens— the pig to consume "the waste growth of his garden," the cow to provide "tender food for his growing ones," and the chickens to supply "a fresh egg every day [for] breakfast." Raising domestic animals, historian John R. Stilgoe points out, was also widely viewed as morally uplifting. As Andrew Jackson Downing wrote, "he who will educate a boy in the country without a 'chicken' is already a semi-barbarian." Catharine E. Beecher, a leading authority on domestic life, and her sister, Harriet Beecher Stowe, best known as the author of *Uncle Tom's Cabin,* agreed. There was no better way for children to learn responsibility, they argued, than to tend to horses, cows, and other domestic animals, to provide "for their sustenance and for their protection from injury and disease."[66]

This consensus retained much of its strength through the late nineteenth century—and, to a lesser degree, into the early twentieth. By then, it was widely acknowledged, few suburbanites had space for cows or other livestock, but as Francis E. Clark, a Protestant minister, wrote in 1907, "there is room for a couple of rabbits and a few bantams" on the "tiniest" of lots. Even on a small scale, poultry farming was worthwhile, its advocates insisted. If a family consumed the eggs and meat, it reduced its expenses; if it sold them to neighbors or local grocers, it generated income to help with the costs of commuting (and possibly with the payments on the lot). Poultry farming was educational too, Clark claimed. "What a vast education a boy can find in a flock of these feathered bipeds!" he wrote. "They teach him mathematics, economics, hygienics, and rudiments of I do not know how many other sciences." Poultry farming, its champions pointed out, gave the family "a common object of interest." At once "sufficiently manual to divert the overtaxed brain of a business or professional man, and sufficiently intellectual to refresh the mind," it provided relief for "nerve-wracked commuters." It gave housewives a way to earn some extra money and children "a chance," in Stilgoe's words, "to experience something of farm-life responsibility." During World War I it was also deemed as patriotic to raise chickens and rabbits on a suburban lot as to grow vegetables in a Victory Garden.[67]

Along with rising food prices, these views gave rise to what Stilgoe calls "the great suburban poultry-raising fad." Before long suburbia had hundreds of thousands, if not millions, of chicken coops, henhouses, and rabbit hutches. The fad caught on in every region and among every social class. At one extreme were the very wealthy—among them Henry Howard Houston, whose fifty-two-acre estate in Philadelphia's Chestnut Hill contained a deer park, vegetable gardens, and a small farm with cows, pigs, horses, chickens, and other fowl. At the other extreme were working people, many of them first- and second-generation immigrants, who raised chickens, rabbits, pigeons, and even goats, cows, and mules in such Los Angeles suburbs as South Gate and Home Gardens. In between were middle- and upper-middle-class families who lived in suburbs like Chevy Chase, where in its early years, one resident later recalled, "nearly everyone kept chickens." Well aware of this fad, more than a few subdividers of low- and middle-income tracts stressed that their lots were large enough not only to grow vegetables and fruit but also to raise chickens and rabbits. As one ad said, "All of the fruit, vegetables, rabbits, poultry, etc., which can be consumed by the average family of six people, can be produced [on your lot]." And as another put it, "the income from poultry, fruits and vegetables can easily be made to pay for the property and add $600 to $1000 a year to your earnings."[68]

Why then did Duncan McDuffie believe poultry farming was not "appropriate for the kind of subdivisions that we are engaged in building"? Why did he, Walter H. Leimert, and John North Willys put a chicken coop, a rabbit hutch, a pigpen, and a cattle yard in the same category as a slaughterhouse, quarry, foundry, and crematory? Why, in other words, did so many subdividers of upper-middle-class tracts prohibit homeowners from keeping livestock, poultry, rabbits, and, in some cases, pigeons and "raucous" parrots? (There were, it is true, some conspicuous exceptions. Joel Hurt and Robert Jemison did not ban domestic animals. And Edward H. Bouton did not ban animals other than pigs at Roland Park; not until he subdivided Guilford did he extend the ban to all livestock and poultry. But many subdividers who did not ban domestic animals imposed other restrictions on them. At The Uplands, for example, residents could keep cattle— though not swine or poultry—but only if they owned at least five acres, which meant at least two or more lots, and made sure the animals were "well screened." At Avalon, a posh subdivision in Great Neck on Long Island, domestic animals could be kept, but only with the consent of the property owners' association, and fowl yards and the like were permitted only if they were "in good taste in a high class residence neighborhood" and in no way "unsightly or repulsive" to the neighbors.)[69]

According to the Olmsteds and other Americans, domestic animals should be kept out of suburbia because they attracted vermin, did a lot of damage, and made a good deal of noise. Cows, said the Olmsteds, leave droppings in which flies breed, and flies carry "germs to food and other things by means of which they may enter the human system." (Cowsheds and stables were "breeding places for rats" too, added a resident of Roland Park.) People who lived in a "first-class suburb" should be protected from "such a disgusting and unsanitary nuisance." Chickens and other poultry get loose from time to time, wrote the Olmsteds, and trespass on the neighbor's land, where, said another resident of Roland Park, they scratch up the vegetable and flower seeds and otherwise make "a nuisance of themselves." Above all, domestic animals make noise at the worst possible time. How annoying, wrote the Olmsteds, "to be awakened early in the morning by the crowing of a healthy rooster." How indeed, a resident wrote to the *Los Angeles Record* in the late 1920s. On one side of his lot, he complained, were goats, rabbits, chickens, roosters, dogs, and guinea hens, on the other chickens and roosters. "These roosters and goats crow and blat all night, making it impossible to sleep at all after 1:30 A.M." Under the law, the livestock had to be kept twenty feet from his home. "But that is nothing [for] the roosters [who] can be heard a block [away]." "Oh," he lamented, "if there was only a law to prevent crowing roosters and blatting goats."[70]

As the Olmsteds advised the subdividers, there were two other reasons to impose a ban on domestic animals. One was to make the subdivision more attractive to prospective buyers. While some might be driven away if they could not raise animals, the Olmsteds believed, more might be driven away if their neighbors could. How prospective purchasers felt was revealed by Arthur D. Foster, a lawyer who lived in Roland Park. Writing in 1915, he said, "while I might like to have chickens—and there is plenty of space for a chicken run on my lots—I can see that my neighbors might prefer to keep ducks or guinea hens, and so I am perfectly willing, in the interest of securing a quiet, peaceful neighborhood, to forgo the pleasure it might give me to raise my own chickens." The other reason to impose a ban was to prevent conflict among residents. As John Charles Olmsted told the subdividers of The Uplands in 1907, "the keeping of poultry and swine on comparatively small residence lots is a prolific source of dissatisfaction and quarreling among neighbors." "Only a few days ago," he wrote, "I read an account of a lawyer who had shot a neighbor's rooster." The rooster's owner was furious, and what started out as a quarrel among neighbors ended up as a nasty lawsuit.[71]

The Olmsteds were aware that many well-to-do Americans wanted fresh eggs for breakfast (and maybe freshly killed meat for dinner). They were also aware that many of them took pleasure in raising domestic animals (or, more likely, in watching their wives and children raise them). But if subdividers imposed a ban on animals, the Olmsteds contended, these Americans had other options. As John Charles Olmsted advised H. J. Slaker, anyone who wants to reside at Scarborough-on-the-Hudson, which banned domestic animals, "can buy some land on the other side of the street or a little distance off where he can keep poultry without annoying [the residents of] this particular community." Perhaps nowhere did the Olmsteds spell out their position more clearly than in a letter to the subdividers of The Uplands in 1907. After stressing that in the long run a ban on domestic animals will "add perceptibly to the value of the remaining land," they went on to say: "Persons desiring to keep poultry have two courses open to them: either they can buy an area of five acres or more, in which case the poultry will be very much less likely to be objectionable to persons living on adjoining lots as designed: or they can buy unrestricted land in the vicinity of The Uplands to be occupied by their gardener or man-of-all-work, who would take care of the poultry and thus supply the family with chickens and fresh eggs."[72]

There is no doubt that many Americans considered domestic animals a nuisance. But neither is there any doubt that many found household pets objectionable. Dogs, declared a Baltimore doctor, are a public health menace, as out of place in a city or suburb as pigs. They root through garbage cans, scattering refuse to the winds. Even worse, "You can never tell when a dog is going to bite you," possibly transmitting rabies (and even diphtheria and scarlet fever). Much like chickens, dogs dig holes in nearby gardens, remarked a Roland Park resident, destroying the neighbor's rows of "succulent beets and tomatoes" and "delicate lettuce and parsley," not to mention his shrubs and flowers. As another Roland Park resident complained, one dog recently came to his house, "amused himself by chasing my pullets, incidentally killing two; chased every young child coming down our lane to go to school, and remained half a day to terrorize the community." Many a resident feels "a warm sense of sympathy and compassion" for well-behaved and affectionate dogs, wrote the *Roland Park Review*, a community newsletter. But anyone who is awakened in the "wee" hours of the morning "by a prolonged howl on the other side of the way, followed by an answering snarl and thereafter by a chorus of discordant yelps," is likely to wish that "the breed might be removed by violent means from the face of the earth."[73]

Cats are even more objectionable than dogs, said another Roland Park resident. They kill so many birds each year that "very soon I fear Roland Park will be without any of the beautiful birds that have been one of the great attractions here in the spring and summer." (Dogs, which he also disliked, have "one thing in their favor—they occasionally kill a cat, thus saving the lives of a lot of birds, and occasionally a few pullets, thus saving some one's beautiful flower garden.") According to one expert cited by the *Roland Park Review,* cats "not only destroy birds but [also] break the peace." What he called their "caterwauling at night" should not be permitted in "a well governed" community. "A person," he added, "has no more right to inflict a cat on the neighborhood than to inflict a goat or rabbits or any other nuisance." The *Roland Park Review* agreed. Saying that it was time to get rid of cats, it declared, "These animals are members of a fierce and merciless tribe. Despite hundreds of years of domestication, their predatory instincts assert themselves whenever a smaller or weaker creature comes within their reach." Besides birds, they kill chipmunks, rabbits, and other "charming reminders of the free and untrammeled pathways of nature." "We are quite willing to acknowledge that 'pussy has her place,' and is, in it, a useful and valuable animal," wrote the *Review;* "but we do not believe that Roland Park should be allotted as one of her places."[74]

One Roland Park resident made fun of the crusade against household pets, saying that it was time to move from dogs and cats to squirrels. Pointing out that these "little pests" scatter "fragments of nuts and hulls over the smooth pavements that are our just pride," he wrote that they had no place "in our high-class suburb." They were dangerous too. "Only last fall a dear, worthy old maiden lady was scared nearly into hysterics by being pelted on her bonnet by a hickorynut that one of these irresponsible squirrels let fall from his careless grasp." "Next month, if *The Review* will be so kind as to grant sufficient space, I hope to take up the subject of pigeons and human infants, both of which seem unnecessarily prevalent in our exclusive suburb." But the animosity to household pets was no laughing matter. To the dismay of pet owners, another resident of Roland Park suggested that the way to deal with barking dogs was to put out "a liberal portion of 'juicy meat salted with effective poison.'" (Indeed, several years later someone used strychnine to kill six dogs, all of them household pets, not strays.) At the same time the *Roland Park Review* instructed its readers how to trap cats and where to bring unclaimed ones for asphyxiation. Before long the Maryland Society for the Prevention of Cruelty to Animals charged that residents of Roland Park were putting stray cats in bags and drowning them, a practice that its general secretary branded "wholesale and unlawful slaughter."[75]

The controversy grew so heated that the Roland Park Civic League felt compelled to set up a special committee to look into the matter. In an attempt to find a middle ground between the pet owners and their antagonists, it stressed that it was not planning to wage war against household pets. "There may be a decided difference of opinion as to the advisability of keeping [them]; but the committee recognizes that their owners have rights which must be respected." It also drew a distinction between the household pet, which should be treated kindly, and "the homeless tramp, the prowling vagrant, the unattached tramp, be he cat or canine," which should not. To solve the problem, it urged pet owners to hang a bell around their cat's neck. "The [bell] would serve a double purpose," it wrote. "It would protect the cats from the cat-catcher and the birds from the cats." Other residents favored more draconian measures. Some—even some who thought it was "little short of sacrilege" to put dogs, "the friend of man, whose fidelity has been tried and proven in a hundred instances," in the same category as pigs—were willing to permit pets in Roland

Park, but only if they were barred from roaming at will. Others wanted them to be taken to the pound or perhaps sent to the country. And still others preferred to dispose of them—humanely, if possible, by whatever means necessary, if not.[76]

Joel Hurt, one of the many subdividers who turned to the Olmsted brothers for advice about restrictions, knew that while some dogs were well behaved, others were, in the Olmsteds' words, "an incessant nuisance," barking loudly, often at "inopportune" times, and "running round and digging up flower beds, chasing other people's pet cats and the like." So did other subdividers. But with very few exceptions—among them one who allowed "nonvicious dogs" and another, wrote the Olmsteds, who placed "a general prohibition against keeping dogs, to which exceptions are made so long as the dogs are not objectionable"—the subdividers did not impose restrictions on dogs. Or, for that matter, on cats. A case in point was H. S. Kissell, one of the leading subdividers in the Midwest. Although he was aware that "people like cats," he believed most of them "like birds even better." And so each year he sent a notice to the residents of Ridgewood, his fashionable subdivision in Springfield, Ohio, about "BANISHING THE CAT." "If a cat is kept in the neighborhood," the notice warned, "it will be next to impossible to get birds to make their nests in your shrubbery." But that was as far as Kissell went. He did not forbid residents to keep cats, much less impose a restriction banning them. (Apparently the notice was enough. "There are 200 homes in the subdivision," he reported, "and not a single cat.")[77]

Why then did many of the leading subdividers impose restrictions on domestic animals but not on household pets? Why, for example, did A. D. Halliwell, head of the company that developed Hycliff, an exclusive subdivision in Stamford, Connecticut, ban poultry, fowl, and livestock, but not cats and only vicious dogs? Why did these subdividers believe the restrictions should deal, in the Olmsteds' words, "more gently" with household pets than with domestic animals?[78] Part of the answer is that by the early twentieth century affluent Americans were more likely to have dogs and cats than chickens and rabbits. And to most of them, the Olmsteds pointed out, neighbors' household pets were ordinarily less objectionable than their domestic animals. Pet owners were also likely to have a stronger attachment to their dogs and cats than poultry farmers had to their chickens and ducks, which would sooner or later be served for dinner anyway. Moreover, it was one thing for would-be poultry farmers to buy a lot knowing that they could not raise chickens and rabbits there, and quite another for pet owners to do so knowing that they would have to get rid of the family dog or cat. As the subdividers saw it, a ban on domestic animals would drive away some prospective purchasers, but a ban on household pets would drive away many more. When dealing with this issue, the subdividers always had to bear in mind that the more stringent the restrictions the more limited the market.

The other part of the answer is that by the early twentieth century most Americans had come to believe that while poultry farming and other forms of animal husbandry were appropriate in some places, Roland Park, St. Francis Wood, and Devonshire Downs were not among them. These activities, it was widely held, were not objectionable in working-class suburbs, to which many first- and second-generation immigrants were driven to move, not by "an aesthetic of romantic pastoralism," to quote historian Becky Nicolaides, but by the day-to-day struggle for economic survival. By raising chickens, rabbits, goats, and pigeons—and by selling backyard produce, taking in boarders, and running small businesses out of their homes—the newcomers generated a steady stream of income that helped protect their families against the hazards of the market economy. But the upper-middle-class suburbanites did not need the extra income, nor did they want to live next door to anyone who did. Hence prospective purchasers who had to raise domestic animals to make ends meet were not welcome in Roland Park and other fashionable suburbs. In August 1904, for example, E. C. Shriver sent a handwritten (and barely legible) postcard to the Roland Park Company asking if it had any houses "with a lot large enough for chickens and our Vegetable Garden" for less than eighteen dollars a month. On behalf of the company, James E. Green replied, politely but brusquely, "We have no property for sale or rent that would fulfill those requirements."[79]

Poultry farming and other forms of animal husbandry, it was also widely held, were not objectionable in the country either. There was much to be said in favor of raising domestic animals, said a resident of Roland Park, but a suburbanite who wanted to "should go clear out into the country and get him a little farm." (John Charles Olmsted agreed. Suburbanites who wanted what he called "the luxury" of raising domestic animals and producing their own eggs, milk, and butter should buy "a small ranch" somewhere else.) To the residents of places like Roland Park, the suburb was an alternative not only to the city but also to the country. Just as these well-to-do suburbanites did not want saloons, gas stations, and apartment houses going up, so they did not want "pigs, cows and chickens running around," to quote another resident of Roland Park. Suburbia appealed to them because it was natural, as opposed to agricultural. And domestic animals were out of place in a natural setting, albeit a man-made one. They were as out of place in Palos Verdes Estates, which was designed by the Olmsted brothers, as in Central Park, which was designed by their father. Indeed, during his term as superintendent of the park, its Board of Commissioners banned not only cows, horses, pigs, goats, sheep, and geese, but also dogs, "unless led by a chain or proper dog-string [or leash], not exceeding five feet in length."[80]

Oil Wells, Billboards, and Fear of the Market

At the heart of many of the restrictions was something the subdividers and their prospective purchasers were afraid of more than chickens and rabbits. By this I mean they were afraid that in the absence of restrictions even the best laid out tracts would be subject to the fundamental law of the real estate market, according to which land would always be put to its highest and best use. And highest and best meant most profitable.[81] Suppose, for example, someone bought a lot in an unrestricted tract for five thousand dollars. And suppose a few years later, before or even after a home was built there, someone else who thought the lot a good site for an apartment house, grocery store, or gas station offered twenty-five thousand dollars for it. According to real estate economists, the owner would sell, no matter what the impact on the nearby property. To prevent people from putting their lots to the highest and best use, the subdividers barred them from using the lots in all sorts of potentially profitable but allegedly objectionable ways. And among those ways that have not yet been discussed were drilling for oil (and other minerals) and putting up billboards (and other signs).

As late as the 1920s, when the United States was producing more than half the world's petroleum, few cities (and even fewer suburbs) had oil wells. There were, however, exceptions, the most conspicuous of which was Los Angeles. Prospectors had been drilling for "black gold" in and around Los Angeles since the 1860s. By the late 1880s about one hundred wells were operating outside the city. In the early 1890s Edward L. Doheny, best known today for his role in the Teapot Dome scandal, and his partner Charles A. Canfield struck oil in one of the many tar pits in Los Angeles. Soon afterward Doheny and others found oil in nearby Whittier and Fullerton. By 1912 greater Los Angeles was producing 4.4 million barrels a year. Several years later Standard, Shell, Union, and other major oil companies, convinced that only a small fraction of the region's oil had yet been tapped, began sinking wells. Early in the 1920s they made the spectacular strikes at Huntington Beach, Signal Hill, and Santa Fe Springs that one petroleum geologist hailed as "the greatest outpouring of mineral wealth the world has ever known." By the mid-1920s a small section twenty to thirty miles south-southeast of downtown Los Angeles was producing hundreds of millions of barrels a year, roughly one-fifth of all the oil produced in the country, and petroleum had replaced agriculture as California's leading industry.[82]

As oil poured out, wrote journalist Albert W. Atwood, investors poured in, "by the tens, the scores[,] perhaps even the hundreds of thousands," most of whom had "money to spend." Some spent it on "units" (or shares) in what they hoped would be the next great strike. Their profits would come from sales. The promoters to whom they entrusted their money ranged from out-and-out swindlers, who were netting one hundred thousand dollars a week in southern California, according to U.S. Department of Justice investigators, to legitimate prospectors. By far the most flamboyant was C. C. Julian, who, writes his biographer, was "the prince of oil promoters." In an effort to raise money, he told prospective investors that he held a lease on four acres *"in the very heart [of] the greatest oil field* in America." Once he struck oil, they could count on "a return of not less than *100% each month.*" Other investors preferred to buy lots on what they hoped would be the site of the next great strike. Their profits would come from royalties. These investors were inspired by stories not only of a few large landowners in places like Signal Hill, but also of the many ordinary folks like themselves—barbers, streetcar conductors, and, said Atwood, "widows living off the proceeds of diminutive chicken yards"—who happened to own property in the right place at the right time. Of the many people, wrote another journalist, "who, by years of effort, had managed to get legal title to a bungalow and a twenty-five-foot lot [and then] found on Tuesday that their income [from oil royalties], beginning Monday, was a hundred dollars a day—or three thousand, or any other incredible figure."[83]

A good many subdividers were eager to capitalize on the demand for oil lots. Hearing news that a wildcatter was about to begin drilling, they swung into action. Setting up shop near the future oil field, they acquired tracts that had languished for years, subdivided fields of cabbages and sugar beets, and then hung signs reading "Oil Lots for Sale." To get potential investors to the site, they chartered buses, which left from downtown Los Angeles (as well as Long Beach and other nearby cities). Along with free rides, they provided free lunches, usually sandwiches, coffee, and cookies. At the site some subdividers set up tents, which, writes historian Jules Tygiel, resembled "the tabernacles of traveling evangelists." "Sucker tents," local residents called them.

Others operated from automobiles parked along the roadside. Most salesmen made the same pitch. "Why don't you play safe, boys," one said to Atwood and his companions, "and buy one of these nice lots, eighty by twenty feet, instead of oil stock or units? You get all the oil there is under the lot and own the land besides, all for $685." The subdividers hammered away at the same point in their ads. West-Man Heights, a tract several miles southwest of downtown L.A., was under lease to a major oil company, said Potter & Smith, a firm that specialized in oil property. If oil was found, investors would share in the royalties; if not, they had a homesite that was bound to rise in value. Sunset Heights, not far from Santa Monica, offered "Choice Ocean-View Lots With Big Possibilities of OIL!" said Taft Realty.[84]

As cabbage fields gave way to oil fields—or to put it another way, as the owners put the land to its highest and best use—property values soared. For many landowners the result was a windfall, the size of which boggled the mind. But those who lived near the oil fields paid a high price for the strikes (and the speculative mania that swept through Los Angeles in their wake). As visitors observed, the oil fields were as bleak, noisy, noxious, and dangerous as any place on earth. The derricks, which sometimes stood only thirty or forty feet apart, devastated the landscape, stripping it of homes, trees, and grass. They also made a fearful din. As novelist Upton Sinclair wrote in 1926, "All day and all night the engine labored, and the great chain pulled, and the rotary-table went round and round, and the bit ate into the rock." As bad as the noise was what a group of residents called the "noxious vapors, smoke, noisome smells, fumes, [and] stench," which were extremely disagreeable (and possibly toxic). The oil fields were very dangerous too, especially when, as a result of the high pressure to which the machinery was subjected, a well had a blowout, gasser, explosion, or geyser. These accidents often set the fields on fire, tore up telegraph poles, and, in Atwood's words, spewed "a sea of mud over large portions of the landscape." At few times were the fields more dangerous than when a drill struck oil. Suddenly, wrote Sinclair, "the inside of the earth seemed to burst through that hole; a roaring and rushing, as Niagara, and a black column shot into the air, two hundred feet, two hundred and fifty—no one could say for sure—and came thundering down to earth as a mass of thick, black, slimy, slippery fluid."[85]

According to observers, conditions were only slightly less dismal on the outskirts of the oil fields. The roads were jammed, not only with trucks full of lumber and drilling equipment, but with buses full of sightseers. Bombarded by newspaper ads to "SEE THE GUSHERS AT SANTA FE SPRINGS," thousands made what Tygiel calls "the sightseeing tour to the oil fields." They came, wrote Sinclair, to look at the derricks and listen to "the monotonous grinding of the heavy drill." If lucky, they might see a gusher. Besides the oil fields, the visitors saw the tent cities, the oil fields' version of a western boom town. In the jerry-built structures that catered to the needs of the roughnecks were saloons, creating, Tygiel writes, "a free-flowing oasis" in the desert of Prohibition; bordellos, in which, said one observer, the girls were "as bare as the walls"; and gambling dens, full of slot machines, roulette wheels, and poker and blackjack tables. In a place, wrote Atwood, where speculators "buy an acre of land . . . one day for $5,000 and sell it the next day for $30,000," everything was up for grabs. "Why should anybody put up a decent building [near the fields] yet?" asked a character in *The Boosters,* a novel about Los Angeles in the 1920s. "There might be oil underneath."[86]

Unlike Potter & Smith and Taft Realty, a good many other sub-dividers, some of the region's most prominent among them, were mindful of the downside of oil exploration. Although they knew the discovery of oil could be a gold mine for some landowners, they also knew it could be a death knell for upper-middle-class residential suburbs. A case in point is E. G. Lewis. Before he pur-chased Palos Verdes from Frank A. Vanderlip, Lewis had gone wildcatting in Montana, Wyoming, and California. And after he launched the Palos Verdes Project, he reserved a portion of the peninsula, located near Long Beach and known as the Panhandle, for oil exploration. Under it, he told investors, was "one of the great oil fields of California," even greater than Signal Hill. But at the same time Lewis was looking for oil in the Panhandle, he was banning drilling at Palos Verdes Estates. There was no place for derricks, no matter how much oil they might produce, at "the Riviera [sic] of the Pacific Coast." Another case in point is Henry E. Huntington, a real estate and transit magnate and one of the largest subdividers in greater Los Angeles. Huntington was especially active in and around San Marino, where he banned drilling on many of his upper-middle-class tracts. He was also a member of a syndicate that formed the Amalgamated Oil Com-pany in 1900. It bought the thirty-three-hundred-acre Hamel and Denker ranch northwest of downtown L.A. and began pros-pecting for oil. When not enough was found, the Amalgamated was reorganized in 1906 as the Rodeo Land and Water Com-pany, which subdivided the property and named it Beverly Hills. Among the affluent subdivision's many stringent restrictions was one that barred the lot owners, one of whom was Edward L. Doheny, from drilling for oil and other hydrocarbons.[87]

Few Los Angeles subdividers had as much firsthand experience with oil as Alphonzo E. Bell. Born in East Los Angeles in 1875,

Bell was the son of one large landowner and the nephew of another. In 1896 he inherited from his uncle 110 acres south of the city that he later subdivided into 5-acre (or smaller) lots. With the profits from this and other ventures Bell bought more than 150 acres in nearby Santa Fe Springs in 1908. For a while he was content to plant alfalfa, cabbage, and orange and lemon trees. But in time he began to suspect his property might be sitting on an oil field, and so he signed leases with Standard Oil in 1916 and Union Oil in 1917. On October 30, 1921, Union made one of the greatest strikes in history, making Bell rich beyond his dreams. By year's end he was getting royalties of $20,000 to $300,000 a month, a vast sum at the time, and one experienced oilman estimated that he would eventually receive at least $6 million and as much as $12–15 million. When a blowout set off a raging fire, Bell was forced to leave his home—which was subsequently moved to another site and turned into a saloon. He moved his family into the posh Beverly Hills Hotel, and with his newfound wealth he bought 1,760 acres in the Los Angeles hills from Daisy Canfield, the daughter of Charles A. Canfield and wife of Jake Danziger, another associate of Edward L. Doheny. Bell then set out to make what he named Bel-Air into one of the most exclusive suburbs in the country. He spared no expense on landscaping, even putting the utilities underground, which was rarely done. He also imposed a host of stringent restrictions, among which was a ban on drilling. By imposing this ban, Bell was making sure that no one could do at Bel-Air what he had done at Santa Fe Springs— to wit, put his land to its highest and best use. Prospective purchasers, Bell was saying, need have no fear that a derrick would spoil this "Community of Gentlemen's Estates," no fear that the market would ruin "The Suburb Supreme."[88]

For every oil well, there were perhaps a thousand billboards, a manifestation of the phenomenal growth of the outdoor advertising industry in the late nineteenth and early twentieth centuries. Once found in only a few places, they were now found just about everywhere—on country roads as well as city streets. They were so common that in 1906 N. W. Ayer, one of the country's leading advertising agencies, estimated that 30 million Americans saw its billboards every day. By 1908, the nation's billboards stretched 8.5 million linear feet, or 1,610 miles, half again the distance from New York to Chicago. The Windy City alone had 500,000 linear feet, or close to a hundred miles. Once used mainly to promote freak shows and patent medicines, billboards were now used to advertise everything from motorcars to men's underwear, from cereal and soap to tobacco and liquor, from Wrigley's Spearmint Gum to Cecil B. DeMille's *The Ten Commandments*. Once small (and fairly unobtrusive), many were now enormous. Lea & Perrins promoted its Worcestershire Sauce on a sign that ran more than four-tenths of a mile along a breakwater facing New York harbor. And Schlitz plastered its beer signs, the largest of which covered roughly half an acre, on eight grain elevators in Chicago. Not as large, though more spectacular, were the electric (and later neon) signs that lit up Times Square and urban America's other "Great White Ways" at night.[89]

There was no escaping the billboard, said painter Emory Albright. It "follows us to the right and left as we go from our homes in the morning, . . . dances along our pathways on every side, . . . nags and goads us every time we look from a street car window, . . . follows us to the country in our automobile rides." Harry F. Lake, a New Hampshire lawyer, agreed. "You have an option as to whether you will attend [an indecent] play," he wrote, "but unless you walk with your eyes closed . . . you cannot exercise an option as to whether you will see the advertisements." (How unpleasant, he added, "to behold all these suggestions and commands about the clothes we should wear, the tobacco we smoke or chew, the whiskey and beer that is the best to drink, or the worst, the kind of codfish we should eat because boneless, the kind of soap that is 99.44 percent pure and floats, the particular sort of breakfast food that will increase our efficiency by half, and the places we must go to if we would be happy.") Crying out, said Olmsted, Jr., "as loud as color and form and size can be made out to cry, 'Here we are! You can't get away from us! Look here! Look here! Look here!'" billboards were "one more unnecessary and undesirable pin prick in the great series which makes life so nervously exhausting."[90]

The proliferation of billboards appalled a good many Americans, most of them middle- and upper-middle-class professionals and businessmen who thought of themselves as Progressives. On their own—or through the American Civic Association (ACA), the American Park and Outdoor Art Association (APOAA), and local civic art associations—they issued a scathing indictment. According to historian William H. Wilson, the indictment charged that billboards did more than hinder the ongoing efforts to beautify the city and to preserve what was left of the natural landscape. They also undermined the morals of the young, tempting them to drink, smoke, and attend lurid plays and movies featuring sex and violence. Billboards, the indictment charged, despoiled the parks, boulevards, churches, and public buildings that were supposed to provide Americans a "haven," in Wilson's words, from the secular and highly materialistic world around them. They jeopardized public safety as well. If made of wood, they were likely to go up in flames and spread the fire to nearby buildings; if made of iron they would probably collapse on the sidewalks and injure passers-by. Billboards even provided a perfect place behind which lowlifes could carry out what a contemporary called "their dissolute and immoral practices." To critics, billboards were more than an eyesore. They were a nuisance. If possible, they should be banned; if not, they should be strictly regulated.[91]

Spokesmen for the outdoor advertising industry vigorously defended the billboard against these charges—whose authors they derided as "a little band of art enthusiasts," "a few long-haired professors and short-haired women," and "a few mentally lopsided aesthetes." Billboards, they argued, were not eyesores. At best they were attractive, stylish, and colorful, "a wonderful art [form]," said one of their supporters, "a poor man's gallery of art," said another. At worst they were more attractive than the otherwise vacant lots, "strewn," in Wilson's words, "with rubbish and rusting cans." Some billboards are "inartistic," conceded one advertising man, but so are many houses. "Shall we wipe out miles and miles of these houses, simply because they are inartistic?" The outdoor advertising industry had done much to foster public morals, argued Albert de Montluzin, manager of the U.S. Lithograph Company. It had refused to post ads for anything lewd or obscene. It had also offered free posters to civic and religious groups, some of which, wrote the manager of the Gospel Publicity League, found billboards "to be their best pullers." The *Billposter,* a trade journal, was happy to report that even the sponsors of a lecture by J. Horace McFarland, president of the ACA, were not above using billboards to attract a large audience. Billboards, their defenders claimed, had never been much of a threat to public safety. Now that they were made of steel and fireproof materials, they were not a threat at all. And they could hardly be held responsible for vicious activities that took place in their vicinity. By no reasonable criteria was the billboard a nuisance.[92]

Spokesmen for the outdoor advertising industry did more than defend the billboard. They celebrated it. They hammered away at the point that billboards, in Wilson's words, were "the hand-maidens of commerce," one of the few ways by which businesses could reach consumers who did not read newspapers and maga-zines. As de Montluzin put it, billboards "are an indication of business; they mean business; they make business." Firms need the billboard because "it brings more business per dollar spent than any other method of advertising—two to one, three to one, five to one." The advertisers and advertising agencies were not the only beneficiaries of the billboard, its defenders pointed out. As Frank Warren, a member of the Bill Posters' Union, noted, upward of a million men were employed in the outdoor advertis-ing industry. If billboards were banned, he asked, "what would become of the artists who are making the posters; what would become of the bill posters, the printers, the stereotypers, and the other workmen employed in the business?" A ban would also have a severe impact on lumberyards, paper mills, ink manufac-turers, and a host of other businesses and their employees. Bill-boards are here to stay, declared their supporters. They were as much a part of modern life as streetcars, telephones, and auto-mobiles. They were better today than ten years earlier. And they would be better still ten years hence. What made them better were the efforts of industry leaders, not the attacks of municipal art leagues and the threats of local and state officials.[93]

The debate over the billboard raged in newspapers, periodicals, city halls, state capitols, and state and federal courts for roughly thirty years. But gradually a consensus emerged on a few points, not the least of which was that billboards were a nuisance when they were, in the words of the *National Real Estate Journal,* "out of place." And other than on the parkways—which, as Olmsted, Jr., wrote, provided "a region of quiet rural sylvan scenery to which people can escape [from] the ceaseless turmoil of city life"—nowhere were billboards as out of place as in residential districts, and especially in fashionable residential suburbs. They were out of place there in a way that they were not in commercial and industrial districts precisely because, as de Montluvin said, they "mean business." And business, it was widely held, had no place in residential neighborhoods. As San Jose City Attorney Jackson Hatch explained, a "glaring billboard" is as offensive to the neighbors as "a pig-sty," "a stone-breaking machine," or "the chime of hoarse bells." Speaking of billboards in much the same way other people spoke of African- and Asian-Americans, Edward T. Hartman, a member of the Massachusetts Civic League, wrote that when they "invade a residence district people desire to get away." And when people move, property values fall. Before long the whole neighborhood deteriorates.[94]

Many subdividers agreed that billboards and other signs were out of place in the suburbs. As Bouton said, "a sign in itself is a disfigurement." "If you are going to have signs," even ones that read "Save the flowers," he told his fellow subdividers, "you should make them as inoffensive as possible." To the Olmsteds, the issue was clear-cut. "It would be decidedly objectionable to residents in the suburbs to have any portion of it disfigured by advertising signs or posters," they told the developers of The Uplands. Homeowners would probably refuse to give anyone permission to put up a billboard on their property. But what about the owners of a vacant lot? Revealing their fear that even the well-to-do might be swayed by the market, they pointed out that one might well give permission if offered enough money. For the benefit of others, "such practices should be prohibited." The Olmsteds were confident that few prospective purchasers would be driven away by restrictions against billboards and other signs. So were many subdividers. Hence many forbade lot owners to post anything other than a doctor's or dentist's doorplate and "For Sale" or "For Rent" signs. Some also regulated their size, color, and design. And a few required that lot owners obtain prior approval before erecting one.[95]

The subdividers who imposed restrictions on drilling for oil and putting up billboards were sending two messages to prospective purchasers. One was that the community would not in time be covered with derricks and, in the words of Hugh E. Prather, developer of Highland Park, "plastered with signs." The other was that they could not one day lease their property to an oil company or outdoor advertiser even if, in their judgment, that was its highest and best use. Given that the subdividers were among the principal players in the market, it is paradoxical that they imposed these restrictions. (The ambivalence toward the market explains why some of the subdividers who banned billboards used signs to advertise their property. Without them, "We couldn't do business," said Paul A. Harsch, a member of the firm that developed Ottawa Hills, a subdivision whose owner retained the right to prohibit signs and even to "summarily remove and destroy" unauthorized ones.) Given that the prospective purchasers were among the principal beneficiaries of the market, it is also paradoxical that they went along with these restrictions. After all, it was with the proceeds from oil exploration that Edward L. Doheny bought a lot in Beverly Hills on which no one could drill for oil or other minerals. And, wrote de Montluzin, it was with the profits from outdoor advertising that industry leaders built "the splendid homes in the suburbs in which they are living today," alongside many of which no one could put up billboards or other signs.[96]

Seeking "A Safe Middle Course"

By now it should be clear why so many subdividers imposed stringent restrictions on how prospective purchasers could use their property (and, to a lesser degree, dispose of it). It should also be clear why so many prospective purchasers—for most of whom private property was close to sacrosanct, wheeling and dealing in real estate was second nature, and a man's home was "his castle"—were willing to buy highly restricted property. It should be clear too why the subdividers and their prospective purchasers viewed restrictions as a means of protection. And it should be clear who the restrictions were meant to protect, what they were meant to protect them against, and how a belief that protection was needed arose out of a host of deep-seated fears that permeated much of American society in the late nineteenth and early twentieth centuries. What is unclear is why the subdividers did not impose more stringent restrictions—why, in other words, they did not do more to keep "undesirable" people and activities out of their "bourgeois utopias."

To give a few examples, if most subdividers banned African- and Asian-Americans, what kept all but a few from banning Italians, Russians, Slavs, Poles, Romanians, Greeks, Armenians, Persians, Syrians, Mexicans, and Puerto Ricans? If some kept out Jews, why did they let in Catholics? If, as the Olmsteds told Joel

Hurt, the higher the minimum cost requirement, the more desirable the neighborhood, why did many subdividers set it at only five thousand or ten thousand dollars?[97] What kept them from raising it to twenty thousand, as the developers of Hycliff did, to twenty-five thousand, as the subdividers of Berkley, a subdivision in Scarsdale, did, or to fifty thousand dollars as J. C. Nichols did on some of the choicest lots in the Country Club District? Why did some subdividers impose setbacks of ten or fifteen feet while others fixed them at thirty-five or fifty feet? Why did a few refrain from putting limits on how high a house could rise or how much of the lot it could cover? Why did some impose loose architectural controls, or none at all, while others imposed tight ones? If fences were out of place in a residential park, why did some subdividers allow them? If signs were, as Bouton said, "a disfigurement," what stopped some subdividers from regulating or banning them? And why did some subdividers who kept out domestic animals let in household pets?

The subdividers also refrained from taking less obvious steps to keep "undesirable" people and activities out of their tracts. To most of them, few things were as inimical to permanence as speculation, the buying and selling of lots by people who had no intention of building houses, much less of living in them and handing them down to their children. Speculators were "a positive detriment to any development," declared King G. Thompson. "Speculators NOT Desired," said an ad for Lankershim Park, a San Fernando Valley subdivision. Why then did so few subdividers include in the restrictions a provision that lot owners had to start and finish construction within a year or two of closing, a provision that Olmsted, Sr., and others believed would do much to drive away speculators? To most subdividers, moreover, few things were as crucial to permanence as homeownership. They fully subscribed to the conventional wisdom that homeowners contributed to neighborhood stability in a way that tenants did not. Unlike what a Palos Verdes Estates promotional pamphlet called the "transient element," homeowners had "an interest in society," claimed the *Detroit News*. It made them better citizens —more responsible, more law-abiding, more public spirited. A homeowner was "a patriot," said a Wilmington subdivider, "a true man," wrote a popular author.[98] Why then did none of the subdividers include in the restrictions a provision that residents could not rent their homes, a provision that would have barred tenants?

The subdividers were aware that even in suburbs where lots were sold only to people "of the very best material," a few were likely to behave in offensive ways. In Roland Park, for example, some dumped ashes on the street instead of putting them in cans. Often they blew all over the place. Others left buckets outdoors reeking of old rags and garbage. Still others dumped bottles, tin cans, wire, nails, and even oyster shells on the roads, turning them into a dump and making them a menace to motorcars. Children were also a source of trouble, wrote a Roland Park resident. They built dams in gutters, creating "a breeding place" for mosquitoes and washing out the roads. Worst of all, some residents made a lot of noise. As the Olmsteds observed, restrictions protected suburbanites against such "nerve racking noises" as "factory whistles," "crowing poultry," and "peddlers['] cries." But what about phonographs, whose "shriek," said another Roland Park resident, was among the most "exquisite" of "miseries?" ("There are doubtless many people who would prefer to live next to a store than next to a private dwelling occupied by lovers of music," wrote a New Jersey judge.) And what about the wagons, most with iron bottoms and few with rubber tires, that the children ride up and down the streets? "[A] steam engine would not make any more noise than they do," said one suburbanite, who declared, "there is no reason why the property owners should have to submit to such a nuisance."[99] Given that the subdividers could have anticipated such complaints, what kept them from including in the restrictions provisions about offensive behavior as well as about objectionable land use?

To put it another way, why were the subdividers reluctant to broaden the definitions of "undesirable" people and activities and impose whatever restrictions were necessary to bar them? The answer is that, much as the subdividers were afraid of the market, much as they were willing to go to great lengths to prevent the lot owners from putting their property to its highest and best use, they were well aware that they were deeply enmeshed in the market. And a fiercely competitive market too. As J. C. Nichols, whose Country Club District dominated the suburban real estate market in Kansas City to a degree that subdividers in other cities could only dream about, said in 1916, "we have miles of good competing residence property in our city." If Nichols felt that the Kansas City real estate market was competitive, imagine how R. C. Gillis, head of the Santa Monica Land and Water Company, must have felt about the Los Angeles real estate market. During the early and mid-1920s, at the peak of the second great real estate boom in the city's history, more than a thousand subdivisions came on the market each year. (The market was so frenetic, one historian has written, that all over southern California white-collar clerks gave up "good office jobs to become real estate salesmen.") So much land was subdivided before the boom collapsed that by the late 1920s more than half of the roughly one million lots in Los Angeles County were vacant.[100]

The market put the subdividers in a bind. In order to attract what Olmsted, Jr., called the discriminating buyer, the buyer who would not close on a lot unless it was protected from undesirable people and activities, the subdividers had to impose stringent restrictions. But as Nichols put it, "the more carefully you restrict your property, the more you lessen the number of people that can buy." Edward A. Loveley, a Detroit developer, made the same point. So did H. A. Lafler, who worked for Walter H. Leimert on Sather Park, a restricted subdivision in Oakland. Leimert, Lafler wrote, stood a better chance of selling the lots if he imposed minimum cost requirements no higher than $4,500 to $5,000 for "the choicest sites" and as low as $3,000 or even $2,500 for "the poorer lots." Nichols was sad to say that he could point to a good many subdividers of "high class" tracts who failed because their "courage and vision" led them to impose restrictions that were too stringent for the market. To Nichols, few things were worse than setting prices so high or imposing restrictions so tough that the subdividers were left with what he called "those straggling unsold lots," the carrying charges on which might well wipe out the profits from previous sales.[101]

Olmsted, Jr., was as well aware of this bind as anyone. Writing in 1909 to William H. Grafflin, president of the Guilford Land Company, which later joined with the Roland Park Company to develop Guilford, he pointed out:

> As a general proposition one of the difficulties in handling this matter of restrictions is to make them sufficiently broad and explicit to prevent objectionable developments, without at the same time seeming to tie up and hamper the possible use of the prop-

erty in such a way as to scare off timid purchasers. If the restrictions are numerous and sweeping a great many people hesitate to buy the land, not because they want to use it for anything which the restrictions forbid but because they do not know what changes may come about in the course of 10 or 20 or 40 years which might make some of the elaborate restrictions a serious encumbrance on the land.

"The problem in drawing up restrictions," Olmsted went on, "is always that of hitting a safe middle course which will assure the purchaser that his neighbors will not be likely to do anything to injure or depreciate the character of the neighborhood and yet will not frighten him by the number and rigidity of the restrictions placed upon his freedom."[102] This safe middle course would have to do more than just prevent a lot owner from putting up, in the words of Olmsted, Sr., "a dram-shop on [the] right, or a beer-garden on [the] left." It would also have to allay two deep-seated fears—the purchasers' fears that things would change, that undesirable people and activities would move in, and the subdividers' fears that things would not change, that no one would move in, that no one would buy the lots.

As Olmsted, Jr., knew, it was hard to find a safe middle course. It was hard to tell when the restrictions were so stringent that they were likely to drive away not only undesirable people but virtually everyone else. Also, what might be a safe middle course in one subdivision might be anything but in another. Over time, however, a consensus emerged among the subdividers, according to which a ban on African-Americans and other racial minorities fell into a safe middle course, but a ban on Italian-Americans did not. A ban on Jews was somewhat problematic; a ban on Catholics was much more so. A minimum cost requirement was not too stringent unless it was set above fifteen to twenty thousand dollars. Also falling into a safe middle course were setback regulations—though, outside the most expensive subdivisions, not height limits and architectural controls. Given that investors made up a sizable portion of the market—about 15 to 25 percent in Chicago, according to a local subdivider, and much more in Los Angeles, where wheeling and dealing in real estate was a way of life—it was too risky to discourage speculating and prohibit renting. It was also too risky to impose restrictions on offensive behavior. J. C. Nichols urged residents of the Country Club District, "Please don't! . . . burn your trash in a place offensive to your neighbors . . . place your garbage cans in a place conspicuous from your neighbor's lawn . . . leave your garage doors open toward the street." He even asked them, "Won't you prevent your dog from becoming a neighborhood nuisance?"[103] But afraid he might "scare off timid purchasers," Nichols did not incorporate these norms into his restrictions. Still, that he and other subdividers imposed so many other sweeping and stringent restrictions on their tracts was striking evidence of how much many Americans were willing to put up with to solve the problem of unwanted change spelled out by Olmsted, Sr., two generations earlier.

Epilogue

On March 11, 1992, Mindy Felinton, a resident of Charleston Place, a posh subdivision in Boca Raton, Florida, brought her five-year-old dog Lucky to the North Boca Animal Hospital. Lucky was not sick, just big—so big that the Charleston Place homeowners' association filed a lawsuit accusing Felinton of violating a restriction that banned dogs weighing more than thirty pounds. With Felinton, her lawyer, two representatives of the association, and a court reporter looking on, Lucky was put on a scale. In the balance was whether Felinton would have to choose between giving up her dog and moving out of her home. Fortunately for her, the results of the weigh-in were inconclusive, largely, wrote a reporter, because "Lucky kept moving around." A few days later the association withdrew its suit and allowed Lucky to stay. A decade later and three thousand miles away, Melinda and Joe Bula found themselves in a similar bind. Six years after moving into El Dorado Hills, a rapidly growing suburb of Sacramento, California, they decided to repaint their home yellow. Even though the house was yellow when they bought it, the Design Review Committee, a group of residents that, in another reporter's words, dealt with "all things aesthetic," denied the Bulas permission. As John Loveless, the head of the committee, pointed out, the El Dorado Hills restrictions stipulated that "no primary colors—yellow, red, or blue—are allowed." Unlike another resident, who agreed to repaint her yellow house in an "earth tone" if the committee would permit her to replace her roof, the Bulas appealed the decision to the El Dorado Hills board and threatened to go to court. In the meantime the committee flagged the Bulas' white picket fence as a violation because it was made of plastic.[1]

As Felinton and the Bulas learned (and millions of Americans already knew), restrictive covenants have not gone the way of the streetcars and interurban railways that opened up the suburbs in the late nineteenth and early twentieth centuries. Three-quarters of a century after Charles E. Clark observed that they were becoming "the rule, rather than the exception," nearly a century and a half after Frederick Law Olmsted, Sr., spelled out the problem they were designed to solve, these covenants are still around. Although they caught on at a time when private land-use controls were virtually nonexistent, they proliferated even after the passage of local zoning ordinances that regulated what landowners could do with their property. And though they took hold in the age of the subdivider, they retained their grip when subdividers gave way to builders after World War II. The postwar builders not only laid out the lots but also put up the houses, leaving the buyers little say about the siting and design of their homes. Thus during the third quarter of the twentieth century restrictions were found just about everywhere in suburbia, even in the large-scale planned communities that were among the hallmarks of the postwar landscape. A case in point was Levittown, Long Island, the first of William J. Levitt's huge middle-class suburbs on the East Coast, which imposed racial covenants and more than a dozen other restrictions. They were also found in Bear Creek, Washington, and the many other gated communities that went up in the late 1980s and 1990s. Known as CC&Rs (for Covenants, Conditions, and Restrictions), the restrictions are as integral a feature of these communities today as the gates that are supposed to protect residents from outsiders.[2]

Restrictions nowadays seldom include minimum cost requirements. Some real estate developers began to question the value of these restrictions in the aftermath of World War I, during which time the cost of single-family houses more than doubled. (It was obvious, they believed, that a requirement of, say, five thousand dollars that was imposed in the early 1910s would not prevent the erection of a shoddy house in the early 1920s.) And even before World War II, which set off another round of inflation, many real estate professionals considered these requirements obsolete. Starting in the 1930s, a few subdividers therefore decided to impose minimum-square-footage requirements, which served the same purpose as minimum cost requirements but were not affected by inflation. This approach was recommended by the National Association of Home Builders in the early 1950s and adopted by many developers soon after. Most developers were also forced to abandon racial and ethnic covenants after 1950. In 1948, after a long drawn out campaign by the NAACP, the U.S. Supreme Court ruled in *Shelley v. Kraemer* that these covenants were unenforceable. Without explicitly repudiating *Corrigan v. Buckley,* it held that a subdivider could include a racial covenant in a deed, but that the courts could not order a buyer to abide by it without violating the Fourteenth Amendment. *Shelley v. Kraemer* did not end residential segregation, as Gunnar Myrdal thought it would. But it did force developers to find other ways to keep African-Americans and other minority groups out of the suburbs. Levitt, for example, did not impose a racial covenant in Levittown II, which was started in Bucks County, Pennsylvania, in the early 1950s. But his salesmen assured prospective purchasers that houses would be sold "to whites only."[3]

The passing of minimum cost requirements and racial covenants notwithstanding, restrictions nowadays are more or less what they were three-quarters of a century ago. In some ways they are even more sweeping and more stringent. They are still designed to exclude "undesirable" people—a category that includes anyone under fifty-five (or even forty-eight) in some retirement communities—and "undesirable" activities. Ordinarily they prohibit nuisances of all sorts and, if they do not ban them altogether, keep workshops and stores out of residential neighborhoods and apartment houses away from single-family homes. They impose setback regulations and architectural guidelines too. Fences are regulated, if not prohibited. So are billboards and other signs. Many restrictions include a ban on domestic animals. Some also set a limit on the number and size of household pets, and a few prohibit them. Unlike Nichols and other subdividers, some developers nowadays impose restrictions on offensive behavior as well as objectionable land use. Many restrictions forbid residents to leave garage doors open, park vehicles other than automobiles on the street, hang laundry on exposed clotheslines, and leave trash cans and garbage bags in the front yard. Others bar residents from letting children play on a swing set, even in the back yard, planting cherry trees, strawberry bushes, and anything else that produces soft fruit, and, in one case, flying the American flag on Flag Day. A few even prohibit bothersome noise. To enforce these restrictions, nearly all developers set up a homeowners' (or property owners') association.[4]

Restrictive covenants are still around largely because the fears of unwanted change that gave rise to them in the late nineteenth and early twentieth centuries continued to plague Americans in the mid and late twentieth. Among the many who voiced these fears was F. Emerson Andrews, director of publications at the Russell Sage Foundation. Writing in *House Beautiful* in 1943, he urged prospective purchasers of suburban property to "look all around your proposed building site and consider what might happen ten or twenty years after you move into that dream house." Unless the lots next door and across the street are restricted to single-family homes, they may be used "some sorry day" to store a contractor's dump trucks or house "a small but self-advertising sauerkraut factory!" A gas station, store, or tavern may spring up on the corner. The home "across from you" may be converted into a boarding house or torn down and replaced by "a bustling apartment house." In "a huff" or out of "pure selfishness," the next-door neighbor may erect "a blank garage wall" along the property line "clear out to the pavement," blocking "that lovely view of yours." Or the house may be turned into a funeral home, "its long and lugubrious processions" passing by your home every day and leaving you nowhere to park much of the time. "Things like these have happened," Andrews warned, "and will continue to." It did not matter whether the prospective purchasers were thinking about moving to River Oaks, Levittown, or Bear Creek. As long as many of them were plagued by fears of unwanted change— as long as they were afraid, a resident of Phoenix said in 2003, "that you can't trust your own neighbor"—subdividers and builders would be under pressure to provide some sort of protection against undesirable people and activities.[5]

Other than to employ restrictive covenants, they had few options. Zoning, where it existed, offered homeowners some protection, especially against the encroachment of factories, stores, apartment houses, and, in some places, even two- and three-family homes. It had the added advantages that the regulations were imposed on the whole community and enforced by public officials. But zoning had severe drawbacks as well. Under *Buchanan v. Warley* it could not be used to exclude African-Americans and other racial minorities. Based as it was on the police power, the state's power to promote public health, safety, and welfare, it could not include minimum cost requirements. Nor, as Olmsted, Jr., pointed out, could it incorporate "aesthetic ideals."[6] Zoning might have been more elastic than covenants, as one of its advocates claimed, but it was not more permanent. The officials who wrote the ordinances could revise them. Under pressure from unhappy property owners, they could grant variances and exceptions as well. Building, as opposed to subdividing, also offered homeowners some protection. By putting up the houses as well as laying out the lots, Levitt and others could prevent the initial buyers from building anything but a single-family home, putting up something cheap, tacky, or ugly, and placing it up against the property line. But in the absence of restrictions, they could not stop them from raising chickens and rabbits or putting up a tall fence or a large sign. In communities without zoning, they could not keep them from turning their homes into stores, saloons, or gas stations, much less from building additions that went beyond the setback lines. As little control as builders like Levitt had over the initial buyers, they had even less over the subsequent owners.

Subdividers and builders were also under pressure to employ restrictive covenants from several influential organizations. The President's Conference on Home Building and Home Ownership endorsed them in the early 1930s, as did the National Association of Real Estate Boards. Only through these covenants was it possible to maintain the "quality of homes and stability of values," wrote two of the conference's consultants. Even more influential was the Federal Housing Administration, a New Deal agency that was empowered by the National Housing Act of 1934 to insure residential mortgages. The FHA strongly supported racial covenants and other restrictions (as well as, in the words of its *Underwriting Manual,* "effective provisions for the enforcement thereof"). To qualify for mortgage insurance, wrote the *Wilmington Morning Star,* a house had to be located in a neighborhood "protected against the encroachment of undesirable elements [meaning people of different racial groups and social classes] and improper use of property by deed restrictions and zoning ordinances." In the wake of *Shelley v. Kraemer,* the FHA stopped requiring racial covenants, but not other restrictions. After World War II the National Association of Home Builders joined the fold, arguing that "well drawn" restrictions were necessary even in low-cost neighborhoods. Even in zoned communities, residential stability and property values could not be preserved without "adequate protective restrictions," it declared. Not long after, the Department of Housing and Urban Development, which was established in 1965, gave its blessings to restrictive covenants.[7]

Subdividers and builders might have withstood these pressures if the restrictive covenants did not work. But they did. By and large, they prevented unwanted change. During a century in which other features of the built environment have changed almost beyond recognition—a century in which department stores have moved from the central business district to outlying shopping centers, expressways and freeways have replaced electric railways, and cities have razed "blighted areas" in the name of urban redevelopment—even the oldest of the highly restricted suburbs have remained much the same. Described by a journalist as "neighborhoods that can't be spoiled," these suburbs have long been regarded as models of the "bourgeois utopia." Late in the 1930s *Good Housekeeping* awarded its Shield (later known as its Seal of Approval) for "all that is best in building practice" to J. C. Nichols's Country Club District. The Shield was also displayed at Roland Park and a dozen other highly restricted communities. Shortly after, the Urbanism Committee of the National Resources Council praised the Country Club District and Roland Park, including Guilford and Homeland, as "perhaps the finest examples of integrated large-scale real estate development to be found in the United States" and hailed Palos Verdes Estates as "one of the [country's] best planned and carefully restricted real estate developments."[8] Nearly seventy years later Roland Park and the Country Club District are still considered the most attractive suburbs in their metropolitan areas. And along with Bel-Air, Oak Knoll, and Beverly Hills, Palos Verdes Estates still stands, in the words of Olmsted, Jr., *"head and shoulders"* above other residential subdivisions in greater Los Angeles.

I spent a day in Palos Verdes Estates in November 2001, a few months after starting work on this book. It was the first time I had been there since the early 1960s, when I spent a year in Los Angeles doing research for my doctoral dissertation. More than anything else, I was struck by how little it had changed (or, to be more precise, how little it seemed to have changed). If not, in E. G. Lewis's words, "a great Acropolis," it was still, as Charles H. Cheney wrote, "a model residential suburb." Its spectacular site —high in the hills, overlooking the Pacific on three sides—was much as I remembered it. So was its picturesque landscape—the winding streets that fit into the contour of the hilly site, the spacious lots that preserved the breathtaking views, and the string of parks and open spaces that enhanced the natural setting. I saw no refineries or other noxious industries, no factories, no strip malls, indeed no malls of any kind—only a few small and tasteful shopping centers, with pharmacies, bookstores, and real estate offices. Nor did I see any saloons, oil wells, billboards, domestic animals, or apartment houses—only a few clusters of garden apartments, which served as a buffer between the shopping centers and the single-family homes. As far as I could tell, the homes were large and well designed, the grounds covered by shade trees and, even in the midst of one of southern California's long droughts, well-tended lawns. Palos Verdes Estates was designed for *"stability* and *permanence,"* wrote Olmsted, Jr. And if, as he believed, the absence of undesirable activities is a sign of these traits, it is an unqualified success.

From the viewpoint of Olmsted, Cheney, and Lewis, I later learned, Palos Verdes Estates was almost as successful in its efforts to bar undesirable people as undesirable activities. From the start the developers attempted to exclude all but Caucasians, all but members of what Lewis called "the greatest race that has ever lived." And through World War II virtually all the residents were white. In the aftermath of *Shelley v. Kraemer,* the civil rights movement, and the emergence of a small but growing number of well-to-do African-Americans, Hispanics, and Asian-Americans, it became harder to segregate racial and ethnic minorities. Still, for reasons that go beyond the scope of this book, as late as 2000, by which time African-Americans, Hispanics, and Asian-Americans outnumbered Caucasians in Los Angeles County, only 1 percent of the residents in Palos Verdes Estates was African-American.

And though one of every seven residents was Asian-American, only 2 percent were Hispanic. From the start the developers also attempted to exclude all but the well-to-do and, in Cheney's words, "to group the people of more or less income together." If anything, things worked out better than expected. As of 2000 the median household income in Palos Verdes was almost $125,000, about three times the median household income in Los Angeles County. More than six of every ten households earned over $100,000, nearly three of every ten over $200,000. And the median value of the homes was close to $800,000, about four times the median value in the county. Nearly nine of every ten were worth more than $500,000, nearly three of every ten more than $1 million.[9]

Palos Verdes Estates has succeeded so well "in shutting out all din and confusion of modern metropolitan life," as one of its promotional brochures put it, that on my brief visit it was hard to remember that I was in Los Angeles, that on the other side of the hills, up and down the coast, lies the second largest metropolis in the nation. A metropolis with oil refineries, assembly plants, and sweatshops, a port whose size boggles the mind, and a network of freeways that has to be seen to be believed. A metropolis with a huge African-American ghetto, the site of two of the worst riots in American history, and whole communities in which English is the second language, and Spanish not necessarily the first. On the day I spent in Palos Verdes—a balmy, sunny, and dry day, the sort Lewis assured prospective investors and purchasers they could count on all year long—it was also hard to remember that the community was inspired not only by dreams, but also by nightmares, not only by hopes, but also by fears. Fears of people of different races and classes. Fears of people like themselves, people

who, in the words of Olmsted, Sr, might be moved, by "ignorance, incompetence, bad taste, or knavery," to sell their property
to objectionable people or to use it in objectionable ways. Fears
of change, fears of the market, fears of much of what had been
going on in American society for a century and a half.
Even so, I saw some signs of these fears. I saw them in the
Palos Verdes Public Library, which keeps the restrictions, and in
the Palos Verdes Homes Association, which enforces them. Had
I been making a longer visit, had I been paying less attention
to the spectacular site, I might have seen other signs, the sort
a *New York Times* reporter glimpsed in the mid-1970s. A family
that had just moved to Palos Verdes Estates was watching the
movers unload their belongings, he wrote, "when a well-dressed,
middle-aged woman arrived and silently attached a red cardboard
tag to the[ir] home." Asked what it meant, she answered that the
design for a railing around the front porch had not yet been approved by the Art Jury. Nor did the house have a "drying yard," a
"screened-off area" that was required because the restrictions forbade residents to hang laundry "outside the home that was visible
to others."[10] Such incidents are common not only in Palos Verdes
Estates but also in other highly restricted suburbs all over the
country. As Felinton and the Bulas found, they sometimes lead
to protracted conflicts and expensive lawsuits. Some suburbanites have complained that the restrictions are unreasonable and
intrusive in some cases, picayune in others. But as Larry Horner,
then president of a league of homeowners' associations in Westlake Village, a planned community about forty miles north of Los
Angeles, said, if the residents were not willing to abide by the restrictions they should not have moved there. But move there they
did—and not only to Westlake Village, but also to Roland Park

and St. Francis Wood, to Levittown, and to Charleston Place and El Dorado Hills. That so many people have been willing to submit to so many restrictions for so many years is the most telling sign of the deep-seated fears of unwanted change that have plagued Americans since the mid-nineteenth century, the most telling sign of the persistence of the dark side of the "bourgeois utopia."

Notes

Introduction

1. Delane Morgan, *The Palos Verdes Story* (Palos Verdes, 1982), pages 7–8; Hallock F. Raup, "Rancho Los Palos Verdes," *Historical Society of Southern California Quarterly*, March 1937, pages 9–13; U.S. Bureau of the Census, *Abstract of the Fourteenth Census of the United States: 1920* (Washington, D.C., 1923), pages 24, 38. See also Frank A. Vanderlip, *From Farm Boy to Financier* (New York, 1935).

2. Vanderlip, *From Farm Boy to Financier*, pages 249–251; Ralph Jester, "Interview with F. A. Vanderlip, Jr.," March 9, 1976, Local History Collection, Palos Verdes Library District, Palos Verdes Estates, California; *Boston Evening Transcript*, July 18, 1914; Augusta Fink, *Time and the Terraced Land* (Berkeley, 1966), pages 105–109.

3. James Sturgis Pray, "John Charles Olmsted," *Landscape Architecture*, April 1922, page 130; Frank A. Vanderlip to Olmsted Brothers, January 27, 1913, Records of the Olmsted Associates (hereinafter cited as Olmsted Records), Job File 5816, Manuscript Division, Library of Congress; *Boston Evening Transcript*, July 18, 1914; Samuel Swift, "Community Life in Tuxedo," *House and Garden*, August 1905, pages 61–71; Olmsted Brothers to W. H. Kiernan, October 18, 1914, Olmsted Records, Job File 5950.

4. *Boston Evening Transcript*, July 18, 1914; Fink, *Time and the Terraced Land*, page 109; Donald K. Lawyer, "Resume of Work Done by Olmsted Brothers," a memo dated February 25, 1926, page 2, Olmsted Records, Job File 5950; Vanderlip, *From Farm Boy to Financier*, pages 290–291; Pray, "Olmsted," pages 134–135; Edward Clark Whiting and William Lyman Phillips, "Frederick Law Olmsted—1870–1957," *Landscape Architecture*, April 1958, page 148.

5. Walter V. Woehlke, "The Champion Borrower of Them All," *Sunset Magazine*, September 1925, pages 17, 19, November 1925, pages 28–

31, 62–63, 73. See also Susan Waugh McDonald, "Edward Gardner Lewis: Entrepreneur, Publisher, American of the Gilded Age," *Missouri Historical Society Bulletin*, April 1979, pages 154–163.

6. E. G. Lewis, *Palos Verdes* (Atascadero, 1923), page 11; *A Report of Proceedings and Addresses [at the] Meetings of Underwriting Subscribers of Palos Verdes Project* (Los Angeles, 1922), pages 12, 16; Fink, *Time and the Terraced Land*, pages 110–111.

7. Fink, *Time and the Terraced Land*, pages 111–112; *Atascadero News*, June 15, 1923, unidentified newspaper, June 18, 1923, *Los Angeles Express*, June 18, 1923, *Los Angeles Times*, June 18, 1923, Local History Collection, Palos Verdes Library District.

8. *Judging Palos Verdes as a Place to Live*, undated promotional brochure, page 23. See also Frederick Law Olmsted, Jr., "Palos Verdes Estates," *Landscape Architecture*, July 1927, pages 257–258; Charles H. Cheney, "A Great City-Planning Project on the Pacific Coast," *American City*, July 1922, page 47; Charles H. Cheney, "Palos Verdes Estates—A Model Residential Suburb," *Pacific Coast Architect*, April 1927, page 14; *Los Angeles Times*, November 25, 1923, January 27, March 20, 1924; Frederick Law Olmsted to Charles H. Cheney, undated letter, Palos Verdes Homes Association, Palos Verdes Estates, California.

9. *Los Angeles Times*, February 10, 17, and 24, March 30, June 4, July 29, 1923, January 6, 13, and 27, February 3 and 10, March 2, 1924. See also *Judging Palos Verdes*, pages 3–31.

10. *Los Angeles Times*, March 18, June 24, July 29, December 2 and 9, 1923, January 13 and 27, March 2, 13, and 20, 1924. See also *Judging Palos Verdes*, pages 3, 13.

11. Olmsted Brothers, "Restrictions for Real Estate in Deed Form," a memo dated Fall 1915, Olmsted Records, Job File 5816; H.V.H., "Land Subdivision Restrictions," *Landscape Architecture*, October 1925, table following page 54; Lewis, *Palos Verdes*, page 22; *Meetings of Underwriting Subscribers*, pages 7–8, 34–35; Olmsted Brothers, "Restrictions for Residential Subdivisions and Related Matters," a report dated January 1925, Appendix, Loeb Library, Harvard University; Fukuo Akimoto, "California's Garden Suburbs: St. Francis Wood and Palos Verdes," a

paper delivered at the 9th International Conference on Planning History, Espoo-Helsinki, Finland, August 20, 2000, pages 8–12.

12. *Protective Restrictions, Palos Verdes Estates, Los Angeles, California* (1923), pages 4, 17, 28; *Meetings of Underwriting Subscribers*, page 11; *Trust Indenture, Palos Verdes Project, Between E. G. Lewis and Title Insurance and Trust Company Trustees* (Los Angeles, 1921), page 2; Robert M. Fogelson, *The Fragmented Metropolis: Los Angeles, 1850–1930* (Cambridge, 1967), pages 120–125.

13. *Protective Restrictions, Palos Verdes Estates*, pages 3–5, 9–10, 22–25, 30–32, 34–35; *Meetings of Underwriting Subscribers*, page 35; *Palos Verdes Bulletin*, December 1925, page 4; Myron Hunt, "The Art Jury of Palos Verdes Estates," *California Southland*, May 1925, page 13. On the need for architectural review at Palos Verdes, see John Charles Olmsted to Jay Lawyer, March 20, 1914, Olmsted Records, Job File 5950.

14. *Protective Restrictions, Palos Verdes Estates*, pages 4–5, 18, 35–36.

15. *Protective Restrictions, Palos Verdes Estates*, pages 3–4, 17–18.

16. *Protective Restrictions, Palos Verdes Estates*, pages 2–3, 5–6, 18–23, 37–40.

17. Robert V. Hines, *California's Utopian Colonies* (Berkeley, 1990); Ian S. Haberman, *The Van Sweringens of Cleveland: The Biography of an Empire* (Cleveland, 1979), pages 6–17; Susan L. Klaus, *A Modern Arcadia: Frederick Law Olmsted, Jr., and the Plan for Forest Hills Gardens* (Amherst, Massachusetts, 2002); Eugenie Ladner Birch and Deborah S. Gardner, "The Seven Percent Solution: A Review of Philanthropic Housing, 1870–1910," *Journal of Urban History*, August 1981, pages 403–438; *Los Angeles Times*, April 1, 1924.

18. *Meetings of Underwriting Subscribers*, pages 8, 34–35; *Los Angeles Times*, March 18, June 24, October 28, November 25, December 9, 1923, January 24, February 10, 1924; James Clifford Findley, "The Economic Boom of the 'Twenties in Los Angeles" (Doctoral dissertation, Claremont Graduate School, 1958), chapter 5; *Judging Palos Verdes*, page 30.

19. *Ignaciunas v. Risley*, 121 A. 783, quote on page 785; Marc A. Weiss, *The Rise of Community Builders: The American Real Estate Industry and*

Urban Land Planning (New York, 1987), pages 80–101; Jules Tygiel, *The Great Los Angeles Swindle: Oil, Stocks, and Scandal During the Roaring Twenties* (New York, 1994), page 13; Mark Lee Luther, *The Boosters* (Indianapolis, 1923), page 181; Olmsted, Jr., "Palos Verdes Estates," pages 257–258; Nathan William MacChesney, *The Principles of Real Estate Law* (New York, 1927), pages 153–156, 160–163, 173; Lawrence J. Vale, *From the Puritans to the Projects: Public Housing and Public Neighbors* (Cambridge, 2000), page 121.

20. *Los Angeles Times,* November 5 and 12, December 3, 1922, February 25, April 15 and 22, May 20, October 27, November 4, December 16 and 30, 1923, January 6 and 27, 1924. See also Jean Strouse, *Morgan: American Financier* (New York, 2000), page 206.

21. Willard Huntington Wright, "Los Angeles—The Chemically Pure," in *The Smart Set Anthology,* ed. Burton Rascoe and Graff Conklin (New York, 1934), page 96; Bruce Bliven, "Los Angeles: The City that Is Bacchanalian in a Nice Way," *New Republic,* July 13, 1927, page 13; H.V.H., "Land Subdivision Restrictions," table following page 54; *Meetings of Underwriting Subscribers,* pages 7–8; Palos Verdes Homes Association, *The Palos Verdes Protective Restrictions* (Palos Verdes Estates, ca. 1925), page 5; *Country Life in America,* November 1, 1911, page 3, August 1920, page 17; *Kansas City Star,* October 3, 1909, March 6, 1910; *Houston Post,* April 12, 1925.

22. A novel form of multifamily housing in which each resident owned his or her apartment (or, more precisely, a corresponding block of shares in the building), cooperative apartment houses first appeared in the late nineteenth century, but they did not catch on until after World War I, when a severe housing shortage sent rents skyrocketing. In an effort to escape from "profiteering" landlords, many well-to-do tenants moved to the suburbs. Some, however, preferred to stay in the city, even if it meant living in an apartment. For them a cooperative provided, as a New York real estate agent said, "a home, not simply an apartment," a home that needed fewer servants and less upkeep than a single-family house. To ensure exclusivity, stability, and permanence, the by-laws gave current residents what the *New York Times* called

a "controlling voice" in the management of the building, especially in the selection of future residents. Although the prices excluded all but the very rich, the coop boards required business and social references from prospective purchasers, and these references, wrote one journalist, "are followed up and run down, at least in the more expensive cooperative developments, until every fact which has a bearing on the desirability of the applicant as a neighbor is revealed." As well as congenial neighbors, a cooperative gave city-dwellers a home of their own. "His home is HIS," read an ad for several Manhattan cooperative apartments: "to do with as he likes; to live in, to hand down to his children and grand children; to alter; to sell or to lease, subject only to restrictions agreed upon by the co-owners to maintain the high character and value of the common property." *New York Times,* June 18, 1922, February 11, March 25, April 15, May 20, October 21, 1923, January 11, 1925; Elmer A. Claar, "Why the Cooperative Plan of Home-Ownership Is Popular," *National Real Estate Journal,* May 18, 1925, pages 46–48; Howard MacDougall, "Cooperative Apartments," *Buildings and Building Management,* July 23, 1925, page 25; *Annals of Real Estate Practice: 1926,* volume 8, page 10.

23. Robert Fishman, *Bourgeois Utopias: The Rise and Fall of Suburbia* (New York, 1987), page 4.

Part 1: Suburbia, 1870–1930

1. Olmsted worked in California in the 1860s and again in the 1880s, but as far as I can tell he never spent time in Los Angeles. See Charles E. Beveridge and Paul Rocheleau, *Frederick Law Olmsted: Designing the American Landscape* (New York, 1995), pages 25–26, 182–191. See also *Los Angeles Times,* March 24, 1924.

2. Robert Fishman, *Bourgeois Utopias: The Rise and Fall of Suburbia* (New York, 1987), pages 127–129; Olmsted, Vaux & Co., "Preliminary Report Upon the Proposed Suburban Village at Riverside, Near Chicago (1868)," *Landscape Architecture,* July 1931, pages 260–262; Beveridge and Rocheleau, *Olmsted,* page 99.

3. Olmsted, Vaux & Co., "Riverside," page 262, 268–270; Frederick Law Olmsted to B. L. Ramsey, November 1884, Frederick Law Olmsted Papers, Manuscript Division, Library of Congress (hereinafter cited as Olmsted Papers).

4. "Prospectus for the New Suburban District of Tarrytown Heights," in *The Papers of Frederick Law Olmsted*, volume 6, *The Years of Olmsted, Vaux & Company, 1865–1874*, ed. David Schuyler and Jane Turner Censer (Baltimore, 1992), pages 503–505; Frederick Law Olmsted et al., "Report to the Staten Island Improvement Commission of a Preliminary Scheme of Improvements," in *Landscape Into Cityscape: Frederick Law Olmsted's Plans for a Greater New York*, ed. Albert Fein (New York, 1967), pages 178, 184–185.

5. Olmsted et al., "Report to the Staten Island Improvement Commission," pages 185–190.

6. Frederick Law Olmsted to Henry H. Elliott, August 27, 1860, in *The Papers of Frederick Law Olmsted*, volume 3, *Creating Central Park, 1857–1861*, ed. Charles E. Beveridge and David Schuyler (Baltimore, 1983), page 262; Walter Firey, *Land Use in Central Boston* (Cambridge, 1961), pages 60–68, 297–299, 315–316, 319; Margaret Supplee Smith, "Between City and Suburb: Architecture and Planning in Boston's South End" (Doctoral dissertation, Brown University, 1976), pages 2–3, 91–100; Lyle W. Dorsett, *The Pendergast Machine* (New York, 1968), pages 5–6; F. A. Cushing Smith, "The Glory of Shaker Village," *American Landscape Architect*, July 1929, page 22.

7. Ronald Dale Karr, "The Evolution of an Elite Suburb: Community Structure and Control in Brookline, Massachusetts, 1770–1990" (Doctoral dissertation, Boston University, 1981), pages 234–236; *Report of the Board of Park and Boulevard Commissioners of Kansas City, Missouri* (Kansas City, 1893), pages 13–14; Jesse Clyde Nichols, "When You Buy a Home Site," *Good Housekeeping*, February 1923, page 39.

8. Olmsted et al., "Report to the Staten Island Improvement Commission," pages 188–189. See also John Archer, "Country and City in the American Romantic Suburb," *Journal of the Society of Architectural Historians*, May 1983, pages 131–156.

9. Alexander von Hoffman, *Local Attachments: The Making of an American Urban Neighborhood, 1850–1920* (Baltimore, 1994), page 47; David R. Contosta, *Suburb in the City: Chestnut Hill, Philadelphia, 1850–1990* (Columbus, Ohio, 1992), pages 97–98; Dennis P. Sobin, *Dynamics of Community Change: The Case of Long Island's Declining "Gold Coast"* (Port Washington, New York, 1968), pages 25–37; E. J. Kahn, *Jock: The Life and Times of John Hay Whitney* (Garden City, New York, 1981), pages 16, 30–34; Stephen Richard Higley, "The Geography of the Social Register" (Doctoral dissertation, University of Illinois at Urbana-Champaign, 1992), page 69; Hugh J. McCauley, "Visions of Kykuit: John D. Rockefeller's House at Pocantico Hills, Tarrytown, New York," *Hudson Valley Regional Review* (1973), pages 2, 4–5, 38–39.

10. Frank J. Scott, *The Art of Beautifying Suburban Home Grounds of Small Extent* (New York, 1886), pages 27–29. See also Fred. Law Olmsted, "Report Upon a Projected Improvement of the Estate of the College of California, at Berkeley, Near Oakland," in *The Papers of Frederick Law Olmsted*, volume 5, *The California Frontier, 1863–1865*, ed. Victoria Post Ranney (Baltimore, 1990), page 553.

11. Samuel Swift, "Community Life in Tuxedo," *Home and Garden*, August 1905, pages 61–71; Samuel Swift, "Llewellyn Park West Orange, Essex Co., New Jersey," *Home and Garden*, July 1903, pages 327–331; *Sticks, Shingles, and Stones: The History and Architecture of Stewart Hartshorn's Ideal Community at Short Hills, New Jersey, 1878–1937* (Millburn, N.J., 1980), pages 2–7; Mary Corbin Sies, "American Country House Architecture in Context: The Suburban Ideal in the East and Midwest, 1877–1947" (Doctoral dissertation, University of Michigan, 1987), pages 229, 388.

12. Scott, *Suburban Home Grounds*, pages 30–31.

13. H. G. Wood, *A Practical Treatise on the Law of Nuisances in Their Various Forms: Including Remedies Therefor at Law and in Equity* (Albany, 1883), pages 1–11, 24–57. See also Andrew J. King, *Law and Land Use in Chicago: A Prehistory of Modern Zoning* (New York, 1986), page 80.

14. Richard M. Hurd, *Principles of City Land Values* (New York, 1903), page 117; Stanley L. McMichael and Robert F. Bingham, *City Growth and*

Values (Cleveland, 1923), page 209; King, *Law and Land Use*, pages 93–94; Wood, *Law of Nuisances*, pages 4, 6–7, 16, 21, 654.

15. R.E.H., "Annotation," 7 *A.L.R.* 749, quotes on pages 749, 756; *Flood v. Consumers Company*, 105 Ill. App. 559, quotes on page 564; Olmsted et al., "Report to the Staten Island Improvement Commission," page 178. See also King, *Law and Land Use*, pages 103–105.

16. *Mulligan v. Nelson*, 51 Ill. App. 441, quotes on page 443; King, *Law and Land Use*, pages 97–98, 105–107; *Oehler v. Levy*, 139 Ill. App. 294, quote on page 301; Wood, *Law of Nuisances*, page 11.

17. "Prospectus for the Suburban District of Tarrytown Heights," page 504; Olmsted to Elliott, August 27, 1860, pages 264–265; Olmsted, Vaux & Co., "Riverside," pages 273–274.

18. Olmsted to Elliott, August 27, 1860, pages 263–265; Olmsted, Vaux & Co., "Riverside," pages 269–271; Frederick Law Olmsted to Francis G. Newlands, November 16, 1891, Olmsted Papers; Charles Mulford Robinson, "Platting of Minor Residence Streets in High-Class Districts," *Real Estate Magazine*, December 1913, pages 48–52; Olmsted Brothers, "St. Francis Wood San Francisco, California," *Home & Grounds*, April 1916, page 106. See also King, *Law and Land Use*, pages 32–33.

19. Olmsted, Vaux & Co., "Riverside," pages 265, 268, 274–275; Olmsted Brothers, "St. Francis Wood," page 105; Swift, "Llewellyn Park," page 328; Olmsted, "College of California," page 288.

20. *National Real Estate Journal*, August 27, 1923, page 28. See also Frederick Law Olmsted to Henry M. Whitney, February 19, 1889, Olmsted Papers.

21. Donald J. Olsen, *Town Planning in London* (New Haven, 1964), pages 14, 22, 99–102; Stefan Muthesius, *The English Terraced House* (New Haven, 1982), pages 31–32; H. J. Dyos, *Victorian Suburb: A Study of the Growth of Camberwell* (Leicester, England, 1961), pages 97, 121. See also William Ashworth, *The Genesis of Modern British Town Planning: A Study of Economic and Social History of the Nineteenth and Twentieth Century* (London, 1954), page 36.

22. *Parker v. Nightingale*, 88 Mass. 341; *Barrow v. Richard*, 8 Paige 351, quotes on pages 352–353; *Tobey v. Moore*, 130 Mass. 448, quote on

page 449; *Jeffries v. Jeffries*, 117 Mass. 184. See also Elizabeth Black-
mar, *Mahattan for Rent, 1785–1850* (Ithaca, 1989), pages 37–38, 41, 92,
100–101; Michael Holleran, *Boston's "Changeful Times": Origins of Pres-
ervation and Planning in America* (Baltimore, 1998), pages 67–68.

23. *Barrow v. Richards*, 8 Paige 351; *Agreements and Deeds Relating Chiefly to
the Back-Bay District of the City of Boston* (Boston, 1883), pages 46, 64;
Annual Report of the [Boston] Public Land Commissioners: 1854, pages
7–8, 11–12; *Allen v. Massachusetts Bonding & Ins. Co.*, 248 Mass. 378,
quotes on pages 383. See also Lawrence W. Kennedy, *Planning the City
Upon a Hill: Boston Since 1630* (Amherst, 1992), pages 62–65.

24. Holleran, *Boston's "Changeful Times,"* pages 69–71. See also Swift,
"Llewellyn Park," pages 327–331; Witold Rybczynski, "How to Build a
Suburb," *Wilson Quarterly*, Summer 1995, pages 118–119.

25. See the annotation to *De Peyster v. Michael*, 57 Am. Dec. 470, quotes
on page 489; *Mandelbaum v. McDonnel*, 29 Mich. 78, quotes on pages
96, 107; *Cowell v. Springs Company*, 100 U.S. 55, quote on page 57;
Real Estate Company v. Serio, 156 Md. 299, quotes on page 231.

26. Holleran, *Boston's "Changeful Times,"* pages 73–74; *Whitney v. Union
Railway Company*, 11 Gray 359, quotes on pages 359, 363; *Cowell v.
Springs Company*, 100 U.S. 55, quotes on page 57. See also William H.
Hamilton, "Restrictive Covenants in a Conveyance of Real Estate,"
Albany Law Journal, July 5, 1884, page 6; Robert T. Devlin, *A Treatise
on the Law of Deeds* (San Francisco, 1897), volume 2, pages 1295, 1322,
1326–1327, 1333, 1337, 1364–1368.

27. *Peabody Heights Co. v. Willson*, 82 Md. 186, especially page 217; *Brouwer v. Jones*, 23 Barbour 153, quote on page 157; *Barrow v. Richard*, 8
Paige 351, especially page 358; *Whitney v. Union Railway Co.*, 11 Gray
359, especially pages 360–361; *Trustees v. Lynch*, 70 N.Y. 440, especially pages 443–445.

28. *Brouwer v. Jones*, 23 Barbour 153, quote on page 162; *Whitney v. Union
Railway Company*, 11 Gray 359, quotes on pages 361, 364. *Brouwer
v. Jones* was foreshadowed by *Barrow v. Richard*, an 1840 decision in
which William T. McCoun, vice chancellor of the New York Court of
Chancery, wrote that a restrictive covenant "follows the land, and be-

comes obligatory upon those who succeed to the same land, whether by descent or purchase." (See *Barrow v. Richard*, 8 Paige 351, quote on page 353.)

29. *Barrow v. Richard*, 8 Paige 351; *Parker v. Nightingale*, 88 Mass. 341, quotes on pages 342, 345, 348. See also Holleran, *Boston's "Changeful Times*," pages 73–74.

30. Charles I. Giddings, "Restrictions upon the Use of Land," *Harvard Law Review*, January 15, 1892, page 284; annotation to *Korn v. Campbell*, 37 L.R.A. (N.S.) 1, especially pages 28–29; *Peabody Heights Co. v. Willson*, 82 Md. 186; *Robinson v. Edgell*, 57 W. Va. 157, quote on page 160; *Boyden v. Roberts*, 131 Wis. 659; King, *Law and Land Use*, pages 33–53; *Hutchinson v. Ulrich*, 145 Ill. 336, quotes on page 342; *Eckhart v. Irons*, 18 Ill. App. 173, quote on page 181.

31. *Dana v. Wentworth*, 111 Mass. 291; *DeGray v. Monmouth Beach Clubhouse Co.*, 24 A. 388, quote on page 390; Giddings, "Restrictions," pages 279–280; *Whitney v. Union Railway Company*, 11 Gray 359, quote on page 367; *Trustees of Columbia College v. Thacher*, 87 N.Y. 311, quotes on pages 320–321; *Jackson v. Stevenson*, 156 Mass. 496, quote on page 502.

32. *Kitchen v. Hawley*, 150 Mo. App. 497, quote on page 503; *Hutchinson v. Ulrich*, 145 Ill. 336, quotes on pages 342, 344; *Jones v. Real Estate Co.*, 149 Md. 271, quote on page 277.

33. Nichols, "When You Buy a Home Site," page 172; *Proceedings of the Seventh National Conference on City Planning: 1915*, page 84; *Stenographic Report of the Third Annual Conference of Developers of High-Class Residence Property* (1919), page 226, Department of Manuscripts and University Archives, Olin Library, Cornell University; *Proceedings of [the] First Annual Conference of Developers [of] High Class Residence Property* (1917), pages 86–87, Department of Manuscripts and University Archives, Olin Library; Edward H. Bouton to S. M. Jarvis, October 13, 1893, Box 298, Roland Park Company Records, Collection 2828, Department of Manuscripts and University Archives, Olin Library.

34. John McC. Mowbray, "After Fifty Years," *Gardens, Houses, and People*, June 1941, page 26; Fletcher Steele, compiler, "Restrictions on Land

to Be Used for Suburban Residential Purposes," a memo prepared for W. H. Manning and dated February 1, 1913, Loeb Library; Thomas Adams, "The British Point of View," *Proceedings of the Third National Conference on City Planning: 1911*, page 34.

35. *Ignaciunas v. Risley*, 121 A. 783, quote on page 785; Robert M. Fogelson, *Downtown: Its Rise and Fall, 1880–1950* (New Haven, 2001), page 29; Sies, "American Country House Architecture," page 87; Becky M. Nicolaides, *My Blue Heaven: Life and Politics in the Working-Class Suburbs of Los Angeles, 1920–1965* (Chicago, 2002), page 17; Lawrence J. Vale, *From the Puritans to the Projects: Public Housing and Public Neighbors* (Cambridge, 2000), page 121; "Why Is a Suburb: By a Woman Who Lives in One," *Countryside Magazine and Suburban Life*, July 1917, page 379.

36. McMichael and Bingham, *City Growth and Values*, page 265; Thorstein Veblen, *Absentee Ownership and Business Enterprise in Recent Times: The Case of America* (New York, 1923), page 143; Fogelson, *Downtown*, page 24; Hurd, *City Land Values*, page 77. See also Holleran, *Boston's "Changeful Times*," chapter 1.

37. John F. W. Ware, *Home Life: What It Is, and What It Needs* (Boston, 1864), page 9. See also Holleran, *Boston's "Changeful Times*," chapter 2; *First Annual Conference*, pages 541, 546; *Third Annual Conference*, pages 235, 249–250; *The Palos Verdes Protective Restrictions* (Palos Verdes Estates, ca. 1925), pages 27–28.

38. Frederick Law Olmsted, Jr., to Karl B. Lohman, April 23, 1917, Olmsted Records, Job File 6536; Robert Pearson and Brad Pearson, *The J. C. Nichols Chronicle* (Kansas City, 1994), page 58; Francis K. Carey to Edward H. Bouton, November 30, 1900, Box 8, Roland Park Company Records.

39. "Portrait of a Salesman: Jesse Clyde Nichols," *National Real Estate Journal*, February 1939, page 22; *Barrow v. Richard*, 8 Paige 351, quote on page 353; Charles H. Cheney, "Progress in Architectural Control," in National Conference on City Planning, *Architectural Control of Private Property* (1927), page 6.

40. Wm. Seton Gordon, "Building Restrictions—Right to Enforce," *Al-*

bany *Law Journal,* May 2, 1891, page 349; Olmsted, Vaux & Co., "Riverside," page 274; Frederick Law Olmsted to Henry M. Whitney, February 19, 1889, Olmsted Papers; Steele, Semmes & Carey to Roland Park Company, December 1, 1892, Box 2, Roland Park Company Records.

41. William S. Worley, *J. C. Nichols and the Shaping of Kansas City* (Columbia, Missouri, 1990), pages 29–30; Rebecca Moudry, "Gardens, Houses, and People: The Planning of Roland Park, Baltimore" (Master's thesis, Cornell University, 1990), pages 49–50.

42. Edward H. Bouton to S. M. Jarvis, October 13, 1893, Box 290, Roland Park Company Records; Worley, *Nichols,* pages 31–33; Moudry, "Roland Park," pages 45–50, 61–69, 74–84, 163; James W. Waesche, *Crowning the Gravelly Hill: A History of the Roland Park-Guilford-Homeland District* (Baltimore, 1987), pages 46–47.

43. *Proceedings of the General Sessions of the National Association of Real Estate Boards at the Seventeenth Annual Conference: 1924,* page 21; Mowbray, "After Fifty Years," page 26; Waesche, *Crowning the Gravelly Hill,* pages 66–67; Worley, *Nichols,* pages 33–34; *Baltimore News,* July 2, 1892, June 7, 1893, Box 296; Schmucker & Whitelock to Edward H. Bouton, October 5, 1893, Box 2; Edward H. Bouton to Roland R. Conklin, January 18, 1894, Box 290, Roland Park Company Records.

44. *Baltimore News,* July 2, 1892, June 7, 1893; *Baltimore American,* June 18, 1893, Box 296; unidentified ad, probably from the Baltimore *Sun,* September 1895, Box 3; Richard W. Marchant, Jr., to William R. Abbott, March 25, 1905, Box 21; F.H.P. to A. N. Martin, June 24, 1913, Box 81, Roland Park Company Records.

45. Edward H. Bouton, "Development of Roland Park, Baltimore," *Proceedings of the General Sessions of the National Association of Real Estate Boards at the Seventeenth Annual Conference: 1924,* page 24; Moudry, "Roland Park," pages 49–50, 352–353; unidentified newspaper dated January 17, 1915, Box 296; J. C. Nichols to Edward H. Bouton, December 12, 1912, Box 83, Roland Park Company Records.

46. Thomas Adams, "An American Garden Suburb: Roland Park, Baltimore," *Architectural Review,* November 1911, pages 290–291; *Baltimore American,* April 13, 1913, Box 296, Roland Park Company

Records; Arthur Tomalin, "Houses that Blend in with Their Surroundings," *Suburban Life*, April 1913, page 232; Baltimore *Sun*, May
9, 1915; *Roland Park Review*, April 1911, page 6; Mowbray, "After
Fifty Years," page 26; Arthur B. Cranford, "A Suburb Conforming to
Architectural Standards, Roland Park, Baltimore, Maryland," *Brick-
builder*, August 1914, pages 191–192; Steele, Semmes, Carey & Bond
to Edward H. Bouton, March 9, 1897, Box 6, Roland Park Company
Records; Worley, *Nichols*, page 34; Adams, "The British Point of View,"
page 34; *Baltimore Herald*, October 1, 1904.

47. Waesche, *Crowning the Gravelly Hill*, chapter 3; *Deed and Agreement
Between the Roland Park Company and Edward H. Bouton Containing
Restrictions, Conditions, Charges, Etc. Relating to Guilford* (1923), pages
1–23; *Third Annual Conference*, page 698; Bouton, "Development of
Roland Park," page 28; *First Annual Conference*, page b53.

48. Baltimore *Sun*, May 19, 1913, July 8, 1914, April 18, May 9, 16, 23, and
30, 1915. For other ads, see Box 296, Roland Park Company Records.

49. J. C. Nichols Investment Company, *Country Club District[:] 3000 Acres
Restricted* (Kansas City, 1924), pages 3–5, 16, 23, J. C. Nichols Collection, Western Historical Manuscript Collection, University of Missouri–Kansas City Archives; Nichols, "When You Buy a Home Site,"
page 172; J. C. Nichols, *Real Estate Subdivisions: The Best Manner of
Handling Them* (Washington, D.C., 1912), page 7; J. C. Nichols, "Housing and the Real Estate Problem," *Annals of the American Academy
of Political and Social Science*, January 1914, page 139; J. C. Nichols
to Edward H. Bouton, July 30, 1913, Box 83, Roland Park Company
Records; Worley, *Nichols*, page 126.

50. *Pleasants v. Wilson*, 125 Md. 237, quote on page 242; Samuel S. Thorpe,
"The More Restrictions the More Buyers," *National Real Estate Jour-
nal*, July 27, 1925, pages 44–46; Nichols, "Housing and the Real Estate
Problem," page 132; Frederick Law Olmsted, "Deed Restrictions that
Affect Houses in Planned Neighborhoods," *Architectural Record*, No-
vember 1940, page 32; Charles E. Clark, *Real Covenants and Other
Interests Which "Run with Land"* (Chicago, 1947), page 170. See also
Susan Mulcahey Chase, "The Process of Suburbanization and the

Use of Restrictive Deed Covenants as Private Zoning, Wilmington, Delaware, 1900–1941" (Doctoral dissertation, University of Delaware, 1995), page 260.

51. Alexander S. Taylor, "Districting Through Private Effort," *Proceedings of the Eighth National Conference on City Planning: 1916,* page 178; Iranaeus Shuler, "Subdivision Control and Standards," *Annals of Real Estate Practice: 1925,* volume 3, page 238; Hugh E. Prather, "Planning, Platting, and Improving the Subdivision," ibid., page 158; Chester S. Chase, "A Well Planned and Well Planted Community," *House Beautiful,* September 1926, page 264.

52. Charles K. Farrington, "When You Buy Your Building-lot," *Suburban Life,* February 1911, page 90.

53. *Kansas City Star,* October 3, 1909; Baltimore *Sun,* May 9, 1913; *Houston Post-Dispatch,* February 5, 1926; Chase, "Restrictive Deed Covenants," page 265; St[.] *Francis Wood: A Great Civic Achievement,* Loeb Library; Olmsted, "Deed Restrictions," pages 32, 34; Thorpe, "The More Restrictions the More Buyers," page 46; Henry Clarke, "Protective Deed Restrictions," *National Real Estate Journal,* June 1932, page 42.

54. *Gasoline Stations or Brendonwood* (ca. 1920), Loeb Library; Holleran, *Boston's "Changeful Times,"* chapter 3; "Raymond Village Tract," Ephemera Collection, Henry E. Huntington Library, San Marino, California; *Los Angeles Times,* December 3, 1922.

55. *Gasoline Stations or Brendonwood; Kansas City Star,* October 3, 1909; *River Oaks: A Pictorial Presentation of Houston's Residential Park,* Loeb Library; *A Summer's Reverie and Dream of a Brendonwood Owner,* Loeb Library; St[.] *Francis Wood and Home,* Loeb Library; Holleran, *Boston's "Changeful Times,"* page 83.

56. Eloise L. Morgan, ed., *Building a Suburban Village: Bronxville, New York, 1898–1998* (1998), page 18; *Why You Should Choose the Location for Your Next Home in Brendonwood* (1920), Loeb Library; *Los Angeles Times,* March 11 and 25, December 23, 1923, February 17, 1924; *Country Life in America,* March 1910, page 505, June 1, 1911, page 7. See also James A. Mayo, *The American Country Club: Its Origins and Develop-*

ment (New Brunswick, 1998), and Peter W. Cookson, Jr., and Caroline Hodges Persell, *Preparing for Power: America's Elite Boarding Schools* (New York, 1995).

57. "A Boston Subdivision," *National Real Estate Journal*, November 15, 1926, pages 23–29. See also Waesche, *Crowning the Gravelly Hill*, page 113.

58. J. C. Nichols Investment Company, *Country Club District*, pages 3–5, 23; Smith, "The Glory of Shaker Village," pages 21–26; Paul A. Harsch, "Ottawa Hills," *Wildwood Magazine*, Summer 1916, pages 7–8, 10; William Pitkin, Jr., and Frederick L. Trautman, "The Greatest Suburban Development Ever Undertaken," *Real Estate Magazine*, October 1914, pages 24–28; Michael H. Ebner, *Creating Chicago's North Shore: A Suburban History* (Chicago, 1988).

59. W. H. Gardner to Olmsted Brothers, March 11, 1907; Cornelius Vanderbilt, Jr., "Uplands, Victoria's Residential Park," *The Spur*, June 1, 1921, page 67, Olmsted Brothers, Job File 3276; L. D. McCann, "Planning and Building the Corporate Suburb of Mount Royal, 1910–1925," *Planning Perspectives*, July 1996, page 276; Duncan McDuffie to Olmsted Brothers, September 10, 1912, Olmsted Records, Job File 5658; St[.] *Francis Wood: A Great Civic Achievement*; Robert M. Fogelson, *The Fragmented Metropolis: Los Angeles, 1850–1930* (Cambridge, 1967), chapter 7.

60. Don Riddle, "'Homes to Last for All Time': The Story of Houston's River Oaks," *National Real Estate Journal*, March 4, 1929, page 23. See also *Suburban Life*, November 1911, page 3.

61. William B. Friedricks, *Henry E. Huntington and the Creation of Southern California* (Columbus, Ohio, 1992), pages 88–89; Patricia Burgess, *Planning for the Private Interest: Land Use Controls and Residential Patterns in Columbus, Ohio, 1900–1970* (Columbus, Ohio, 1994), pages 52–58; *Los Angeles Times*, December 31, 1922, January 4, February 25, April 15 and 22, September 2, October 28, November 4, 1923, February 3, 1924.

62. Pearson and Pearson, *The J. C. Nichols Chronicle*, page 93; Nichols, "Housing and the Real Estate Problem," pages 134–136; *Annals of Real*

Estate Practice: 1925, volume 3, pages 211, 213; Baltimore *Sun*, May 11, 1913.

63. Robert Phelps, "The Search for a Modern Industrial City: Urban Planning, the Open Shop, and the Founding of Torrance, California," *Pacific Historical Review*, November 1995, pages 503–535.

64. Dana W. Bartlett, "Torrance," *American City*, October 1913, pages 310–314; Nicolaides, *My Blue Heaven*, pages 14–35; Nancy Quan-Wickham, "'Another World': Work, Home, and Autonomy in Blue-Collar Suburbs," in *Metropolis in the Making: Los Angeles in the 1920s*, ed. Tom Sitton and William Deverell (Berkeley, 2001), pages 123–141; Richard Harris, *Unplanned Suburbs: Toronto's American Tragedy, 1900 to 1950* (Baltimore, 1996), chapter 8; Johanna von Wagner to Frederick Law Olmsted, Jr., January 29, 1912, Olmsted Records, Job File 5354.

65. *Protective Restrictions for Devonshire Downs* (1929), "Explanatory Note" and pages 4–21, Loeb Library.

66. *First Annual Conference*, page b112; *Hutchinson v. Ulrich*, 145 Ill. 336; *Deutsch v. Mortgage Securities Co.*, 122 S.E. 793; *Saratoga Building Co. v. Stables Co.*, 146 Md. 152; *Kitchen v. Hawley*, 150 Mo. App. 497, quote on page 503.

67. *Tobey v. Moore*, 130 Mass. 448, quotes on pages 449, 451; *Kitchen v. Hawley*, 150 Mo. App. 497, quote on page 504; *Hutchinson v. Ulrich*, 145 Ill. 336, quotes on pages 339, 342, 344.

68. 175 *A.L.R.* 1191, especially pages 1194–1202; *Restrictions Relating to Guilford*, page 5; *Protective Restrictions for Devonshire Downs*, page 4; *Warranty Deed, Country Club District, Fairway Section*, Loeb Library; *Protective Restrictions, Palos Verdes Estates*, page 17; *Munsey Park[:] A Restricted Community of Homes at Manhasset, L.I.* (1927), pages 1–2, Loeb Library; William A. Woodbury, "Restrictions: Good in Youth—Dangerous in Age," *Real Estate Magazine*, December 1915, page 30.

69. *Barrow v. Richard*, 8 Paige 351, quote on page 352; *Agreement for Sale [Between] The Uplands, Limited, and H. R. Ferriss, July 31, 1912*, Loeb Library; *Declaration of Restrictions and Covenants Affecting the Property Known as St[.] Francis Wood, San Francisco, California* (1912), page 3, Bancroft Library, University of California at Berkeley. See also Helen

Monchow, *The Use of Deed Restrictions in Subdivision Development* (Chicago, 1928), pages 27–33.

70. *Third Annual Conference,* pages 533–527, 601–602, 613; *Hycliff Standards[:] A Declaration of Protections and Restrictions for Hycliff, Section Two* (1929), page 5, Loeb Library; Worley, *Nichols,* pages 209–210, 223–224, 248–249.

71. Devlin, *Law of Deeds,* volume 2, page 1364; *Sharp v. Ropes,* 110 Mass. 381; *Hycliff Standards,* page 6. See also Monchow, *Deed Restrictions,* pages 37–45.

72. *Sharp v. Ropes,* 110 Mass. 381; *Jackson v. Stevenson,* 156 Mass. 496; *Protective Restrictions, Palos Verdes Estates,* pages 30–31. See also Monchow, *Deed Restrictions,* pages 27–31, 37.

73. Devlin, *Law of Deeds,* volume 2, pages 1362–1368; Pearson and Pearson, *The J. C. Nichols Chronicle,* page 58; *Jones v. Northwest Real Estate Company,* 149 Md. 271, quote on page 277; Worley, *Nichols,* page 126; Chase, "Restrictive Deed Covenants," pages 262–263; Steele, compiler, "Restrictions on Land," page 3. The figures for Wilmington are based on deeds that had at least one restriction.

74. H.V.H., "Land Subdivision Restrictions," table following page 54; *Bacon v. Sandberg,* 179 Mass. 396; Monchow, *Deed Restrictions,* pages 28, 31, 37; Burgess, *Planning for the Private Interest,* pages 45, 47; Chase, "Restrictive Deed Covenants," pages 274, 278; Carol A. O'Connor, *A Sort of Utopia: Scarsdale, 1891–1981* (Albany, 1983), pages 46–48; *Building Restrictions and Regulations [for] Chelmsleigh Addition to the Country Club Estates* (1926), Loeb Library. See also *Proceedings of the General Sessions of the National Association of Real Estate Boards at the Seventeenth Annual Convention: 1924,* page 19.

75. *Baltimore News,* July 12, 1913, Box 292, Roland Park Company Records. See also Frank L. Meline, "Advantages of Architectural Harmony in Subdivisions," *Annals of Real Estate Practice: 1925,* volume 3, page 166; Olmsted Brothers to W. H. Kiernan, October 9, 1914; John Charles Olmsted to Jay Lawyer, March 20, 1914, Olmsted Records, Job File 5950.

76. J. C. Nichols to E. H. Bouton, July 30, 1913, Box 83, Roland Park Com-

pany Records. See also *Peabody Heights Co. v. Willson,* 82 Md. 186, quote on page 195; Olmsted, Vaux & Co., "Riverside," page 274; Monchow, *Deed Restrictions,* pages 34–35; *Proceedings of the General Sessions of the National Association of Real Estate Boards at the Seventeenth Annual Convention: 1924,* page 21; Steele, compiler, "Restrictions on Land," page 13–15.

77. Monchow, *Deed Restrictions,* pages 28–31, 34–35; Chase, "Restrictive Deed Covenants," pages 281–282; Olmsted Brothers, "Restrictions for Residential Subdivisions and Related Matters," a report dated January 1925, pages 3–15, Loeb Library; *Shaker Village Standards,* pages 12–14, Loeb Library; Olmsted, "Deed Restrictions," pages 34–35; *Proceedings of the General Sessions of the National Association of Real Estate Boards at the Seventeenth Annual Convention: 1924,* page 19; Bouton, "Development of Roland Park," pages 24–25; *Third Annual Conference,* pages 698, 701.

78. Beveridge and Rocheleau, *Olmsted,* page 107; H.V.H., "Land Subdivision Restrictions," table following page 54; undated Great Neck Improvement Company deed, Loeb Library; undated Andrews Land Company Declaration of Restrictions, Loeb Library; *Declaration of Conditions, Covenants, and Charges Affecting St[.] Francis Wood Extension No. 2, San Francisco, California* (1917), page 4, Bancroft Library.

79. H.V.H., "Land Subdivision Restrictions," table following page 54; *Sharp v. Ropes,* 110 Mass. 381; Chase, "Restrictive Deed Covenants," pages 298, 302–303; *Warranty Deed, Country Club District, Fairway Section; Hycliff Standards,* page 8; *Protective Restrictions for Devonshire Downs,* page 12.

80. Chase, "A Well Planned and Well Planted Community," page 267. See also H.V.H., "Land Subdivision Restrictions," table following page 54; Monchow, *Deed Restrictions,* pages 28–31, 33–34; Beveridge and Rocheleau, *Olmsted,* page 107; undated Great Neck Improvement Company deed.

81. Karr, "Evolution of an Elite Suburb," page 265; *Ringgold v. Denhardt,* 136 Md. 136, quote on page 139; Sam B. Warner, Jr., *Streetcar Suburbs: The Process of Growth in Boston, 1870–1900* (Cambridge, 1962), page 122; Arthur B. Darling, ed., *The Public Papers of Francis G. New-*

lands (Boston, 1932), volume 1, pages 296–297; William R. Rowley, *Reclaiming the Arid West: The Career of Francis G. Newlands* (Bloomington, 1966), pages 139–144, 154–155; Elizabeth Jo Lampl and Kimberly Prothro Williams, *Chevy Chase: A Home Suburb for the Nation's Capital* (Crownsville, Maryland, 1998), page 56.

82. Worley, *Nichols*, pages 147–148; Chase, "Restrictive Deed Covenants," page 311; *Third Annual Conference*, page 580; Schmucker & Whitelock to Edward H. Bouton, October 5, 1893, Box 2, Roland Park Company Records; L. S. Knight, "Restrictions for the Subdivision," *Proceedings of the First Annual Convention Conferences of the Homebuilders' and Subdividers' Division of the National Association of Real Estate Boards: 1923*, page 53; McMichael and Bingham, *City Growth and Values*, page 200.

83. Kenneth Fox Graham, "Urban Space, Racial Covenants, and the Origins of Racial Residential Segregation in a U.S. City, 1900–1950," *Journal of Urban and Regional Research*, September 2000, page 621. See also U.S. Bureau of the Census, *Fourteenth Census of the United States Taken in the Year 1920*, volume 2, *Population: 1920* (Washington, D.C., 1922), pages 47–49; Garrett Power, "Apartheid Baltimore Style: The Residential Segregation Ordinances of 1910–1913," *Maryland Law Review*, 1983, pages 297–298; Ronald M. Johnson, "From Romantic Suburb to Racial Enclave: LeDroit Park, Washington, D.C., 1880–1920," *Phylon*, December, 1984, pages 264–270.

84. *Buchanan v. Warley*, 245 U.S. 60, quotes on page 81; Michael Jones-Correa, "The Origins and Diffusion of Restrictive Covenants," *Political Science Quarterly*, Winter 2000–2001, pages 547–550; Power, "Apartheid Baltimore Style," pages 298–306; David Delaney, *Race, Place, and the Law, 1836–1948* (Austin, 1998), pages 105–114, 119–147; Chase, "Restrictive Deed Covenants," page 313.

85. *Gandolfo v. Hartmann*, 49 Fed. 181, quote on page 182; *Queensborough Land Co. v. Cazeaux*, 67 So. 641, quote on page 643; *Koehler v. Rowland*, 275 Mo. 573, quote on page 585; *Corrigan v. Buckley*, 271 U.S. 323, quotes on pages 327, 330; *Appellants' Points*, a brief submitted to the U.S. Supreme Court in the case of *Corrigan v. Buckley*, page 41, Harvard Law Library; Clement E. Vose, *Caucasians Only: The Supreme*

Court, the NAACP, and the Restrictive Covenant Cases (Berkeley, 1959), pages 17–24.

86. *Title Insurance & Trust Co. v. Garrott*, 183 P. 470, quotes on page 473; *Los Angeles Inv. Co. v. Gary*, 186 P. 596; Knight, "Restrictions for the Subdivision," page 63; *Parmalee v. Morris*, 218 Mich. 625; *Porter v. Barrett*, 206 N.W. 532; *White v. White*, 150 S.E. 531; Vose, *Caucasians Only*, pages 21–22.

87. Worley, *Nichols*, page 148; Garrett Power, "The Covenants of Roland Park" (1991), an unpublished paper made available to me by Professor Power; *Washington Post*, February 15, 1999; Lampl and Williams, *Chevy Chase*, page 141; Monchow, *Deed Restrictions*, page 49; Burgess, *Planning for the Private Interest*, page 57; Charles Orson Cook and Barry J. Kaplan, "Civic Elites and Urban Planning: Houston's River Oaks," *East Texas Historical Journal*, 1977, page 31; Chase, "Restrictive Deed Covenants," pages 304–305; *Protective Restrictions for Devonshire Downs*, page 11; *Los Angeles Times*, May 20, November 4, 1923; Kevin Starr, *Material Dreams: Southern California Through the 1920s* (New York, 1990), page 87; Bouton, "Development of Roland Park," page 28.

88. U.S. Immigration Commission, *Report of the Immigration Commission*, volume 5, *Dictionary of Races and Peoples* (Washington, D.C., 1911), page 3; Matthew Frye Jacobson, *Whiteness of a Different Color: European Immigrants and the Alchemy of Race* (Cambridge, 1998), page 95; *White v. White*, 150 S.E. 531; Olmsted Brothers to Walter H. Leimert, September 27, 1917, Olmsted Records, Job File 5945; William C. Miller, "Modern Trends in Subdividing," *Annals of Real Estate Practice: 1930*, page 300; *Shelley v. Kraemer*, 334 U.S. 1; Burgess, *Planning for the Private Interest*, page 45; Ross Peterson, "Creating the Packaged Suburb: The Evolution of Planning and Business Practices in the Early Land Development Industry, 1900–1914," in *Suburbia Reexamined*, ed. Barbara M. Kelly (Westport, Connecticut, 1989), page 127; undated Land Purchase Contract, Lake Shore Club District, Loeb Library.

89. J. C. Nichols, "A Developer's View of Deed Restrictions," *Journal of*

Land & Public Utility Economics, May 1929, pages 139–140; Charles S. Ascher, "Reflections on the Art of Administering Deed Restrictions," ibid., November 1932, pages 374, 377; *Roland Park Review*, February 1909, page 4; Pearson and Pearson, *The J. C. Nichols Chronicle*, page 59; Richard Longstreth to Robert M. Fogelson, March 6, 2004, author's files; Edward H. Bouton to James A. Burgess, November 14, 1908, Box 33, Roland Park Company Records.

90. Nichols, "A Developer's View," page 139; Paul Kinkead, "This Is the House that Jesse Built," *Liberty*, October 23, 1927, page 89; *Palos Verdes Bulletin*, December 1924, pages 1–2.

91. Nichols, "When You Buy a Home Site," page 175; Steele, compiler, "Restrictions on Land," page 32; *Roland Park Review*, February 1909, page 4; Charles E. Merriam, *Building Districts and Restrictions* (Chicago, 1919), pages 39–40; Ascher, "Administering Deed Restrictions," pages 373–374.

92. *Roland Park Review*, February 1909, pages 3–4; Nichols, "When You Buy a Home Site," page 175; Frederick Law Olmsted, Jr., to F. P. Smith, February 7, 1903, Olmsted Records, Job File 2385; John Charles Olmsted to J. H. Oldfield, May 21, 1907, Olmsted Records, Job File 3276; Worley, *Nichols*, page 168; *First Annual Conference*, pages b100–b101; Pearson and Pearson, *The J. C. Nichols Chronicle*, page 59; *Palos Verdes Bulletin*, December 1924, pages 1–2; Monchow, *Deed Restrictions*, pages 62–65, 69–71. Since it included tenants as well as homeowners, the Roland Park Roads and Maintenance Association was, strictly speaking, a residents' rather than a property owners' association. On Bouton's decision to include tenants in the association, see *Stenographic Report of the Second Annual Conference of Developers of High Class Residence Property* (1918), pages 265–268, Department of Manuscripts and University Archives, Olin Library.

93. *Sharp v. Ropes*, 110 Mass. 381; *Jackson v. Stevenson*, 156 Mass. 496; Olmsted Brothers to Joel Hurt, May 16, 1903, Olmsted Records, Job File 71; "Restrictions Create Values in the Country Club District," *National Real Estate Journal*, February 1939, page 37; Joel Hurt to Olmsted Brothers, May 13, 1905, Olmsted Records, Job File 71.

94. Monchow, *Deed Restrictions,* page 59; Pearson and Pearson, *The J. C. Nichols Chronicle,* page 57; J. C. Nichols, "Financial Effects of Good Planning in Land Subdivision," *Proceedings of the Eighth National Conference on City Planning: 1916,* pages 108–109; John Charles Olmsted to J. H. Oldfield, May 21, 1907, Olmsted Records, Job File 3276; *Zinn v. Sidler,* 268 Mo. 680, especially page 683; *Proceedings of the General Sessions of the National Association of Real Estate Boards at the Seventeenth Annual Convention: 1924,* page 26; Nichols, "A Developer's View," page 135; *Proceedings of the First Annual Convention Conferences of the Homebuilders' and Subdividers' Division of the National Association of Real Estate Boards: 1923,* page 70.

95. Nichols, "A Developer's View," page 135; H.V.H., "Land Subdivision Restrictions," table following page 54; Monchow, *Deed Restrictions,* pages 56–59; Worley, *Nichols,* pages 127–128; John Charles Olmsted to J. H. Oldfield, May 21, 1907, Olmsted Records, Job File 3276.

96. "Restrictions Create Values," page 37; Pearson and Pearson, *The J. C. Nichols Chronicle,* pages 57–59; Worley, *Nichols,* page 131; Nichols, "Good Planning in Land Subdivision," pages 109–110; *Proceedings of the Annual Convention Conferences of the Homebuilders' and Subdividers' Division of the National Association of Real Estate Boards: 1923,* pages 70–71; Monchow, *Deed Restrictions,* pages 59–62.

97. Monchow, *Deed Restrictions,* page ii; Marc A. Weiss, "Richard T. Ely and the Contribution of Economic Research to Home Ownership and Housing Policy," MIT Center for Real Estate Development Working Paper No. 19 (February 1989), pages 1–2; Olmsted Brothers, "St. Francis Wood, Westgate Park, San Francisco, California," a memo dated March 1916, Olmsted Records, Job File 5658.

98. Fukio Akimoto, "Charles H. Cheney of California: His Thoughts and Practices," a revised version of a paper that appeared in the *City Planning Review of Japan,* October 1999, page 10.

99. *Palos Verdes Protective Restrictions,* page 8; Clarke, "Protective Deed Restrictions," page 42; Prather, "Planning, Platting, and Improving the Subdivision," page 158; Shuler, "Subdivision Control and Standards," page 238.

100. McMichael and Bingham, *City Growth and Values*, pages 200, 256; undated brochure, Box 296, Roland Park Company Records; Pitkin, Jr., "Lessons in Subdivision Restrictions," page 38; Marc A. Weiss, "Urban Land Developers and the Origins of Zoning Laws: The Case of Berkeley," *Berkeley Planning Journal* (1986), pages 8-9; Chase, "Restrictive Deed Covenants," pages 267-268.

101. Lawrence Veiller, "Districting by Municipal Regulation," *Proceedings of the Eighth National Conference on City Planning: 1916*, page 149; Weiss, "Origins of Zoning Laws," pages 8-9; Vose, *Caucasians Only*, pages 8-9, 17; Robert H. Whitten, "Zoning and Living Conditions," *Proceedings of the Thirteenth Annual Conference on City Planning: 1921*, page 22.

102. Merriam, *Building Districts and Restrictions*, page 39; Holleran, *Boston's "Changeful Times,"* page 207; Lawrence Veiller, "Protecting Residential Districts," *Proceedings of the Sixth National Conference on City Planning: 1914*, page 93; Veiller, "Districting by Municipal Regulation," pages 149-150.

103. Merriam, *Building Districts and Restrictions*, page 41; Nichols, "A Developer's View," pages 133-134; *The Country Club District[:] The 1000 Acres Restricted*, J. C. Nichols Company Scrapbooks, volume ?, J. C. Nichols Collection; Harsch, "Ottawa Hills," page 8.

104. Veiller, "Districting by Municipal Regulation," page 156; Merriam, *Building Districts and Restrictions*, page 41; Edward M. Bassett, "Zoning Versus Private Restrictions," *Civic Comment*, October 29, 1921, pages 5-6; Monchow, *Deed Restrictions*, page 78.

Part 2: Bourgeois Nightmares

1. *Stenographic Report of the Second Annual Conference of Developers of High Class Residence Property* (1918), pages 1-2, 164-168, Department of Manuscripts and University Archives, Olin Library, Cornell University. See also *National Real Estate Journal*, April 5, 1921, pages 30-31.

2. *Second Annual Conference*, pages 534-537.

3. *Second Annual Conference*, pages 542-543, 545-546; *Stenographic Re-*

port of the Third Annual Conference of Developers of High-Class Residence Property (1919), pages 245–246, Department of Manuscripts and University Archives, Olin Library.

4. *Proceedings of the Eighth National Conference on City Planning: 1916,* page 176; *Second Annual Conference,* page 532; *Third Annual Conference,* pages 245–246.

5. *Second Annual Conference,* page 546; *Los Angeles Times,* January 21, 1923.

6. Daniel Mark Epstein, *Nat King Cole* (New York, 1999), pages 177–182. See also *Los Angeles Times,* November 5 and 26, 1922, December 10, 1923.

7. Olmsted Brothers, "Restrictions for Residential Subdivisions and Related Matters," a report dated January 1925, page 16, Loeb Library, Harvard University. See also Jon M. Kingsdale, "The 'Poor Man's Club': Social Functions of the Urban Working-Class Saloon," *American Quarterly,* October 1973, pages 472–488.

8. Olmsted, Vaux & Co., "Preliminary Report Upon the Proposed Village at Riverside, Near Chicago (1868)," *Landscape Architecture,* July 1931, page 276.

9. J. C. Nichols, "The Lessons of a Lifetime of Land Developing," *National Real Estate Journal,* February 1939, page 28; *Proceedings of the First Annual Convention Conferences of the Homebuilders' and Subdividers' Division of the National Association of Real Estate Boards: 1923,* page 160; *Los Angeles Times,* November 26, December 3, 1922, March 11, July 8, October 21, December 22, 1923; undated ad, Box 296, Roland Park Company Records, Collection 2828, Department of Manuscripts and University Archives, Olin Library; Eloise L. Morgan, ed., *Building a Suburban Village: Bronxville, New York, 1898–1998* (1998), page 18; *Country Life in America,* December 1909, page 118, November 1923, page 10, March 19, 1926, page 16c; *Kansas City Star,* October 3, 1909.

10. Elmer A. Claar, "Why the Cooperative Plan of Home-Ownership Is Popular," *National Real Estate Journal,* May 18, 1925, page 47.

11. *White v. White,* 150 S.E. 531, quote on page 532; Charles Abrams, *Forbidden Neighbors: A Study of Prejudice in Housing* (New York, 1955),

page 158; "Transcript of Testimony" in the case of *City of Louisville v. Arthur Harris*, November 14, 1914, pages 67–68, in *Records and Briefs, Buchanan v. Warley*, 245 U.S. 68, Harvard Law Library; L. S. Knight, "Restrictions for the Subdivision," *Proceedings of the First Annual Convention Conferences of the Homebuilders' and Subdividers' Division of the National Association of Real Estate Boards: 1923*, page 63; Olmsted Brothers to Joel Hurt, April 4, 1902, Records of the Olmsted Associates (hereinafter referred to as Olmsted Records), Job File 71, Manuscript Division, Library of Congress.

12. U.S. Immigration Commission, *Reports of the Immigration Commission*, volume 5, *Dictionary of Races and Peoples* (Washington, D.C., 1911), page 3; John Modell, *The Economics and Politics of Racial Accommodation: The Japanese of Los Angeles, 1900–1942* (Urbana, 1977), pages 56–66; *Proceedings of the First Annual Convention Conferences of the Homebuilders' and Subdividers' Division of the National Association of Real Estate Boards: 1923*, page 69; *Protective Restrictions, Palos Verdes Estates, Los Angeles, California* (1923), page 17.

13. *Deed and Agreement Between the Ottawa Hills Company and John North Willys Containing Restrictions and Conditions Relating to Plat Number One, Ottawa Hills* (1916), page 6; U.S. Bureau of the Census, *Fourteenth Census of the United States Taken in the Year 1920*, volume 2, *Population: 1920* (Washington, D.C., 1922), pages 58–59. See also Claar, "Cooperative Plan of Home-Ownership," page 47; "Transcript of Testimony" in the case of *City of Louisville v. Arthur Harris*, pages 66–67.

14. Matthew Frye Jacobson, *Whiteness of a Different Color: European Immigrants and the Alchemy of Race* (Cambridge, 1998), page 199; Garrett Power, "The Residential Segregation of Baltimore's Jews," *Generations* (Fall 1996), page 6; Abrams, *Forbidden Neighbors*, pages 154–156; Susan L. Klaus, *A Modern Arcadia: Frederick Law Olmsted Jr. and the Plan for Forest Hills Gardens* (Amherst, 2002), page 116; Charles Orson Cook and Barry J. Kaplan, "Civic Elites and Urban Planning: Houston's River Oaks," *East Texas Historical Journal* (1977), page 36.

15. *Proceedings of [the] First Annual Conference of Developers [of] High Class*

Residence Property (1917), pages b53–b54, Department of Manuscripts and University Archives, Olin Library; *Third Annual Conference*, pages 565–580.

16. *First Annual Conference*, pages b53–b54; *Third Annual Conference*, pages 565–580. See also John R. Freeman to Katherine McNamara, August 4, 1931, Loeb Library; "Transcript of Testimony" in the case of *City of Louisville v. Arthur Harris*, pages 66–67; Richard Albert Farnum, Jr., "Prestige in the Ivy League: Meritocracy at Columbia, Harvard, and Penn, 1870–1940" (Doctoral dissertation, University of Pennsylvania, 1990), pages 95–100, 187–196.

17. Madison Grant, *The Passing of the Great Race or the Racial Basis of European History* (New York, 1918), pages 65–66; Ian F. Haney Lopez, *White by Law: The Legal Construction of Race* (New York, 1996), pages 61–68, 203–208; U.S. House Committee on Immigration and Naturalization, *Hearings Relative to the Further Restriction on Immigration and Naturalization* (Washington, D.C., 1913), part 2, pages 77–78; John R. Freeman to Katherine McNamara, August 4, 1931; Epstein, *Cole*, pages 177–182; *Third Annual Conference*, page 579.

18. See Introduction, note 22, above.

19. Olmsted Brothers to Joel Hurt, April 4, 1902, Olmsted Records, Job File 71; Edward A. Loveley, "Fundamental Principles in Developing High-Grade Subdivisions," *Annals of Real Estate Practice: 1925*, volume 3, page 69.

20. John Charles Olmsted to Messrs. Oldfield, Kirby & Gardner, August 2, 1907, Olmsted Records, Job File 3276; Olmsted Brothers to Joel Hurt, April 4, 1902, Olmsted Records, Job File 71.

21. John Charles Olmsted to J. H. Oldfield, May 21, 1907, Olmsted Records, Job File 3276; Edward H. Bouton to James B. Ladd, August 3, 1916, Box 291, Roland Park Company Records; *Third Annual Conference*, pages 698–701; Olmsted Brothers, "Restrictions for Residential Subdivisions," pages 24–25.

22. U.S. Bureau of the Census, *Historical Statistics of the United States: Colonial Times to 1970*, Part 1 (Washington, D.C., 1975), page 301; Margaret Marsh, *Suburban Lives* (New Brunswick, 1990), page 133; Becky

M. Nicolaides, *My Blue Heaven: Life and Politics in the Working-Class Suburbs of Los Angeles, 1920–1965* (Chicago, 2002), pages 188–189.

23. Frederick Law Olmsted, Jr., "Palos Verdes Estates," *Landscape Architecture,* July 1927, pages 257–258; *Monthly Labor Review,* October 1920, pages 98–99, June 1922, pages 69–73, June 1923, pages 111–115, October 1924, pages 69–82, June 1926, pages 61–63, August 1931, pages 383–385.

24. Robert M. Fogelson, *The Fragmented Metropolis: Los Angeles, 1850–1930* (Cambridge, 1967), page 324; "Final Report of the Commissioners of Central Park: 1870," in *Frederick Law Olmsted, Landscape Architect, 1822–1903,* ed. Frederick Law Olmsted, Jr., and Theodora Kimball (New York, 1970), volume 2, page 406.

25. U.S. Bureau of the Census: *Fifteenth Census of the United States: 1930, Population,* volume 6, *Families* (Washington, D.C., 1933), pages 181–184; *First Annual Conference,* pages b53–b54; *Third Annual Conference,* pages 567–568; Cook and Kaplan, "River Oaks," page 36; Power, "Residential Segregation of Baltimore's Jews," pages 5–7; Carey McWilliams, *Southern California Country: An Island on the Land* (New York, 1946), page 328.

26. *Pacific Palisades,* a 1920s pamphlet, Ephemera Collection, Huntington Library, San Marino, California.

27. *Palos Verdes Bulletin,* April 1929, page 4; *Kansas City Star,* July 16, 1916; Frederick Law Olmsted, Jr., to Clinton B. Miller, September 26, 1922, Olmsted Records, Job File 8001; Charles H. Cheney, "The Benefits of Community Planning," *House Beautiful,* August 1926, page 146; E. H. Bouton, "Development of Roland Park, Baltimore," *Proceedings of the General Sessions of the National Association of Real Estate Boards: 1924,* page 24. The observations of Olmsted, Jr., can also be found in Olmsted Records, Job File 3276, portions of which were kindly sent me by Professor Larry D. McCann, Department of Geography, University of Victoria.

28. *Los Angeles Times,* March 2, 1923; River Oaks Corporation, *A Few Homely Preachments Concerning Homes and Homesites,* undated pamphlet, Loeb Library; *Why You Should Choose the Location for Your Home*

in Brendonwood, undated pamphlet, Loeb Library; *Sunset Hill of the Country Club District, "1000 Acres Restricted," Planned-Developed and Offered Exclusively by J. C. Nichols* (1916), J. C. Nichols Collection, Western Historical Manuscript Collection, University of Missouri–Kansas City Archives.

29. Robert M. Fogelson, *Downtown: Its Rise and Fall, 1880–1950* (New Haven, 2001), page 10.

30. Witold Rybczynski, *A Clearing in the Distance: Frederick Law Olmsted and America in the Nineteenth Century* (New York, 1999), page 43; Thorstein Veblen, *Absentee Ownership and Business Enterprise in Recent Times: The Case of America* (New York, 1923), page 143; Kenneth Jackson, *Crabgrass Frontier: The Suburbanization of the United States* (New York, 1985), page 134; Albert T. Atwood, "Money from Everywhere," *Saturday Evening Post,* May 12, 1923, pages 144, 147; Erik H. Monkkonen, *America Becomes Urban* (Berkeley, 1988), page 7.

31. Jules Tygiel, *The Great Los Angeles Swindle: Oil, Stocks, and Scandal During the Roaring Twenties* (New York, 1994), page 13; *Los Angeles Times,* November 5, 12, and 26, 1922, January 14, March 4, June 10, October 28, 1923; *Country Life in America,* June 1909, page 40.

32. J. C. Nichols, "Suburban Subdivisions with Community Features," *Proceedings of the General Sessions of the National Association of Real Estate Boards at the Seventeenth Annual Convention: 1924,* page 17.

33. Alexis de Tocqueville, *Democracy in America* (New York, 1959), volume 2, pages 144–145; George William Pierson, "The Moving Americans," *Yale Review,* Autumn 1954, pages 102–104; William Dean Howells, *Suburban Sketches* (Boston, 1875), page 16.

34. Stephan Thernstrom and Peter R. Knights, "Men in Motion: Some Data and Speculations About Urban Population Mobility in Nineteenth-Century America," *Journal of Interdisciplinary History,* Autumn 1970, pages 7–37; Howard P. Chudacoff and Judith E. Smith, *The Evolution of American Urban Society* (Englewood Cliffs, 1994), pages 101–102, 136–143. See also Monkkonen, *America Becomes Urban,* pages 194–197.

35. John F. W. Ware, *Home Life: What It Is, and What It Needs* (Boston,

1864), page 9; J. C. Nichols, "Financial Effects of Good Planning in Land Subdivision," *Proceedings of the Eighth National Conference on City Planning: 1916,* pages 102–103.

36. Kevin Starr, *Material Dreams: Southern California Through the 1920s* (New York, 1990), page 71. See also William S. Worley, *J. C. Nichols and the Shaping of Kansas City: Innovation in Planned Residential Communities* (Columbia, Missouri, 1990), chapter 9.

37. Alexander von Hoffman, *Local Attachments: The Making of an American Urban Neighborhood, 1850–1920* (Baltimore, 1994), page xv; Pierson, "Moving Americans," page 110.

38. Fogelson, *The Fragmented Metropolis,* chapter 4; Willard Huntington Wright, "Los Angeles: The Chemically Pure," in *The Smart Set Anthology,* ed. Burton Rascoe and Graff Conklin (New York, 1934), page 93; McWilliams, *Southern California Country,* page 135; Sarah Comstock, "The Great American Mirror," *Harper's Monthly Magazine,* May 1928, page 723.

39. Atwood, "Money from Everywhere," pages 11, 134, 140; *A Report of Proceedings and Addresses [at the] Meetings of Underwriting Subscribers of Palos Verdes Project* (Los Angeles, 1922), page 17; McWilliams, *Southern California Country,* pages 165, 170.

40. Samuel Swift, "Community Life in Rochelle Park," *House and Garden,* May 1904, page 243.

41. Frederick Law Olmsted, Jr., to Joel Hurt, April 4, 1902, Olmsted Records, Job File 71. See also Mark Stewart Foster, "The Decentralization of Los Angeles During the 1920s" (Doctoral dissertation, University of Southern California, 1971), pages 230–231.

42. Robin L. Einhorn, *Property Rules: Political Economy in Chicago, 1833–1872* (Chicago, 1991), page 154; Kingsdale, "The 'Poor Man's Club,'" pages 472–488; James H. Timberlake, *Prohibition and the Progressive Movement, 1900–1920* (Cambridge, 1966), page 94.

43. John Marshall Barker, *The Saloon Problem and Social Reform* (Boston, 1905); Timberlake, *Prohibition,* page 58; Robert T. Devlin, *A Treatise on the Law of Deeds* (San Francisco, 1897), volume 2, page 1322; 51 *A.L.R.* 1454; John Charles Olmsted to Messrs. Oldfield, Kirby & Gardner, Au-

gust 2, 1907, Olmsted Records, Job File 3276; *Hatcher v. Andrews*, 5 Bush 561. See also Joseph R. Gusfield, *Symbolic Crusade: Status Politics and the American Temperance Movement* (Urbana, Illinois, 1963).

44. John Charles Olmsted to Walter H. Leimert, June 28, 1917, Olmsted Records, Job File 5945; Frederick Law Olmsted, Jr., to Joel Hurt, April 4, 1902, Olmsted Records, Job File 71; "The Uplands Limited: Prospectus Revised by Messrs. Olmsted Bros.," November 2, 1908, Olmsted Records, Job File 3276; *State v. Houghton*, 158 N.W. 1017; Richard M. Hurd, *Principles of City Land Values* (New York, 1903), page 117; Henry Clarke, "The Real Estate Business—Today and Tomorrow," *National Real Estate Journal*, May 1932, page 36.

45. *Third Annual Conference*, pages 601, 605–610; *State v. Houghton*, 158 N.W. 1071, quote on page 1022. See also *Trustees of Columbia College v. Thacher*, 87 N.Y. 311.

46. Andrew J. King, *Law and Land Use in Chicago: A Prehistory of Modern Zoning* (New York, 1986), page 80; *Report of the Board of Park and Boulevard Commissioners of Kansas City, Mo.* (Kansas City, 1893), page 14; Country Club Homes Association, *Report of Activities for the Year Nineteen Twenty-Eight*, J. C. Nichols Company Scrapbooks.

47. Joel Schwartz, "Evolution of the Suburbs," in *American Urban History*, ed. Alexander B. Callow, Jr. (New York, 1982), page 502; Fogelson, *Downtown*, page 323; Homer Hoyt, *One Hundred Years of Land Values in Chicago* (Chicago, 1933), page 136; *Second Annual Conference*, pages 552–553; *Third Annual Conference*, pages 226, 234–235, 528–533, 544–545, 559–560.

48. Kenneth Baar, "The National Movement to Halt the Spread of Multifamily Housing, 1890–1926," *Journal of the American Planning Association*, Winter 1992, pages 39–48; Elmer S. Forbes, "Housing Conditions in Small Towns," *Proceedings of the First National Conference on Housing: 1911*, pages 71–72; *City of Bismarck v. Hughes*, 208 N.W. 711, quote on page 717; Lawrence Veiller, "Protecting Residential Districts," *Proceedings of the Sixth National Conference on City Planning: 1914*, pages 103–104; *City of Jackson v. McPherson*, 138 S.E. 604; Otto W. Davis, "Shall We Encourage or Discourage the Apartment House?"

Proceedings of the Fifth National Conference on Housing: 1915, pages 334, 345; *Proceedings of the Third National Conference on Housing: 1913*, page 213; *City of Youngstown v. Kahn Bros. Bldg. Co.*, 148 N.W. 842.

49. *City of Youngstown v. Kahn Bros. Bldg. Co.*, 148 N.W. 842, quote on page 845; Ware, *Home Life*, pages 15–16; Bernard J. Newman, "Shall We Encourage or Discourage the Apartment House?" *Proceedings of the Fifth National Conference on Housing: 1915*, pages 158–159; Davis, "Shall We Encourage or Discourage the Apartment House?" pages 336–337; Gwendolyn Wright, *Building the Dream: A Social History of Housing in America* (New York, 1981), page 151.

50. *Brendonwood* (1920), a pamphlet in the Loeb Library; Otto W. Davis, "How Can We Keep Our City a City of Homes?" *Proceedings of the Third National Conference on Housing: 1913*, page 208; Walter Firey, *Land Use in Central Boston* (Cambridge, 1946), page 277; *Lewis v. Gollner*, 29 N.E. 81; Forbes, "Housing Conditions in Small Towns," page 72; *Proceedings of the Third National Conference on Housing: 1913*, page 347; *State v. Houghton*, 176 N.W. 159; *Third Annual Conference*, pages 546–547.

51. *Miller v. Board of Public Works*, 234 P. 381, quotes on page 387; Wright, *Building the Dream*, pages 148–149; *Proceedings of the Fifth National Conference on Housing: 1915*, page 348; Davis, "How Can We Keep Our City a City of Homes?" pages 207–208.

52. Charles H. Cheney, "Removing Social Barriers by Zoning," *Survey*, May 22, 1920, page 277; *Miller v. Board of Public Works*, 234 P. 381, quote on page 387; *Third Annual Conference*, pages 534–535; John Charles Olmsted to Walter H. Leimert, June 28, 1917, Olmsted Records, Job File 5945; James Frederick Dawson to Walter H. Davis, March 17, 1920, Olmsted Records, Job File 6562; *Euclid v. Ambler*, 272 U.S. 365, quote on page 395.

53. Olmsted Brothers to Messrs. Oldfield, Kirby & Gardner, November 5, 1908, Olmsted Records, Job File 3276.

54. Fletcher Steele, compiler, "Restrictions on Land to Be Used for Suburban Residential Purposes," a memo dated February 1, 1913, pages 5–6, Loeb Library; Jackson, *Crabgrass Frontier*, pages 58–60; Olmsted

Brothers to Joel Hurt, April 4, 1902, Olmsted Records, Job File 71; Duncan McDuffie to James F. Dawson, July 7, 1913, Olmsted Records, Job File 5658; Robert Fishman, *Bourgeois Utopias: The Rise and Fall of Suburbia* (New York, 1987), pages 146–147.

55. Duncan McDuffie to James F. Dawson, July 7, 1913, Olmsted Records, Job File 5658; Olmsted Brothers to Joel Hurt, April 4, 1902, Olmsted Records, Job File 71; Frederick Law Olmsted, "Deed Restrictions That Affect Houses in Planned Neighborhoods," *Architectural Record,* November 1940, page 33.

56. F. A. Cushing Smith, "The Glory of Shaker Heights," *American Landscape Architecture,* July 1920, pages 21–26; J. C. Nichols, "Suburban Subdivisions with Community Features," *Proceedings of the General Sessions of the National Association of Real Estate Boards at the Seventeenth Annual Conference: 1924,* page 18; *Palos Verdes Bulletin,* March 1929, page 7.

57. Frank L. Meline, "Advantages of Architectural Harmony in Subdivisions," *Annals of Real Estate Practice: 1925,* volume 3, page 166; Chester S. Chase, "A Well Planned and Well Planted Community," *House Beautiful,* September 1926, page 267; Richard W. Marchant, Jr., to Charles A. Platt, December 30, 1902, Box 10, Roland Park Company Records; John Charles Olmsted to Jay Lawyer, March 24, 1914, and Olmsted Brothers to W. H. Kiernan, October 9, 1914, Olmsted Records, Job File 5950.

58. John Charles Olmsted to Jay Lawyer, March 20, 1914, Olmsted Records, Job File 5950; Meline, "Architectural Harmony," page 166; *Baltimore News,* May 6, 1896, Box 296, Roland Park Company Records.

59. John R. Stilgoe, *Common Landscape in America, 1550–1845* (New Haven, 1982), pages 191–192; Paul Groth, "Lot, Yard, and Garden: American Distinctions," *Landscape* (1990), pages 32–33; Philip Dole, "The Picket Fence at Home," in *Between Fences,* ed. Gregory K. Dreicer (Washington, D.C., 1996), page 33; David P. Handlin, *The American Home: Architecture and Society, 1815–1915* (Boston, 1979), pages 178–179; Frank J. Scott, *The Art of Beautifying Suburban Home Grounds of Small Extent* (New York, 1886), pages 51, 55, 107.

60. Nathaniel H. Egleston, *The Home and Its Surroundings or Villages and*

Village Life (New York, 1884), pages 134–146. On the village improvement movement, see Handlin, *The American Home*, pages 91–116.

61. Egleston, *The Home and Its Surroundings*, pages 149–150; Julian R. Tinkham, "A Discussion of the Fence Problem: II. A Plea for Fences and Privacy," *Country Life in America*, September 1903, pages 326–327; L. H. Bailey, "A Discussion of the Fence Problem: I. The Philosophy of Fences," ibid., pages 324–325; Ernest Hemmings, "Hedges for the Country or Suburban Estate," *Suburban Life*, September 1907, page 276; Parris Thaxter Farwell, *Village Improvement* (New York, 1913), page 129; Groth, "Lot, Yard, and Garden," page 33.

62. Steele, compiler, "Restrictions on Land," page 17; Mary Harrod Northend and Dorothy Loud, "A Plea for Fences," *House Beautiful*, February 1917, page 147; "On Our Fenceless State," *Atlantic Monthly*, August 1909, pages 283–284; Tinkham, "A Plea for Fences and Privacy," pages 326–327; Hemmings, "Hedges for the Country or Suburban Estate," page 276.

63. Frederick Law Olmsted to *American Gardner*, August 26, 1889, Frederick Law Olmsted Papers, Manuscript Division, Library of Congress (hereinafter cited as Olmsted Papers); Edward H. Bouton to Messrs. Stuart & Young, June 28, 1898, Box 291, Roland Park Company Records; *First Annual Conference*, pages b76–b77; Olmsted Brothers to Joel Hurt, May 16, 1905, Olmsted Records, Job File 71; Olmsted Brothers to Walter H. Leimert, June 28, 1917, Olmsted Records, Job File 5945; Frederick Law Olmsted, Jr., to Edward H. Bouton, December 13, 1911, Olmsted Records, Job File 3391; Olmsted Brothers to Messrs. Oldfield, Kirby & Gardner, November 5, 1908, Olmsted Records, Job File 3276; Edward H. Bouton to James A. Burgess, September 11, 1908, Box 291, Roland Park Company Records.

64. Steele, compiler, "Restrictions on Land," pages 17–19; H.V.H., "Land Subdivision Restrictions," *Landscape Architecture*, October 1925, table following page 54; Olmsted Brothers to Walter H. Leimert, June 28, 1917, Olmsted Records, Job File 5945; Olmsted Brothers to Messrs. Oldfield, Kirby & Gardner, November 5, 1908, Olmsted Records, Job File 3276.

65. Olmsted Brothers to Messrs. Oldfield, Kirby & Gardner, August 2,

1907, Olmsted Records, Job File 3276; W. S. Kies to H. J. Slaker, January 31, 1916, Olmsted Records, Job File 5816; Joel Hurt to Olmsted Brothers, May 13, 1905, Olmsted Records, Job File 71; *Second Annual Conference,* page 700; Steele, compiler, "Restrictions on Land," page 23.

66. *City of St. Louis v. Stern,* 3 Mo. App. 48, quote on page 49; *In re Linehan,* 72 Cal. 114; *Sharp v. Ropes,* 110 Mass. 381; Donald Grant Mitchell, *Out-of-Town Places: With Hints for Their Improvement* (New York, 1884), pages 40, 63; John R. Stilgoe, *Metropolitan Corridor: Railroads and the American Scene* (New Haven, 1983), page 271; Catharine E. Beecher and Harriet Beecher Stowe, *The American Woman's Home* (New York, 1869), chapter 34.

67. Francis E. Clark, "Why I Chose a Suburban Home," *Suburban Life,* April 1907, pages 187–189; Stilgoe, *Metropolitan Corridor,* pages 273–277; H. S. Babcock, "Poultry Breeding in the United States," *Outing,* October 1900, page 44; E. I. Farrington, "Poultry-Yard Patriotism," *Countryside Magazine and Suburban Life,* June 1917, page 316; Henry Lowe, "Rabbit Raising for War-Time Food," *Illustrated World,* July 1918, pages 737–741.

68. Stilgoe, *Metropolitan Corridor,* pages 273–277; David R. Contosta, *Suburb in the City: Chestnut Hill, Philadelphia, 1850–1920* (Columbus, Ohio, 1992), pages 97–98; Johanna Von Wagner to Frederick Law Olmsted, January 29, 1912, Olmsted Records, Job File 5354; *Washington Post,* February 15, 1999; Nicolaides, *My Blue Heaven,* pages 17–18, 26–35; *Los Angeles Times,* April 29, 1923.

69. *Second Annual Conference,* page 699; *Hycliff Standards[:] A Declaration of Protections and Restrictions for Hycliff, Section Two* (1929), page 8; H.V.H. "Land Subdivision Restrictions," table following page 54; deed from Walter W. Davis and Hallie K. Davis to an unidentified buyer, May 14, 1927, Loeb Library.

70. Foster, "Decentralization of Los Angeles," page 38. See also Olmsted Brothers to Messrs. Oldfield, Kirby & Gardner, November 5, 1908, Olmsted Records, Job File 3276; Baltimore *Sun,* May 30, 1915; John Charles Olmsted to H. J. Slaker, February 28, 1916, Olmsted Records, Job File 5816.

71. Olmsted Brothers to Joel Hurt, October 18, 1902, Olmsted Records, Job File 71; Baltimore *Sun*, May 9, 1915; John Charles Olmsted to J. H. Oldfield, May 21, 1907, Olmsted Records, Job File 3276.

72. Olmsted Brothers to Messrs. Oldfield, Kirby & Gardner, August 2, 1907, Olmsted Records, Job File 3276. See also John Charles Olmsted to J. H. Oldfield, May 21, 1907, Olmsted Records, Job File 3276; John Charles Olmsted to H. J. Slaker, February 28, 1916, Olmsted Records, Job File 5816.

73. *Roland Park Review,* March 1909, page 7, April 1909, page 4, June 1909, page 12.

74. *Roland Park Review,* April 1909, pages 3–4, May 1909, page 6, August 1909, page 6, April 1911, page 2.

75. James W. Waesche, *Crowning the Gravelly Hill: A History of the Roland Park-Guilford-Homeland District* (Baltimore, 1987), page 73; *Roland Park Review,* March 1909, page 7, May 1910, pages 2–3, March 1916, page 6.

76. *Roland Park Review,* March 1909, page 7, April 1909, page 4, August 1909, page 6, January 1910, page 5, May 1910, pages 2–3.

77. Olmsted Brothers to Joel Hurt, May 16, 1905, Olmsted Records, Job File 71; *Hycliff Standards,* page 8; Olmsted Brothers to William H. Graf[f]lin, March 22, 1909, Job File 3391; Henry S. Kissell, "Community Features for Suburbs," *Annals of Real Estate Practice: 1925,* volume 3, pages 128–129.

78. *Hycliff Standards,* page 8; Olmsted Brothers to Joel Hurt, May 16, 1905, Olmsted Records, Job File 71.

79. Nicolaides, *My Blue Heaven,* page 13, 29, 33–34, 102; Johanna von Wagner to Frederick Law Olmsted, January 29, 1912, Olmsted Records, Job File 5354; *Los Angeles Times,* January 21, 1923; E. C. Shriver to Roland Park Company, August 1904; James E. Green to E. C. Shriver, August 17, 1904, Box 18, Roland Park Company Records.

80. Baltimore *Sun,* May 9 and 30, 1915; John Charles Olmsted to J. H. Oldfield, May 21, 1907, Olmsted Records, Job File 3276; *Fourth Annual Report of the Board of Commissioners of the Central Park: 1861,* pages 107–108.

81. Hurd, *Principles of City Land Values,* page 77.

82. Fred W. Viehe, "Black Gold Suburbs: The Influence of the Extractive Industry on the Suburbanization of Los Angeles," *Journal of Urban History*, November 1981, pages 6, 11, 13; Dan La Botz, *Edward L. Doheny: Petroleum, Power, and Politics in the United States and Mexico* (New York, 1991), pages 10–11; Tygiel, *The Great Los Angeles Swindle*, pages 14–16, 25–35; Starr, *Material Dreams*, pages 85–87.

83. Albert W. Atwood, "When the Oil Flood Is On," *Saturday Evening Post*, July 7, 1923, pages 4, 96; Tygiel, *The Great Los Angeles Swindle*, pages 36, 40–41, 50; Bruce Bliven, "Los Angeles: The City That Is Bacchanalian—In a Nice Way," *New Republic*, July 13, 1927, page 200.

84. Upton Sinclair, *Oil* (New York, 1926), pages 24–25; Tygiel, *The Great Los Angeles Swindle*, pages 37–39; Albert W. Atwood, "Mad from Oil," *Saturday Evening Post*, July 14, 1923, pages 10–11, 94; *Los Angeles Times*, May 13, July 22, August 5, October 21, 1923.

85. Sinclair, *Oil*, pages 24–25, 65. See also Atwood, "When the Oil Flood Is On," page 89; Martin R. Ansell, *Oil Baron of the Southwest: Edward L. Doheny and the Development of the Petroleum Industry in California and Mexico* (Columbus, Ohio, 1998), pages 30–31; Tygiel, *The Great Los Angeles Swindle*, page 27.

86. Tygiel, *The Great Los Angeles Swindle*, pages 29, 39; Sinclair, *Oil*, pages 24–25; Atwood, "When the Oil Flood Is On," page 93; Mark Lee Luther, *The Boosters* (Indianapolis, 1923), pages 197–198.

87. Walter V. Woehlke, "The Champion Borrower of Them All," *Sunset Magazine*, November 1925, pages 27, 62; *Meetings of Underwriting Subscribers*, page 14; E. G. Lewis to Underwriting Subscribers, a memo dated February 5, 1925, Local History Collection, Palos Verdes Library District, Palos Verdes Estates, California; *Protective Restrictions, Palos Verdes Estates, Los Angeles, California* (1923), page 17; Indenture Between the Huntington Land and Water Company and Lester H. Luhnon and Elizabeth Clark Luhnon, July 3, 1925, Huntington Land Companies Files, which were once in the companies' office in San Marino, California, and, archivist Alan Jutzi tells me, are now in the Huntington Library, which is also in San Marino; Pierce E. Benedict and Don Kennedy, eds., *History of Beverly Hills* (Beverly Hills, 1934), part 1,

pages 60–61; Rodeo Land and Water Company to E. L. Doheny, a deed dated June 8, 1914, Historical Collections, Beverly Hills Public Library, Beverly Hills, California.

88. John O. Pohlmann, "Alphonzo E. Bell: A Biography," part 1, *Southern California Quarterly*, September 1964, pages 197–222, and part 2, ibid., December 1964, pages 315–350; Tygiel, *The Great Los Angeles Swindle*, pages 25–28; Atwood, "When the Oil Flood Is On," pages 99, 101; Pacific Southwest Trust and Savings Bank to Susan Emma Beachy, a deed dated January 15, 1927, Bel-Air Association Files, Bel-Air, California; *Los Angeles Times*, October 28, December 16, 1923.

89. William H. Wilson, "The Billboard: Bane of the City Beautiful," *Journal of Urban History*, August 1987, pages 395–397; Quentin J. Schultze, "Legislating Morality: The Progressive Response to American Outdoor Advertising, 1900–1917," *Journal of Popular Culture*, Spring 1984, pages 37–38; Fogelson, *Downtown*, pages 191–192.

90. Wilson, "The Billboard," pages 397–405; Schultze, "Legislating Morality," pages 38–42. See also W. L. Lawton, "Regulation of Outdoor Advertising," *Planning Problems of Town, City, and Region: Papers and Discussions at the Eighteenth National Conference on City Planning: 1926*, page 88; Everett L. Millard, "What Chambers of Commerce and Realtors Can Do to Help Abate the Billboard Nuisance," *American City*, March 1920, page 276.

91. Wilson, "The Billboard," pages 405–412; "Billboards and Other Forms of Outdoor Advertising," Chicago *City Club Bulletin*, December 16, 1912, pages 395–396, 401–403, 406–407. See also *St. Louis Advertising Co. v. City of St. Louis*, 137 S.W. 929, especially pages 963–968.

92. "Billboards and Other Forms of Outdoor Advertising," pages 394, Harry F. Lake, "The Billboard Nuisance," *American City*, November 1910, pages 221–222; Frederick Law Olmsted, Jr., to Charles H. Loring, June 20, 1900; Frederick Law Olmsted, Jr., to Myron E. Pierce, December 26, 1906, Olmsted Records, Job File 3035.

93. "Billboards and Other Forms of Outdoor Advertising," pages 395–396, 400–403, 406–407. See also Wilson, "The Billboard," pages 405–407.

94. Wilson, "The Billboard," pages 412–419; *American City*, March 1927, page 389; Frederick Law Olmsted, Jr., to Charles H. Loring, June 20, 1900, Olmsted Records, Job File 3035; *Housing*, June 1929, page 130; Clinton Rogers Woodruff, ed., *The Billboard Nuisance*, American Civic Association, series 2, no. 2. (June, 1908), page 6; Edward T. Hartman, *The Billboard Nuisance*, an undated, unpaged pamphlet published by the Massachusetts Civic League, Loeb Library; *Billboard Advertising in St. Louis: Report of the Signs and Billboards Committee of the [St. Louis] Civic League* (St. Louis, 1910), page 17.

95. *First Annual Conference*, pages b95–b96; Olmsted Brothers to Messrs. Oldfield, Kirby & Gardner, November 5, 1908, Olmsted Records, Job File 3276.

96. *Third Annual Conference*, pages 483–486; *Deed and Agreement Between the Ottawa Hills Company and John North Willys Containing Restrictions and Conditions Relating to Plat Number One, Ottawa Hills* (1916), pages 6–7, Loeb Library; "Billboards and Other Forms of Outdoor Advertising," page 395.

97. Olmsted Brothers to Joel Hurt, April 4, 1902, Olmsted Records, Job File 71. See also *Proceedings of the First Annual Convention Conferences of the Homebuilders' and Subdividers' Division of the National Association of Real Estate Boards: 1923*, page 135.

98. *Second Annual Conference*, page 436; *Los Angeles Times*, February 25, 1923; Helen Monchow, *The Use of Deed Restrictions in Subdivision Development* (Chicago, 1928), page 34; Steele, compiler, "Restrictions on Land," page 15; Charles E. Beveridge and Paul Rocheleau, *Frederick Law Olmsted: Designing the American Landscape* (New York, 1998), page 108; *Judging Palos Verdes as a Place to Live*, undated promotional pamphlet, page 29; Fogelson, *Downtown*, page 29; Nicolaides, *My Blue Heaven*, page 17; Susan Mulcahey Chase, "The Process of Suburbanization and the Use of Restrictive Deed Covenants as Private Zoning" (Doctoral dissertation, University of Delaware, 1995), pages 257–258; Jackson, *Crabgrass Frontier*, page 50.

99. Richard W. Marchant, Jr., to John Morrow Adams, February 21, 1907, Box 30; W. L. Tuttle to Richard W. Marchant, Jr., May 9, 1905, Box

19, Roland Park Company Records; Waesche, *Crowning the Gravelly Hill,* pages 72, 74; Richard W. Marchant, Jr., to John Rutledge, May 13, 1908, Box 31, Roland Park Company Records; Olmsted Brothers to Messrs. Oldfield, Kirby & Gardner, November 3, 1908, Olmsted Records, Job File 3276; *Ignaciunas v. Risley,* 121 A. 783, quote on page 785; A. C. F. Judge to Roland Park Company, June 22, 1905, Box 19, Roland Park Company Records.

100. Nichols, "Good Planning in Land Subdivision," page 100; *Eberle Economic Service,* March 28, 1932, page 50; W. W. Robinson, "The Southern California Real Estate Boom of the Twenties," *Historical Society of Southern California Quarterly,* March 1942, page 25; James Clifford Findley, "The Economic Boom of the 'Twenties in Los Angeles" (Doctoral dissertation, Claremont Graduate School, 1968), page 195.

101. Nichols, "Good Planning in Land Subdivision," page 101; Loveley, "Fundamental Principles in Developing High-Grade Subdivisions," page 69; H. A. Lafler to Walter H. Leimert, February 9, 1915, Olmsted Records, Job File 5945; J. C. Nichols, "A Developer's View of Deed Restrictions," *Journal of Land & Public Utility Economics,* May 1939, page 134; Nichols, "Lessons of a Lifetime," page 91.

102. Frederick Law Olmsted to William H. Graf[f]lin, March 22, 1909, Olmsted Records, Job File 3391.

103. *Country Club District Bulletin,* November 1927, page 4. See also C. P. Gray, "Principles in Selecting Land for Subdivision," *Proceedings of the First Annual Convention Conferences of the Homebuilders' and Subdividers' Division of the National Association of Real Estate Boards: 1923,* page 15.

Epilogue

1. *Orlando Sentinel,* March 13 and 17, 1992; *New York Times,* July 24, 2002. See also Evan McKenzie, *Privatopia: Homeowner Associations and the Rise of Residential Private Government* (New Haven, 1994), pages 15–18.

2. J. M. Nolte, "Restrictions for the Man of Moderate Means," *Annals of Real Estate Practice: 1925*, volume 3, page 387; Joseph Laronge, "The Subdivider of Today and Tomorrow," *Journal of Land & Public Utility Economics*, November 1942, page 427; *New York Times*, August 25, 1975, September 5, 1995; John Delafons, *Land-Use Controls in the United States* (Cambridge, 1962), pages 87–89; Edward J. Blakely and Mary Gail Synder, *Fortress America: Gated Communities in the United States* (Washington, D.C., 1995), chapter 1.

3. *Proceedings of the General Sessions of the National Association of Real Estate Boards at the Seventeenth Annual Convention: 1924*, page 19; Laronge, "The Subdivider," page 428; National Association of Home Builders, *Home Builders Manual for Land Development* (Washington, D.C., 1954), pages 252–253; *Shelley v. Kraemer*, 334 U.S. 1; Clement E. Vose, *Caucasians Only: The Supreme Court and the Restrictive Covenant Cases* (Berkeley, 1967), especially chapter 8; Gunnar Myrdal, *An American Dilemma* (New York, 1944), volume 2, page 624; Eugene Rachlis and John E. Marqusee, *The Landlords* (New York, 1963), pages 245, 249–250.

4. McKenzie, *Privatopia*, pages 13–18; Blakely and Snyder, *Fortress America*, pages 20–22; *New York Times*, September 5, 1995, July 24, 2002, July 27, 2003; "America's New Utopias," *Economist*, September 1, 2001, page 25. Scores, if not hundreds, of restrictive covenants are available on the World Wide Web.

5. F. Emerson Andrews, "When Is a *Restriction* Really a *Protection?*" *House Beautiful*, December 1943, page 90. See also *New York Times*, July 27, 2003.

6. Frederick Law Olmsted, "Deed Restrictions That Affect Houses in Planned Communities," *Architectural Record*, November 1940, page 34.

7. John M. Gries and James Ford, eds., *Planning for Residential Districts* (Washington, D.C., 1932), pages 57, 75; Susan Mulcahey Chase, "The Process of Suburbanization and the Use of Restrictive Deed Covenants as Private Zoning: Wilmington, Delaware, 1900–1941" (Doctoral dissertation, University of Delaware, 1995), pages 276–279; Na-

tional Association of Home Builders, *Home Builders Manual,* pages 246–248; John H. Beuscher, Robert W. Wright, and Morton Gitelman, *Cases and Materials on Land Use* (St. Paul, 1976), page 219.

8. Marc N. Goodnow, "Neighborhoods That Can't Be Spoiled," *Survey,* July 1, 1931, page 353; Helen Koues, "Beauty in Community Planning," *Good Housekeeping,* March 1937, pages 50–51; *Urban Planning and Land Policies: Volume 2 of the Supplementary Report of the Urbanism Committee to the National Resources Council* (Washington, D.C., 1939), pages 88–89.

9. These figures were gathered from the 2000 census by my research assistants, Tamam Mango and Diana R. Sherman.

10. *New York Times,* August 25, 1975.

Acknowledgments

If *Bourgeois Nightmares* did not take as long as expected, it's largely because I had so much help.

MIT's Humanities, Arts, and Social Sciences Fund, which supported my last two books, gave me a grant that helped with this one. Additional support came from elsewhere at the Institute, notably from the Center for Real Estate, the Dean's Fund of the School of Humanities, Arts, and Social Sciences, and the Department of Urban Studies and Planning. My thanks to Tony Ciochetti, Marion Cunningham, David Geltner, Phil Khoury, Bill Mitchell, Harriet Ritvo, Bish Sanyal, and Larry Vale.

My research assistants — Kate Fichter, Lita Lee, Tamam Mango, Alison Novak, and Diana Sherman — were of great help. Also of great help were the MIT and Harvard libraries, especially MIT's Rotch and Humanities libraries and Harvard's Loeb, Law, and Widener libraries. Thanks to Margaret de Popolo, head of Rotch, Teresa Tobin, head of Humanities, and their colleagues. Thanks also to the Baltimore Public Library, Department of Manuscripts and University Archives of Cornell's Olin Library, Henry E. Huntington Library, Manuscript Division of the Library of Congress, Palos Verdes Homes Association, Palos Verdes Library District, and Larry McCann of the University of Victoria, who sent me a copy of his files on the Olmsted Brothers firm.

For getting me material from out-of-the-way places (and sparing me several long and arduous trips), I would also like to thank Kelly Davenport, a former student, Elaine Gerdau of the Bel-

Air Association (as well as Tom Gilmore and Greg Fischer, who put me in touch with her), Charlie Halpern, an old friend and former head of the Nathan Cummings Foundation, Alan Jutzi of the Huntington Library, June Lewin of the Beverly Hills Public Library, and Stephanie Willerth, another former student.

Anna Bergren, David Handlin, Langley Keyes, Richard Longstreth, Douglas Rae, and Lloyd Weinreb, all of whom had more than enough other things to do, read one or another draft of *Bourgeois Nightmares*. And many of their suggested revisions were incorporated into the text. Nancy Kirk and Phil King, who edited the manuscript, did a splendid job, as did Lisa Fogelson, who typed the draft, Alexa Selph, who prepared the index, and Nancy Ovedovitz, who designed the book. Many thanks to them—as well as to Anna Bergren, David Boutros, and John Cook for their help with the illustrations.

Thanks also to my agent Ike Williams, his associate Hope Denekamp, and Michelle Komie of Yale University Press, each of whom was a pleasure to work with.

Index